EUROPEAN AIR TRANSPORT LAW AND COMPETITION

Jeffrey Goh

University of Sheffield

JOHN WILEY & SONS

Chichester • New York • Weinheim • Brisbane • Singapore • Toronto

Copyright © 1997 by John Wiley & Sons Ltd,
Baffins Lane, Chichester,
West Sussex PO19 1UD, England

National 01243 779777
International (+44) 1243 779777
e-mail (for orders and customer service enquiries):
cs-books@wiley.co.uk
Visit our Home Page on http://www.wiley.co.uk
or http://www.wiley.com

Other Wiley Editorial Offices

John Wiley & Sons, Inc., 605 Third Avenue,
New York, NY 10158-0012, USA

VCH Verlagsgesellschaft mbH, Pappelallee 3,
D-69469 Weinheim, Germany

Jacaranda Wiley Ltd, 33 Park Road, Milton,
Queensland 4064, Australia

John Wiley & Sons (Canada) Ltd, 22 Worcester Road,
Rexdale, Ontario M9W 1L1, Canada

John Wiley & Sons (Asia) Pte Ltd, 2 Clementi Loop #02-01,
Jin Xing Distripark, Singapore 129809

Library of Congress Cataloging-in-Publication Data

Goh, Jeffrey.
 European air transport law and competition/Jeffrey Goh.
  p. cm. – (Wiley series in European law)
 Includes index.
 ISBN 0-471-96159-0(cloth)
 1. Aeronautics. Commerical–Law and legislation – European Union
countries. I. Title. II. Series.
KJE6920.G64 1997
341.7'567'094–dc21   96–51972
                                                                              CIP

British Library Cataloguing in Publication Data

A catalogue record for this book is available from the British Library

ISBN 0-471-96159-0

Typeset in 10/12pt Baskerville by Poole Typesetting (Wessex) Ltd, Bournemouth, Dorset
Printed and bound in Great Britain by Bookcraft (Bath) Ltd, Midsomer Norton, Somerset
This book is printed on acid-free paper responsibly manufactured from sustainable
forestation, for which at least two trees are planted for each one used for paper production.

To My Family

As we begin to write a new chapter in the fundamental law of the air, let us all remember that we are engaged in a great attempt to build enduring institutions of peace. These peace settlements cannot be endangered by petty considerations or weakened by groundless fears. Rather, with full recognition of the sovereignty and juridical equality of all nations, let us work together so that the air may be used by humanity, to serve humanity.

Franklin D. Roosevelt
International Civil Aviation Conference
Chicago, 1944

CONTENTS

PREFACE

This book marks the dawn of a new era in civil aviation. By April 1997, the European Community will have completed a 10-year process of creating a single air transport market within the Community by harmonising and opening up the air transport markets of 15 Member States to competition. This will be an historic moment. No other organisation of countries so diverse in character can lay claim to such an achievement. Indeed, the uniqueness of the structure and jurisprudence of the European Community and the European Union has no comparable equivalent.

The programme of liberalisation has been both an ambitious and monumental task. It has sought to achieve a common denominator for 15 different air transport markets while at the same time attempting to break down a myriad of traditions and sometimes arcane practices that have characterised air transport since its conception. Yet, as an integral part of the objectives of a unified Europe, the Community cannot avoid the ineluctable dynamism of the air transport industry; an industry which constantly evolves to produce new challenges, no less so than the challenges which are emerging from growing economic regions such as Asia-Pacific. The global village is itself changing, and traditions are being appraised and re-appraised. The Community cannot be oblivious to these. Adjustments must be made accordingly if it is to remain at the forefront of global developments including air transport.

In the course of these 10 years, and in fact beyond, a great deal has happened to change the landscape of Community air transport. Competition, in particular, has been single-handedly responsible for these dramatic changes. No doubt, this is true also in the global context. Indeed, across economies of different complexion, be they social or market economies, competition has come to be regarded as the *sine qua non* of modern industrial policy. It symbolises a new economic and industrial renaissance which has been variously promoted as "re-inventing government" by the Americans, "perestroika" by the Russians and "doi moi" by the Vietnamese. In the Community, competition has been proclaimed as a means for securing an efficient environment, for producing better products and for improving the quality of services. The White Paper of 1993 on Growth, Competitiveness and Employment has stated explicitly that competition underlies sustainable expansion. It is in this regard that I make no apology for delving into the history of the air transport liberalisation programme because to understand the context of the present and where we can go from here, we need to know where we have come from, and how.

This book has been written with two objectives in mind. First, it aims to provide an insight into the liberalisation programme and the regulatory laws which govern the single aviation market including the rules on computer reservation systems, mergers and state aids as they affect competition in air transport. A number of important recent developments have taken place, such as the link-up between Lufthansa and Scandinavian Airlines System, and the controversial State aid to Iberia, which are examined in considerable detail in their respective chapters. However, and short of turning this book into an encyclopedia, the areas covered in this book have been necessarily selective. This is by no means to understate the significance of other harmonisation initiatives from compensation for denied boarding to aircraft noise restrictions. Secondly, this book is intended to mark the historic occasion both in the context of Community pursuits and civil aviation generally. The one major limitation to the objectives of such a book is of course that the exposition has to be stated at a particular point in time. In this case, the law is stated as at 1 December 1996. Indeed and so often, developments in the Community have far outpaced any book that can be written in time to capture their essence. On that ground alone, I have chosen to ignore the political structure of the European Union and to refer throughout the book to the European Community for the sake of simplicity, unless otherwise specified. Likewise, I have not sought to distinguish between the European Community and the European Economic Area, in so far as this is possible.

These tasks could not have been achieved without the assistance, and indeed the perseverance of those many individuals who have efficiently and patiently tended to my persistent requests for answers and documentation. The debts are of enormous proportions. Foremost of all, I want to thank the Civil Aviation Authority, and in particular Cliff Paice, for having been a reservoir of invaluable information and for having commented on various aspects of my work. I must also thank officials of the Department of Transport and the European Commission who took time to respond to my requests. Thanks are also due to Iñigo del Guayo, a dear friend and colleague, whose comments on the style and content were very much valued, and also to Peter Davies who shared with me his delightful thoughts on the chapter dealing with mergers. I am also grateful to David Ong who so often obliged with eleventh-hour requests for help.

On comparative data relating to the deregulated industry of the USA, I have to thank Gary Edles, a valued friend who was formerly at the Civil Aeronautics Board. Others to whom I am indebted are Patrick Murphy, Assistant Secretary at the Department of Transportation, and Dayton Lehman Jr. at the Office of Aviation Enforcement and Proceedings. Thanks are also due to the team at Wiley, and in particular to David Wilson and Suzanne Bracher, who were exemplary in seeing this book to fruition.

For all those individuals who have helped in one way or another, but whose names I have inadvertently failed to mention, I remain eternally grateful. Finally, though not least, my thanks to Judith who spent countless hours reading and re-reading drafts of this book and for her support throughout my commitment to deliver this book. Ultimately, however, responsibility for errors and omissions must remain solely mine.

JEFFREY GOH
December 1996

TABLE OF CASES

Court of Justice Decisions

United Kingdom

United States

TABLE OF LEGISLATION

TABLE OF ABBREVIATIONS

AEA	Association of European Airlines
AOC	Air Operator's Certificate
AOM	Air Outre-Mer
BA	British Airways
BMA	British Midland Airways
CAA	Civil Aviation Authority (UK)
CCP	Common Commercial Policy
CDC-P	Caisse des Dépots et de Consignations-Participations
CDG	Charles de Gaulle
CFI	Court of First Instance
CMLR	Common Market Law Reports
CRS	Computer Reservation System
EC	European Community
ECAC	European Civil Aviation Conference
ECJ	European Court of Justice
ECLR	European Competition Law Review
ECR	European Court Reports
ECSC	European Coal and Steel Community
EEA	European Economic Area
EFTA	European Free Trade Area
EURATOM	European Atomic Energy Community
GATS	General Agreement on Trade in Services
GATT	General Agreement on Trade and Tariffs
GDP	Gross Domestic Product
GVA	Gross Value Added
HDR	High Density Rule
IASTA	International Air Services Transit Agreement
IATA	International Air Transport Association
IATAg	International Air Transport Agreement
ICAO	International Civil Aviation Organization
KLM	KLM-Royal Dutch Airlines
MEIP	Market Economy Investor Principle
MMC	Monopolies and Mergers Commission (UK)
MTF	Mergers Task Force
NUTS	Nomenclature of Statistical Territorial Units
OA	Olympic Airways

PIA	Pakistan International Airways
PPS	Purchasing Power Standards
PSO	Public Service Obligation
SAS	Scandinavian Airlines System
TAP	TAP Air Portugal
TAT	TAT-European Airlines
UTA	Union des Transports Aériens
VLAAMSE	Vlaamse Luchttransportmaatschappij

Part I

INTRODUCTION

Chapter 1

AN OVERVIEW

Air transportation, whether international, European or domestic, is a rapidly   1.1
growing industry. The quality of service and the level of fares have been driven to
such fierce and intense competition on so many routes that pioneers of aviation at
the beginning of the twentieth century would not have anticipated. The thinking
behind the provision of air transport[1] services has changed over the decades. More
emphasis is now placed on competitive solutions rather than bureaucratically pre-
scribed solutions. Airlines with different philosophy, strategies and range of products are emerging, and will continue to do so. The shift in the make-up and the
structural balance of air transport industry has been very considerable. If these are
anything to go by, then air transport in the twenty-first century will have many
more exciting developments in store. This state of affairs, however, would not have
been achieved without a framework which encouraged competition and innovation. Air transportation, as a matter of tradition, has existed under a highly protectionist approach where cartels or monopolies were the norm, and competition the
exception. Various justifications exist for the protectionist philosophy spanning
from the need to control and preserve air space sovereignty, to the protection of
the national flag-carrier and the protection of international trade and economy. As
we shall see in due course, the European air transport sector has not been left
sacrosanct, but has instead been exposed incrementally to competition, under what
is known as the liberalisation policy.

The study and understanding of the air transport industry, quite apart from   1.2
being interesting in its own right, is increasingly becoming necessary as air travel
becomes an important mode of access and means of communication, whether for
business or leisure. The complexities and intricacies of air transport operations
remain a persistent mystery to many, and although this book does not attempt to
unravel them all, it seeks to provide an understanding of the laws and policies
which govern competition in the European industry.

1. The international context

International Civil Aviation Organization

Before plunging into the details of European law for air transport competition, the   1.3
emergence of the industry must be put in perspective. This requires a cursory

---

[1] "Air transport" and "civil aviation" will be used interchangeably in the book

discussion of the regulatory framework for international air transport which was laid down at the International Civil Aviation Conference in 1944[2], in order to gain a better appreciation of the existing European legal framework for air transport and the issues confronting it; European air transport, whether comprising of individual Member States or the European Community *en bloc*, has been, and still is, a part of the international system of civil aviation.

Although the first machine-driven flight took place at the start of the twentieth century, it was not until the conclusion of the Second World War that civil air transport, as an industry, grew with any degree of significance. Much of this was attributed to the aircraft used for the War which were then left idle; pilots too abound, whose training and experience in flying were employed for civil air transport services. This growth, however, was not accompanied by any systematic regulation to ensure fairness nor safety in the air. The latter in particular prompted international concern and there were calls for concerted efforts to establish an orderly way of flying, a matter which individual governments were not likely to have the ability to solve. At the instigation of the UK, a meeting was convened in Chicago to address the concerns among the countries which were major players in the air transport game. This meeting eventually led to the enactment of the Convention on International Civil Aviation 1944[3].

1.4   An insight into the purpose of the Convention is best obtained from its Preamble, which states:

> "WHEREAS the future development of international civil aviation can greatly help to create and preserve friendship and understanding among the nations and peoples of the world, yet its abuse can become a threat to the general security; and
> WHEREAS it is desirable to avoid friction and to promote that co-operation between nations and peoples upon which the peace of the world depends;
> THEREFORE, the undersigned governments having agreed on certain principles and arrangements in order that international civil aviation may be developed in a safe and orderly manner and that international air transport services may be established on the basis of equality of opportunity and operated soundly and economically;
> Have accordingly concluded this Convention to that end."

1.5   The Convention is comprised of two major sections in which the first lays down general legal principles relating to international civil aviation, while the second provides for the establishment of the International Civil Aviation Organization (ICAO), whose permanent seat is in Montreal. The cardinal principle of the Convention (ICAO Convention), indeed of international civil aviation, is stated in Article 1:

> "The contracting States recognise that every State has complete and exclusive sovereignty over the airspace above its territory."

---

[2] An excellent and leading account of the law relating to international air transport can be found in B. Cheng, *The Law of International Air Transport* (1970). For a more historical introduction to air transport, however, see R.E.G. Davies, *A History of the World's Airlines* (1964).
[3] (1944) 15 U.N.T.S. 295. The Convention has 16 Annexes.

This principle is further developed in a later provision which states that:

"No scheduled international air service may be operated over or into the territory of a contracting State, except with the special permission or other authorisation of that State, and in accordance with the terms of such permission or authorisation."[4]

Articles 1 and 6 have been largely responsible for the mass of bilateral agreements which have emerged since then. These bilateral agreements represent the "special permission or other authorisation" which is a pre-requisite under the Convention for airlines of contracting States to operate international scheduled air services into the territory of another contracting State.   **1.6**

Such a permission or authorisation is often granted on the basis of a number of conditions including detailed provisions relating to routes, capacity, tariffs and the manner of their determination, and the designation of airlines by the countries to the agreement. Since Articles 1 and 6, and the practice subsequently adopted by the contracting States, provided a very fertile ground to extract concessions and to secure maximum advantage, the consequence was a highly protectionist approach where routes, capacity and tariffs were regulated by detailed rules contained in those agreements.

An exception to the requirement of such a specific permission or authorisation, however, applies in relation to *non-scheduled* services, and this is recognised by Article 5 of the Convention:

"Each contracting State agrees that all aircraft of the other contracting States, being aircraft not engaged in scheduled international air services shall have the right, subject to the observance of the terms of the Convention, to make flights into or in transit non-stop across its territory and to make stops for non-traffic purposes without the necessity of obtaining prior permission, and subject to the right of the State flown over to require landing . . . Such aircraft, if engaged in the carriage of passengers, cargo, or mail for remuneration or hire on other than scheduled international air services, shall also, subject to the [rules of cabotage], have the privilege of taking on or discharging passengers, cargo, or mail, subject to the right of any State where such embarkation or discharge takes place to impose such regulations, conditions or limitations as it may consider desirable."

Different rights are therefore conferred on non-scheduled international air services such as chartered services or privately operated flights. These services are granted a general exemption from the effect of the provisions in Articles 1 and 6, subject always to the right of the contracting State to impose restrictions on that privilege.[5]   **1.7**

Part II of the Convention creates the ICAO and sets out the provisions dealing with its functions. Article 44 of the Convention charges it:

---

[4] Art. 6.
[5] The rules of cabotage are contained in Article 7. Essentially, cabotage relates to the right to provide domestic air services within the territory of another contracting State.

- to develop the principles and techniques of international air navigation;
- to foster the planning and development of international air transport;
- to ensure the safe and orderly growth of international civil aviation throughout the world;
- to promote the arts of aircraft design and operation for peaceful purposes;
- to promote the development of airways, airports, and air navigation facilities for international civil aviation;
- to promote safe, regular, efficient and economical air transport to meet the needs of the people;
- to encourage the avoidance of economic waste caused by unreasonable competition;
- to promote respect of the rights of contracting States including a fair opportunity to operate international airlines and the avoidance of discrimination between contracting States;
- to promote generally the development of all aspects of international civil aviation.

1.8   Since 1947, the ICAO has been a specialised agency of the United Nations. It is also a parent organisation comprising of the ICAO Assembly, the ICAO Council, and other subsidiary bodies. While the role of the subsidiary bodies is by no means unimportant, it is the ICAO Council as the governing body which carries out important functions of the Organization.[6] It is entrusted with a tripartite function of enacting legislation, adjudicating disputes and administering the regulation of international civil aviation. In this latter regard, the ICAO is responsible for monitoring the implementation of ICAO regulations and directives as well as supervising the compliance of international air service agreements with the Convention. In its legislative capacity, the ICAO Council legislates primarily on technical matters of civil aviation such as navigation, safety, environmental protection and aircraft worthiness, and the emphasis on such matters is well reflected in the technical advancement of civil aviation. Legislating or regulating economic matters is not, and has never been, an easy task at the international level; civil aviation is no exception because whatever the degree of competition adopted as acceptable to guarantee regular and efficient air services, it will not always suffice as a guarantee to the needs of any one country or airline. Although one of its objectives is to "promote . . . efficient and economical" air transport services (which at any rate would not be readily translated into commercial rights such as route, capacity and tariffs), the ICAO itself lacks a strong political disposition such that to legislate on economic matters relating to civil aviation would destroy its *raison d'être* as an institution designed primarily to co-ordinate technical and operational standards in civil aviation. That was the original basis of the

---

[6] These subsidiary bodies, some of which were created by the Convention itself, include the Air Navigation Committee, Air Transport Committee, Committee on Joint Support of Air Navigation Services, Finance Committee, Legal Committee, Personnel Committee and Committee for Unlawful Interference.

Conference; that was the basis of ICAO's existence. The extent to which the participants at the Chicago Conference failed to conclude a multilateral agreement on economic matters, which instead have to be negotiated on a bilateral basis, is also a strong rationale for the avoidance of economic legislation.

Freedoms of the air

Despite this failure, it is still noteworthy that the countries which attended the   1.9
Conference concluded two supplementary agreements which went some way towards bringing about a multilateral agreement on the commercial rights of international civil aviation: the International Air Services Transit Agreement (IASTA)[7] and the International Air Transport Agreement (IATAg).[8] A few observations are in order here. The IASTA is primarily concerned with non-commercial traffic consisting of first, the privilege to fly across the territory of a contracting State without landing, and secondly, the privilege to land for non-traffic purposes such as, for instance, refuelling and repairs. These privileges constitute the first two of what are now commonly known as the "freedoms of the air". The IATAg, on the other hand, deals with the carriage of traffic between the State of registration of the aircraft and another contracting State. This agreement embodies a number of commercial traffic rights or the five freedoms of the air:

(1)   the privilege to fly across the territory of a contracting State;
(2)   the privilege to land for non-traffic purposes;
(3)   the privilege to put down passengers, mail and cargo taken on in the territory of the State whose nationality the aircraft possesses;
(4)   the privilege to take on passengers, mail and cargo destined for the territory of the State whose nationality the aircraft possesses;
(5)   the privilege to take on passengers, mail and cargo destined for the territory of any other contracting State and the privilege to put down passengers, mail and cargo from any such territory.

These rights or privileges are clearly more extensive than those embraced by the   1.10
IASTA and they have a much more obvious bearing on the commercial aspects of international air transport services. The agreement also required its signatories to renounce "all obligations and understandings between them which are inconsistent with its terms, and undertake not to enter into any such obligations and understandings".[9] It is therefore not surprising that, at the conclusion of the agreement, no more than a handful of signatories to the ICAO Convention were also signatories to the IATAg.[10] The lack of interest for multilateralism in the commercial rights of international civil aviation explains the great number of bilateral agreements that exists today, which in most cases would incorporate the provisions of the IATAg. Many nations have persistently felt the need to maintain

---

[7] (1944) 84 U.N.T.S. 389.
[8] (1944) 171 U.N.T.S. 387.
[9] Art. II, s.1.
[10] In 1996, there were 11 States who were signatories to the IATAg, as compared to 111 States in respect of the IASTA. (Source: ICAO).

control over the economic regulation of civil aviation, and no less in domestic civil aviation. This is symbolised by the reluctance to grant the fifth freedom rights which involve the transportation of passengers, mail and cargo between two points not from or to the territory of the State whose nationality the carrier possesses: for example, London–Brussels–Athens.[11]

1.11   The growing importance of international air transport has, however, demanded greater efforts in the co-ordination of international air transport regulation. The ICAO "has undertaken an expanding role as a forum for multilateral discussion of attendant problems and as a source of guidance to States".[12] It is actively engaged, for instance, in developing guidance that may be widely acceptable for the avoidance or resolution of disputes on competition in international air transport services. The progress towards greater globalisation of civil aviation has also seen the gradual emergence of what is called the sixth and seventh freedoms of the air. A sixth freedom, although loosely defined, is a species of the anterior fifth freedom right which permits a carrier to carry traffic between two different countries with a stop in the State in which it is registered, but without express permission under *one agreement*. For instance, a UK air carrier carrying traffic between Canada and Germany, with a stop in the United Kingdom, will be relying on *two agreements* authorising carriage between Canada–United Kingdom and United Kingdom-Germany respectively. The seventh freedom is a highly radical and no doubt controversial privilege which permits the operation of stand-alone services between the originating point and destination without any stop in the territory of the State in which the aircraft is registered. This privilege has been recognised in the most recent draft Bermuda Agreement between the United Kingdom and the USA enabling UK airlines to fly between certain points in the European Community other than the United Kingdom, for example Ireland, Luxembourg, the Netherlands, and the USA.[13] Permission of the relevant Member State, however, must be obtained, without which these seventh freedom rights will be worthless. Under the third liberalisation package, as we shall see, this difficulty will be avoided since the creation of a Single European Air Transport Market coupled with the right of establishment under the Treaty of Rome embodies the seventh freedom as an inherent characteristic. The Spanish carrier, Viva Air, was one of the first air carriers to exercise this right on the Paris–Lisbon route. These seventh freedom rights, however, are not likely to be adopted on a major scale in the context of international civil aviation. Similarly, there is a supreme reluctance to grant eighth freedom rights or cabotage rights which would involve the

---

[11] Existing agreements suggest that the fifth freedom rights can be divided into three different categories: (i) *anterior fifth freedom traffic: e.g.* Canada–UK–Germany, carrying Canadian and UK traffic; (ii) *intermediate fifth freedom traffic: e.g.* UK–Belgium–Germany, with an intermediate stop to pick up Belgian traffic; (iii) *posterior fifth freedom traffic* (also known as "beyond rights"): UK–Germany–Russia, under a UK–Russia agreement with Germany's permission to carry German traffic.

[12] ICAO, *Memorandum on ICAO*, 14th edn. (1990), p.32.

[13] See the Air Service Agreement between the UK and USA, 1993 (yet to be officially published). Also included are points from Belgium, France and Germany. Thanks to Edmund Cullen, Department of Transport for providing a draft copy of the Agreement.

transportation of passengers, mail and cargo within the territory of another State: for example, London–Tokyo–Osaka.[14]

Disputes

From time to time, disputes will arise over the interpretation and application of   1.12
the Convention. On a complaint from an aggrieved party, whether a contracting
State or an airline, the ICAO Council may exercise its jurisdiction to determine
the dispute, provided a number of conditions have been met:

- there is a disagreement between the parties concerned;
- the disagreement relates to the interpretation or application of the Convention or its Annexes;
- the disagreement cannot be settled by negotiation;
- the parties have *locus standi*, that is, parties "concerned in the agreement".[15]

The requirement that the dispute must first be resolved by negotiation reflects   1.13
the need to avoid protracted formal proceedings. Parties to a dispute recognise
the disincentives of referring the dispute to the ICAO Council, since in practice
these disputes are often the "by-product of temporary political frictions between
the parties".[16] The resort to diplomatic negotiations, rather than formal adjudi-
cation, is indicative of a system predicated by a greater degree of informalism than
would otherwise be the case if the ICAO had a stronger political appeal.

International Air Transport Association

The International Air Transport Association (IATA) is a non-governmental   1.14
organisation established in 1919 as the International Air *Traffic* Association, the
year when the first recorded international scheduled air service was operated. The
modern IATA today is a by-product of the international system of civil aviation
which grew out of the 1944 Chicago Convention. The aims of the Association are
many-fold:

- to promote safe, regular, and economical air transport for the benefit of the peoples of the world;
- to foster air commerce, including the study and solving of related problems;
- to provide a forum for discussion and consultation on the problems of the air transport industry, including the provision of centralised services and research;
- to co-operate with the ICAO and other organisations;

---

[14] For an exhaustive treatment of these freedoms, see J. Fox, *The Regulation of International Commercial Aviation: The International Regulatory Structure* (1994).
[15] See Art. 84. The Council may also inquire into a complaint by a contracting State on an action by another contracting State under the IATAg which is causing injustice or hardship to it: see Art. IV, ss.2–3.
[16] T. Buergenthal, *Law-Making in the International Civil Aviation Organization* (1969), p.195.

- to represent an association of airlines committed to air transport competition and free trade.[17]

1.15   Membership of the Association is voluntary and is automatically open to any airline engaged in international services, whose government is also eligible for membership of the ICAO. The governing body of IATA is the Executive Committee, in addition to which there are various standing committees responsible to the Executive Committee such as the Technical Committee; Financial Committee; Traffic Committee. The functions of IATA are organised into three categories, within which a large variety of activities are carried out. Primarily, these functions are:

- *core functions:* government and industry affairs; industry monetary affairs; management of information; technical services; legal services.
- *industry co-ordination activities:* tariff co-ordination; scheduling services; agency administration; fraud prevention.
- *self-financing services:* agency training; revenue accounting training; currency clearance service; market and economic analysis; seminars and symposia.

1.16   The emphasis of IATA's work is now on the setting and co-ordination of tariffs, a task which otherwise would have to be devolved to the often protracted bilateral negotiations. No doubt its other efforts are equally important in their own right. It simplifies the travelling experience by facilitating through-ticketing, even between different airlines, so that air travel reservations can be made through one telephone call and paid in one currency.

1.17   Given the nature and functions of IATA, there appears at first sight to be an incompatibility between IATA and the competition rules of the Treaty of Rome, namely Article 85. It may be incompatible because the agreements concluded under the auspices of the Association may affect trade between Member States and have as their object or effect the prevention, restriction or distortion of competition within the common market, in particular those which "directly or indirectly fix purchase or selling prices". Other activities liable to fall foul of the Article may be the standardisation of products and the use of common selling agencies. On the other hand, however, the importance of IATA and the agreements concluded under its auspices may have the benefit of an Article 85(3) exemption.[18]

1.18   The role of the ICAO and of the IATA, whether independently or in collaboration, has been instrumental in moulding the regulatory framework of international civil aviation. The system which currently exists is deeply indebted to the remarkable progress which has been achieved since the Second World War. Without that, international air transport and its technical developments would have advanced without being accompanied by a systematic framework of regulation that ensures safety, efficiency and economy; the consequences of its absence may be beyond our imagination.

---

[17] See IATA, *IATA: Aims and Objectives* (1991). For a more exhaustive treatment of the role of IATA, see J.W.S. Brancker, *IATA and What It Does* (1977).
[18] See Ch. 3 *infra.*

2. The European context

European Community

European civil aviation is largely governed by those rules applicable on an   1.19
international basis. Since every Member State of the European Community is
a signatory to the Chicago Convention, the laws relating to European air transport are essentially parallel to the international rules to reflect the place of the
Community as a part of the wider international air transport system. For instance,
the Regulations governing aircraft noise set out similar provisions to Annex 16 of
the ICAO Convention requiring Member States to comply with the programme
of phasing out older and noisier aircraft. The two major exceptions to this resem-
blance, of course, are the provisions for the economic regulation of the industry,
namely the competition provisions, which assume a much diluted significance
under the ICAO Convention, and the difference in the legal character of
European law and international law. The legal status of the European framework
for air transport is significantly different from the ICAO framework, given in
particular the obvious political disposition of the Community and, more importantly, the doctrine of supremacy of Community law over the laws of Member
States. This has been so established since 1963 when the European Court of
Justice decided in the well-known case of *Van Gend en Loos* that:

> "The purpose of the EEC Treaty – to create a Common Market, the functioning of
> which directly affects the citizens of the Community – implies that this Treaty is more
> than an agreement creating only mutual obligations between the contracting parties.
> This interpretation is confirmed by the preamble to the Treaty which, in addition to
> mentioning governments, affects individuals . . . We must conclude from this that the
> Community constitutes a new legal order of international law, for whose benefit the
> States have limited their sovereign rights, albeit within limited fields, and the subjects
> of which comprise not only the member-States but also their nationals."[19]

This view was echoed by the Court when it decided the case of *Costa* v *ENEL* in   1.20
which it stated that:

> "As opposed to other international treaties, the Treaty instituting the EEC has created
> its own order which was integrated with the national order of the member-States the
> moment the Treaty came into force; as such it is binding upon them. In fact, by
> creating a Community of unlimited duration, having its own institutions, its own
> personality and its own capacity in law, apart from having an international standing
> and more particularly, real powers resulting from a limitation of competence or a
> transfer of powers from the States to the Community, the member-States, albeit within
> limited spheres, have restricted their sovereign rights and created a body of law
> applicable both to their nationals and to themselves . . . It follows from all these

---

[19] Case 26/62, *N.V. Algemene Transport En Expedite Onderneming Van Gend En Loos* v *Nederlandse
Tariefcommissie* [1963] ECR 1, at 12, CMLR 105 at 129.

observations that the rights created by the Treaty, by virtue of their specific original nature, cannot be judicially contradicted by an internal law, whatever it might be, without losing their Community character and without undermining the legal basis of the Community."[20]

1.21   Therefore, the binding nature of Community law over domestic legal provisions transcends the customary nature of international law and the ICAO Convention, and places the system of European air transport on a significantly different plateau. The central principle of exclusive sovereignty over airspace in international civil aviation, as recognised by Article 1 of the ICAO Convention, would pale into insignificance if the doctrine of supremacy of Community law was to be taken to its logical conclusion.

1.22   Without pre-empting more detailed discussion in subsequent chapters, a number of interesting features in the relationship between air transport and the Community ought to be outlined here. In general terms, the relevant provisions of the Treaty of Rome envisage an efficient system of transportation where barriers to competition would be as low as could be achieved. Competition is seen as the *locus* of greater user choice and industrial progress. The benefits accruing from competition will also be enjoyed by other sectors dependent on transportation such as manufacturers of goods and business passengers. Given, however, that the Treaty itself provided very little policy information to pursue those objectives, it became necessary to establish a common transport policy that would be designed primarily to remove the ills of anti-competitive practices and to inject more competitive values into the transport industry as a whole. Air transport would therefore be a part of this common policy. A Memorandum was subsequently issued by the Commission in 1979 to mark the first steps towards a unified system of air transport within the Community. These issues are developed further in the following chapter.

European Civil Aviation Conference

1.23   Non-governmental organisations have contributed extensively to the process of policy formulation. For example, and in particular, the European Civil Aviation Conference (ECAC) has contributed significantly to the birth of the much-needed Common Air Transport Policy as we shall see in due course. The ECAC was created in 1956 as a regional body to represent the interests of the European air transport industry; it works in close liaison with the ICAO. Indeed, it owes its origins to the efforts of the ICAO in setting up the Co-Ordination Conference on European Air Transport in 1954, requested by the Council of Europe. Frequent meetings are held for the director-generals responsible for the civil aviation of their respective countries to consider recommendations and resolutions, which are usually implemented by the member countries given the collective nature of decision-making between the director-generals.

---

[20] Case 6/64, [1964] ECR 585, at 593, [1964] CMLR 425 at 455–456. See subsequent cases which furthered this doctrine: Case 11/70, *Internationale Handelsgesellschaft* v *Einfuhr und Vorratsstelle für Getreide und Futtermittel* [1970] ECR 1125, [1972] CMLR 255.

Association of European Airlines

The Association of European Airlines (AEA) is a representative body, without   1.24
regulatory powers, for airlines in Europe including those outside the Community.
It is primarily concerned with the economic aspects of air transport such as
matters relating to costs and efficiency, although it concerns itself with technical
matters as well. In any case, the relationship between the economics of operations
and technology often cannot be satisfactorily separated. The main objectives of
the AEA are as follows:

- to serve and to represent the common interests and welfare of its members;

- to promote co-operation amongst its members for the benefit of the
  Association as a whole.

The origin of the Association dates back to 1952 when the leaders of Air   1.25
France, KLM, Sabena and Swissair convened to initiate a study into the economic difficulties encountered by European airlines. The report of this study was
largely responsible for the subsequent setting up of a permanent body in 1954,
the Air Research Bureau. By virtue of its name, it was a body mainly concerned
with research into the efficiency of those airlines which were members of the
Bureau. Its European identity was crystallised when a decision was made to re-
name the Bureau as the European Air Research Bureau in 1963. It was not until
1973 that the Bureau, already with a more obvious European character, was
given its present name. By this time, of course, as was happening throughout the
world, the European air transport industry had grown considerably, and the
logical step was to expand the scope of activities undertaken by the AEA beyond
economic studies and statistical exchanges to formally include commercial,
aeropolitical and technical matters.[21]

---

[21] Under the general auspices of the AEA, several standing committees exist to support its more
specific functions: Trade Practices and Standards Committee; Public Policy Committee; Infrastructure
and Environment Committee; Social Affairs; Technical and Operations Committee.

Chapter 2

FORGING A FRAMEWORK

The purpose of this chapter is to trace the developments which culminated in the   2.1
various liberalisation measures and, in particular, the Single European Air Transport
Market. In doing so, the main policy documents will be examined in order to shed
some light on the basis for the legislative measures subsequently adopted. This background chapter will take us through the Common Transport Policy, the Common
Air Transport Policy, and a number of secondary documents. To understand the
aims and objectives for such a policy framework, however, we need first of all to look
at the relationship between air transport and the Treaties.

1. Air transport and the Treaties

The European Communities were essentially constituted under three separate   2.2
treaties: the European Coal and Steel Community Treaty (ECSC), the European
Atomic Energy Community Treaty (Euratom), and the European Economic
Community Treaty (EEC), which has now been renamed the European
Community (EC) as a result of the Treaty on European Union of 1992. Both the
ECSC and Euratom have little, if any, relevance to the air transport sector. It is
the EC Treaty, otherwise known as the Treaty of Rome, and as amended by
subsequent treaties, which provides for the regulation and development of a single
market in European air transport.

When the Treaty of Rome was concluded in 1957, the ultimate intention was   2.3
to create "an ever closer union among the peoples of Europe".[1] To achieve
this, the Community has established a common market and will progressively
approximate the economic policies of Member States so as to promote throughout the Community:

- a harmonious development of economic activities;

- a continuous and balanced expansion;

- an increase in stability;

- an accelerated raising of the standard of living;

- a closer relationship among the States belonging to it.[2]

---

[1] Preamble to the EC Treaty.
[2] Art. 2. Art. 3 sets out a non-exhaustive list of activities of the Community for the pursuit of the objectives
laid down in Art. 2, which include the adoption of "a common policy in the sphere of transport".

2.4   Entrenched in the EC Treaty are four fundamental freedoms: the free movement of goods; the free movement of persons; the free movement of services; and
the free movement of capital.[3] These foundational principles are pivotal to the
idea of an ever closer union among the peoples of Europe in that they provide
for the removal and prohibition of barriers between members of the Community.
Inherent within them, however, and more particularly in the case of free movement of persons, is the right of establishment. This right is provided for by Article
52 which requires the progressive abolition by Member States of "restrictions on
the freedom of establishment of nationals of a Member State".

2.5   Provisions relating to transport generally are contained in Title IV of Part II of
the EC Treaty. Apart from the strong accent placed on the market economy and
competition, these provisions reflect very significantly the special position of
transport within the Community. Unlike Title II on Agriculture, no provision is
made to extend the concept of a common market to the transport sector, but
instead the objectives of the Treaty are to be pursued "within the framework of
a common transport policy".[4] This special position is attributed to a number of
related factors worthy of mention here. As recognised by Article 75, the transport
sector possesses "distinctive features" which require a separate treatment to avoid
detrimental consequences to the efforts of creating a unified Europe. In particular,
the transport sector embodies public service connotations, and its high suscep-
tibility to fluctuating economic conditions is not always consonant with the public
interest. The founders of the Treaty were well aware of the wide divergence in
the underlying policies and philosophies of the respective national transport industries which magnified the difficulties of stipulating more precise provisions in the
Treaty. The solution was to leave the task of adopting a common policy and
introducing more specific measures to institutions of the Community. But that was
always going to be "a lengthy, laborious and difficult task . . . Great difficulties
are bound to be encountered . . . It is the duty of the political authorities to ensure
that solutions are sought on the Community level and in a European spirit".[5]

2.6   More importantly, air and maritime transport are excluded from Title IV of the
Treaty, underscoring the view that matters on transportation present unique and
no doubt significant challenges to the process of European integration. Article
84(2) provides that:

"The Council may, acting [by a qualified majority], decide whether, to what extent
and by what procedure appropriate provisions may be laid down for sea and
air transport."[6]

It should also be noted that Article 61 of the EC Treaty, which is part of a
chapter dealing with the freedom to provide services, expressly states that such a
freedom in relation to transport "shall be governed by provisions of the Title

---

[3] Goods: Arts. 9–11; persons: Arts. 48–51; services: Arts. 59–66; capital: Arts. 67–73.
[4] Art. 74.
[5] (1960) 5 *EC Bulletin*, pp.5–8.
[6] The original provision of Art. 84(2) required unanimity. The amendment was effected by the Single
European Act 1986: see Art. 16(5).

relating to transport". Therefore, freedom to provide transport services, including air transport, is dependent on the initiatives and measures adopted by the Council. This is a significant observation to make in the light of a land-mark decision of the Court of Justice in *European Parliament* v *EC Council*.[7]

The lack of more specific policy information on air transport is a reflection of the supreme difficulty in reconciling the central principle of air space and territorial sovereignty in international air transport and the idea of a unified, common European air transport market. The latter implies a surrender of that sovereignty which underlies the political character of air transport. Notwithstanding that the air and maritime transport sectors are subject to a special treatment, it will be seen below that certain general provisions of the EC Treaty are nevertheless applicable to both transport sectors, therefore ensuring that both are within the ambit of the competition rules of the Treaty. **2.7**

Given, however, that the general objectives laid down in Article 2 are applicable to the air transport sector, and that it falls within the scope of Article 3 of the Treaty such that it is a means to achieving the aims of Article 2, an air transport policy must be developed in the context of the wider interests of the Community, particularly those set out in the policies applicable to other sectors: industrial policy on the aeronautical sector; regional policy on regional accessibility; environmental policy on noise disturbance and fuel emission.

The creation of a Single European Air Transport Market requires Member States to eliminate any incompatibilities with the EC Treaty. This is particularly relevant in respect of incompatibilities arising from the traditional air service agreements between Member States *inter se* and between Member States and third countries. Although Article 234 preserves the rights and obligations of Member States arising from such agreements which were concluded prior to the Treaty, it places a duty upon them to eliminate agreements which are incompatible with the Treaty. In the context of air transport, particularly international air transport, the common use of the nationality clause, fares and capacity restrictions as well as restricted designation of carriers, potentially contravene the EC Treaty or Community law. Member States must amend such provisions accordingly.[8] **2.8**

2. Common transport policy

Communications of the Commission to the Council

In 1961, the Commission communicated to the Council the general lines on which a common transport policy may be based. Although the Commission recognised that there were still differences in the national transport policies, it was necessary to pursue a common transport policy in order to achieve the aims of the Treaty. It noted that several "common fundamental ideas have nevertheless **2.9**

---

[7] Case 13/83, [1985] ECR 1513, *infra.*
[8] See Ch. 15 *infra.*

crystallized, and these may be regarded as the common denominator for the future".[9] A number of specific objectives were identified for the transport sector in the Communication, alongside which the Commission laid down guiding principles to achieve those objectives, the most important being competition. The Commission argued that actions of the Community must be centred on the aim of removing the special aspects of transport or of neutralising their effects where they continue to operate against that principle.[10]

2.10   Yet another Communication was made by the Commission to the Council in 1967 in which it argued that urgent actions were needed to achieve a common transport policy for the Community.[11] Following the enlargement of the Community in the early 1970s, the Commission took several further steps in an attempt to secure a common transport policy by communicating its opinion to the Council. That Opinion, *Development of the Common Transport Policy* (1971) prioritises the measures which have to be taken over the next five years to create a more harmonised transport system within the Community. It also referred to the need of creating a transport system that guaranteed maximum efficiency while at the same time meeting the aims of integration, of having due regard to the political and social significance of these measures, and of placing the transport system sector within the context of the general Community economy.[12] In 1973, the Communication of the Commission to the Council on *Development of the Common Transport Policy*[13] noted further that the geographic and economic changes have given a new impetus in that direction for which no striking progress has been made in the few years immediately preceding the Communication. The Commission stated that:

> "The practice of adopting at intervals partial and limited measures extracted from the Commission's proposals slows its development. The Community needs, on the contrary, to work out an overall approach enabling it to respond, in the medium and long terms, to the requirements of a society and an economy which are in the midst of profound change."[14]

2.11   More notably, the Commission was concerned with the ways in which developments in the transport sector were becoming more "compartmentalised" as a result of actions taken at the national level. Some of these actions were responsible for the failure to eliminate trade impediments successfully, plunging efforts towards a common transport policy and economic integration into an impasse. Furthermore, there would be repercussions on the free movement of transport services contrary to the provisions of the Treaty. To circumvent these difficulties, the Commission argued that it was necessary that "measures should

---

[9] (1961) 4 *EC Bulletin*, p.5. See further *Programme for Implementation of A Common Transport Policy* (1962), (1962) *EC Bulletin*, Supplement 7, pp.14–16.
[10] *Ibid.*, p.7.
[11] See (1967) *EC Bulletin*, Supplement 3.
[12] See (1971) *EC Bulletin*, Supplement 8.
[13] See (1973) *EC Bulletin*, Supplement 16.
[14] *Ibid.*, p.1.

be taken through the common transport policy to prevent purely national action, however justified it may be".[15]

The Commission stressed in the Communication that the credibility of a common transport policy depended on its ability to relate to the policy objectives identified in other sectors. They included the regional, social, fiscal, industrial, environmental, energy, and external relations policies, all of which have a bearing on the transport sector and *vice versa*.[16] Since transport is a means to achieving social and economic cohesion, its progress cannot ignore its "polycentric" effects, for that would propel the Community in the direction of an unbalanced development. A common transport policy, however, should not have the effect of centralising decision-making nor excessive regulation. On the contrary, the policy should entail layers of responsibility. Broader objectives will be set at Community level, establishing a policy framework within which national authorities of Member States may intervene but only in cases where it is clearly called for, such as the need for corrective measures against anti-competitive forces or for the maintenance of public services. Operational decisions, such as on investments, should be made by undertakings at the market level.[17]

In spite of the numerous Communications from the Commission to the Council since the first blueprint in 1961, little or no action was taken by the latter. Apart from anything else, this lack of action was a manifestation of the inherent difficulties in dismantling strong national transport policies that constitute significant barriers in the struggle for an integrated European transport system. It is therefore important to note that the drive towards a common European transport policy required an intervention that transcended the political arena, particularly where it was evident that the political will had either begun to decelerate or had been prematurely terminated. In the highly important case of *European Parliament v EC Council*,[18] the European Parliament initiated Article 175 proceedings against the Council for failing to introduce a common transport policy, in spite of 16 Commission proposals to that effect, and which therefore amounted to an infringement of the EC Treaty, specifically on the introduction of the freedom to provide transport services. Institutionally, this decision is significant because it clarified the *locus standi* of the European Parliament as regards the initiation of an action under Article 175. On the substantive issues, the European Court of Justice ruled that although the Council retained the discretion to adopt a common position on transport, that discretion was limited by the *requirement to establish* a common transport market and by the *time period* within which it was required to achieve that common position. The margin of discretion was only in relation to the *objectives* and the *means* of achieving a common transport policy. The real significance of this decision lies in the argument that political, technical or economic difficulties cannot constitute an excuse for inaction nor for failure to perform Treaty obligations. The decision provoked a response from the Council

2.12

---

[15] *Ibid.*, p.9.
[16] *Ibid.*, pp.11–14.
[17] *Ibid.*, pp.15–16.
[18] Case 13/83, [1985] ECR 1513.

whose statement indicated that it regarded the decision as "very important and providing an impetus for progress in the development of the common transport policy".[19]

2.13   In 1992, a number of initiatives in respect of a common transport policy were undertaken. In particular, the Commission published a White Paper entitled *Future Development of Common Transport Policy*[20] which addressed, *inter alia*, the ways in which the quality of transportation may be improved, including its role in developing regional accessibility, since an important aim of the common transport policy must be to promote economic and social cohesion within the Community. Also highlighted was the growing problem of infrastructural constraint that must be overcome if a more efficient market structure for transport is to be realised.

A further initiative came from the Committee on Transport and Tourism of the European Parliament, which set a date for the completion of the liberalisation and harmonisation processes and which noted the importance of including within transport costs any social and economic costs.[21]

3. Common air transport policy

2.14   The first signs of a common effort towards an integrated system of European air transport emerged in 1951 when the (then) Consultative Assembly of the Council of Europe called for co-ordination in European air transport, particularly the setting up of "a single European body which would assume the operation of air routes between Member States".[22] In other words, a single European airline. The proposal was prompted largely due to the substantial losses incurred by the airlines of Member countries which were caused by unnecessary competition. The idea was eventually rejected in favour of collaboration and co-operation between the airlines. It was widely felt that the diverse and complicated character of national interests in air transport held little prospect for achieving such an integration, a matter which aroused a further remark from the sponsor of the idea, Mr de Freitas:

> "[I]t is exasperating to encounter what appears to be nothing but selfish nationalism when one is convinced that peace and prosperity can best be served by an international authority."[23]

The idea nevertheless did become instrumental to the inter-governmental agreement between Denmark, Norway and Sweden to set up the Scandinavian Airlines System (SAS). Other efforts to collaborate included those between KLM, Sabena and Swissair.

---

[19] See (1985) 5 *EC Bulletin*, p. 8.
[20] COM(92) 494.
[21] *Horizon 2000: European Transport* [1992] OJ C176/246.
[22] Council of Europe, *Official Report of the Consultative Assembly* (1951) vol.4, p.847.
[23] *Ibid.*, p.850.

In relation to the Community specifically, the first steps towards a common air   2.15
transport policy did not surface until 1970 when the Commission adopted a draft
proposal·for a Council Decision on common action in Community air transport.
No action, however, was forthcoming from the Council although the Assembly
made several observations on the proposal which later became known as the Noe
Report. In particular, the Report pointed to the need for commonality between
Member States when concluding bilateral agreements. The fields of action included, *inter alia*, the "multi-lateralisation" of traffic rights between Member States, the
co-ordination of tariffs at Community level independently of other tariff-setting
fora, and the common negotiation of air service agreements with non-Community
countries. As might be expected, these recommendations struck a sensitive chord
on which international air transport hinged. Traffic rights carried connotations of
territorial sovereignty, while tariff setting was often a matter of great importance
to the success and profitability of a national airline, both of which were issues
charged with political overtones and were always liable to provoke a fierce
opposition from member countries that practised protectionism. The subsequent
retreat of these member countries from the idea of common action necessarily
meant the demise of the Commission proposal and the Noe Report.

First Memorandum of the Commission

While the Common Transport Policy may have set the agenda for the   2.16
formulation and adoption of a common air transport policy, the impetus for such
an action was very much due to the recognition of a need to harmonise the development of economic activities within the Community and to further the development in Community air transport services *per se*. Consequently, the first signs
towards such an end emerged in 1972 when the Commission recommended to
the Council several joint actions in the air transport sector which focused
especially on improving the air service network of the Community, on tariffs, and
on the relationship with third countries. These initial steps would involve a
Community-wide co-operation between the Member States to avoid differences
that would impede the creation of a common European air transport market.[24]

More significantly, the Commission recognised in its First Memorandum,   2.17
Contribution of the European Communities to the Development of Air Transport Services, that
there was a degree of inappropriateness in applying a common transport policy
to the air transport sector, as the inherent characteristics of air transport which
differed from other modes of transportation required specific measures.[25] This
caution was duly reflected in an introductory observation of the Commission:

"In view of the specific characteristics of the sector . . . it is necessary to reflect in
depth on the necessity and the advantages of new measures before their adoption.

---

[24] [1972] OJ C110/6.
[25] Memorandum of the Commission, *Contribution of the European Communities to the development of air
transport services* (1979) *EC Bulletin*, Supplement 5, para. 12.

21

Action is desirable only if it is possible to show the benefits which could follow from Community action." [26]

2.18   Secondly, as we have seen above, international air transport in particular is characterised by highly-charged political overtones. The fundamental principle of international air transport, as recognised in the ICAO Convention, is air space and territorial sovereignty. An air transport policy must necessarily revolve around political considerations since neither are separable without ignoring the history of air transport and distorting the underlying principles that sustain an air transport system.

In the run-up to the adoption of the first specific measures in 1987, the Commission produced three memoranda which set out its vision on the direction of air transport within the Community and beyond. The importance of these documents requires an analysis of their provisions in order to appreciate the underlying basis for subsequent developments in the sector. The First Memorandum was adopted in 1979 to stimulate a dialogue for the future of Community air transport. As a starting point, the Commission deduced four short- to medium-term objectives from the main categories of interest groups, namely users, airlines, employees and the general public.

(1)   A total network unhampered by national barriers with efficient services beneficial to the different categories of users at prices as low as possible without discrimination.

2.19   In respect of the first objective, the Commission identified a number of deficiencies which needed to be addressed. In particular, it saw the high prices as a consequence flowing from the nature of the tariff-setting system and the demand for flexibility and service level by business passengers who form the largest constituent of air transport users. Equally relevant, though, was the wide-spread adherence to the system of bilateral agreements which preserved national barriers and hence restricted innovation both in terms of price and service. Both had the effect of preventing free (or freer) flow of persons and goods while at the same time imposed costs related to such barriers, contrary to the spirit of an ever closer union among the peoples of Europe. [27]

(2)   Financial soundness for the airlines, a diminution of their costs of operation and an increase in productivity.

2.20   Although the First Memorandum acknowledged the fact that those deficiencies would prevent the proper development of Community air transport, it took the view that any measures adopted to remedy them must not prejudice the financial soundness of airlines. Detrimental consequences, whether in the form of losses or ultimately bankruptcies, would benefit neither users nor taxpayers. In addition, the Commission argued that because Community air transport existed within the wider system of international air transport, and its airlines operated in a

---

[26] *Ibid.*, para. 4.
[27] See *ibid.*, paras. 18–22.

world-wide context, it was important to ensure that they were financially able to match the competition from non-Community countries. However, it rejected the appropriateness of state aids as the way to guarantee such financial strength; State intervention must be limited to cases where it was necessary to sustain the services as a matter of social obligation. Airlines must, therefore, seek to improve productivity, and this could be achieved within a coherent framework of competition. The Commission stated that:

> "The purpose of competition through market entry and innovation in tariffs, marketing and type and network of services would be to introduce a commercial deterrent with respect to abuse of dominant positions and to incorporate a pressure towards productivity."[28]

Above all else, there must be strong controls over state aids to eliminate distortions on competition through greater transparency of the State–airline financial relationship, and the existence of a strong policy on air safety.[29]

(3) Safeguarding the interests of airline employees in the context of social progress, including free access to employment.

The basis for this objective stemmed from the freedom of movement of persons provided under the EC Treaty. To facilitate the achievement of this objective, the Commission noted in the First Memorandum that impediments in the form of differences in the issue and recognition of licences or qualifications had to be removed. While the focus on the air transport sector might well be principally on competition, it was also necessary to consider the implications that increased productivity could have on working conditions, especially those which had a bearing on air safety, and on other sectors of the Community including aircraft manufacturing.[30]   2.21

(4) Improving the conditions of life for the general public and respect for the wider interests of the Community.

Air transport is but one of many economic sectors within the Community. It was therefore essential that an air transport policy and any subsequent measures must reflect the objectives of such other sectors, whether in the protection of the environment or human life, or the development of regional accessibility.[31]   2.22

The Memorandum underlined the importance of introducing measures on an evolutionary basis. To approach the harmonisation process by way of highly controversial or rigid measures would have the likelihood of creating disruptive effects and irreparable consequences. Any measure adopted would need to reflect the political character of air transport while at the same time providing for flexibility and innovation in Community air transport.

---

[28] *Ibid.*, para. 31.
[29] See *ibid.*, paras. 23–32.
[30] See *ibid.*, paras. 33–35.
[31] See *ibid.*, para. 36.

Second Memorandum of the Commission

2.23   The First Memorandum failed to propel the Council into taking any significant actions, reflecting again the immense difficulties of achieving consensus in such a sensitive area as air transport. Nevertheless, the Commission communicated to the Council its observations in 1981 that the absence of any measure applying the competition rules of the EC Treaty to air transport was seriously obstructing its role and the realisation of Treaty objectives. In particular, it pointed to the lack of jurisdiction to ensure an effective and uniform application of those rules to the sector. Instead, it had to rely on the co-operation of the competent national authorities since Article 88 vested such a responsibility on them and limited the role of the Commission under Article 89 to that of supervising compliance with Treaty provisions. The Commission further noted that as Articles 88 and 89 were directly applicable in Member States, the lack of progress at Community level ran the risk of facilitating a disjointed body of law evolving between the Member States.[32]

2.24   A Second Memorandum was subsequently adopted by the Commission in 1984 "designed to improve the efficiency and profitability of the air transport industry as well as the quality and price of the product it offers, while at the same time maintaining the significant benefits the present system provides".[33] Although the general underlying impetus for this Second Memorandum was the economic changes which had taken place since the First Memorandum, the Commission was concerned more specifically with the question of whether the air transport industry was serving the interests of users or of the airlines in the longer term. Growing consumer criticism, financial difficulties experienced by the airlines as a result of the prevailing economic recession, and changes in the regulatory structure of the US air transport industry, all combined to place a question-mark on the realisation of the Treaty objectives.

2.25   A central theme of the Second Memorandum was the relationship between the competition policy and the aviation policy of the Community, since a competitive industry was not only the key to industrial efficiency, but also an important means for achieving an internal market within the Community. But the Commission stressed the importance of avoiding a sudden introduction of competitive values into an industry previously dominated by non-competitive practices, thereby causing disruption and risking irreversible damage. The process of shifting to a more competitive industry had to be evolutionary though that could not provide an excuse for postponing efforts to relax the existing system from the anti-competitive constraints. This view was echoed strongly by some of those who submitted responses to the First Memorandum, including the European Parliament, which advocated a gradual and judicious process[34], and the Economic and Social Committee.[35] Other respondents were the ICAO, representative bodies of users,

---

[32] See (1981) 7 *EC Bulletin*, p.15.
[33] Memorandum No.2, *Progress Towards The Development of A Community Air Transport Policy* (COM(84) 72), p.i.
[34] See [1980] OJ C219/65.
[35] See [1980] OJ C230/30.

employee organisations, and representative bodies of airlines, particularly the ECAC whose highly influential report is considered more fully below. The Commission pointed to a number of conditions which prevailed in the sector as calling for such a graduated approach, the most significant of which was the high level of governmental protection accorded to the sector. Several remarks of the Commission are relevant here:

> "Most, if not all, Member States would regard it as unthinkable that their airline should go out of business . . . [The bilateral system] also enables governments to ensure that their airlines do not suffer from the operations of competitors to a degree that they consider unacceptable . . . the ultimate protection afforded by the possibilities of correcting commercial failure by diplomatic negotiations has for long periods reduced the incentive of carriers to apply to their own operations the sort of critical approach that undertakings in a more competitive environment are driven to."[36]

Therefore, any programme of action to make the industry more competitive should concentrate on developing rules which could be operated under the existing system of Community air transport. Such rules would address the effect and content of bilateral agreements, amend the machinery for tariff fixing, and limit the anti-competitive effects of commercial agreements between airlines. The Commission believed that any exemption granted to agreements between airlines under the competition rules could only be justified if reciprocal changes in governmental procedures on bilateral agreements and tariff-fixing were effected.[37] The Commission therefore argued that there needed to be more flexibility in respect of capacity, revenue and tariff between Member States when negotiating bilateral agreements. At the undertakings level, however, exemptions were likely to be granted only to limited spheres of air transport operations: capacity sharing, revenue sharing, joint operations, and tariff consultations.[38]   2.26

- Capacity sharing agreements could only be exempted on the condition that a party was entitled to withdraw from such an agreement on giving notice since they tended to disadvantage more efficient airlines in their ability to provide innovative services.   2.27
- Revenue sharing or pooling agreements often have the effect of restricting competition. In the view of the Commission, a revenue sharing agreement that was designed simply to distribute revenue would fall foul of the competition rules. To qualify for exemption would require not only a strong case to be made out but must be compatible with one or more of the categories of exemption envisaged under the competition rules, such as the ability in return to provide unprofitable services that would benefit the user. Thus, the agreement must be "clearly related to the improvement in air transport services; it must represent the give and take of schedule compromises with the minimum anti-competitive effect".[39]

---

[36] Memorandum No.2, para. 42.
[37] *Ibid.*, para. 46.
[38] See *ibid.*, paras. 50–58.
[39] *Ibid.*, para. 54.

- Agreements relating to joint operations fall into a category that require separate treatment by virtue of the fact that their effect on competition could only be judged according to the circumstances prevailing in each case. Individual exemptions may therefore be granted where perhaps a route in question could only be operated economically by a single airline in order to pass on any benefit to the user.

- *Prima facie*, tariff consultations would restrict competition. The Commission recognised, however, that in most cases the system provided reliable and quality services to the user. In that respect, an exemption would be granted if the exercise did not restrict the effective right of an airline to take independent action on tariffs, and enabled the Member States concerned and the Commission to participate as observers.

2.28   While the virtues of competition can be extolled as a means that would facilitate the attainment of higher productivity and improved services to the user, no significant changes are likely to be seen unless the measures adopted provide at the same time adequate safeguards against practices which have dominated the air transport sector for decades: excessive government protection. Accordingly, the gradual exposure to competition must be balanced by a policy on state aids in order to ensure that the move towards competition within the industry is not distorted by reliance on government subsidies. In the Second Memorandum, the Commission set out its views on state aids in air transport and their compatibility with the relevant provisions of the Treaty.[40] First, the central principle governing state aids is the requirement of transparency such that the Commission would be able to assess the effects of any aid given. Secondly, the Commission would pay particular attention to a case of state aid that had intra-Community implications in order to prevent the difficulties of an air carrier in one Member State being transferred to and imposed on those of other Member States as a result of the aid. By implication, therefore, the Commission would not apply the rules on state aid to put Community air carriers at a competitive disadvantage with non-Community carriers who are the recipients of subsidies or preferential treatment from their State.

2.29   Overall, the Second Memorandum represented a highly important document that sought to set in motion a programme of action towards achieving a common air transport policy upon which progress had been inordinately slow. It provided an opportunity to reflect on the views of interested parties and developments in the air transport sector since the First Memorandum. Ironically, no actions were forthcoming until much later, following a series of cases brought before the European Court of Justice.

Third Memorandum of the Commission

2.30   After two memoranda, the lack of action was increasingly becoming a glaring incompatibility with the objectives of the EC Treaty. The European Court of

---

[40] See *ibid.*, paras. 61–66. See Ch. 12 *infra*.

Justice, in the meantime, had had to decide a case relating to air transport with reference only to provisions of the Treaty in the absence of specific legislative measures governing Community air transport.[41] The Commission therefore adopted a Third Memorandum indicating the need for a fresh impetus to the work of the Council in respect of air transport within the Community.[42] In particular, the Commission referred to its observation made within the White Paper on *Completing the Internal Market* that "if the Council fails to make progress towards the adoption of proposed Regulations, concerning the application of the competition rules to air transport, the Commission intends to take decisions recording existing infringements . . . according to Article 89 of the Treaty".[43]

Two specific matters were referred to in the Third Memorandum: fares and   2.31
capacity. Action was urgently required to remove restrictions that were bearing on the flexibility and freedom of action on the part of the airlines to set fares and decide on capacity. Certain necessary limitations and safeguards would continue to apply, nevertheless, in order to protect the interests of users and airlines. The Commission argued further that an arbitration procedure would also be required to settle disputes between governments on the approval of fares and capacity arrangements. Unless and until effective competition was achieved, the Commission reasoned that it would not have "sufficient grounds based on the provisions of Article 85(3) to grant group or individual exemptions in respect of certain practices normally prohibited by Article 85(1)". In other words, competition was a condition precedent to any exemptions that the Commission would be prepared to grant.

In the years since the First Memorandum of 1979, the Council had only   2.32
produced responses that lacked any real intention to take actions towards the attainment of a common air transport policy. The opinion of the Council in response to the Third Memorandum, however, cast a slightly different light on the progress, reflecting the inevitable pressure that would come to bear on the Council to act. The statement, which deserves to be cited in full:

> "(i) confirmed the need for a coherent Community air transport system based on a balanced set of instruments promoting increased competition in intra-Community air services as regards tariffs, capacity and market entry, in conformity with the competition rules of the Treaty;
> (ii) agreed in this context that such a system should be established gradually. To that end, the Council agreed on an initial period of three years, during which the Council would review developments and take decisions on further steps in order to achieve the objective of the completion of the internal market by the year 1992."[44]

In relative terms, this response signalled an important departure in the attitude   2.33
of the Council from one of neglect to one in which a common air transport policy and market was recognised as an essential component of a unified and integrated

---

[41] Case 209/84, *Ministère Public* v *Asjes* [1986] ECR 1425, also known as the *Nouvelles Frontières* Case. See Ch. 3 *infra*.
[42] Communication by the Commission to the Council, *Civil Aviation* (COM(86) 338).
[43] Com(85) 310, para. 111.
[44] (1986) 6 *EC Bulletin*, p.77.

Europe, given the dependence of other sectors central to the Community on a strong and successful European air transport industry. The die was therefore cast.

The liberalisation measures

2.34   The first measures towards a common policy on air transport were adopted in 1987. These were followed by a second set of measures in 1990, and eventually, the far-reaching set of measures in 1992. Together, these constitute the Common Air Transport Policy.

The first set of measures:

- *Council Regulation 3975/87* laying down the procedure for the application of the rules on competition to undertakings in the air transport sector;
- *Council Regulation 3976/87* on the application of Article 85(3) of the EC Treaty to certain categories of agreements and concerted practices in the air transport sector;
- *Council Directive 87/601* on fares for scheduled air services between Member States;
- *Council Decision 87/602* on the sharing of passenger capacity between air carriers on scheduled air services between Member States and on access for air carriers to scheduled air service routes between Member States.

2.35   The second set of measures:

- *Council Regulation 2342/90* on fares for scheduled air services;
- *Council Regulation 2343/90* on access for air carriers to scheduled intra-Community air service routes and on the sharing of passenger capacity between air carriers on scheduled air services between Member States;
- *Council Regulation 2344/90* amending Regulation 3976/87 on the application of Article 85(3) of the Treaty to certain categories of agreements and concerted practices in the air transport sector.

2.36   The third set of measures:

- *Council Regulation 2407/92* on licensing of air carriers;
- *Council Regulation 2408/92* on access for Community air carriers to intra-Community air routes;
- *Council Regulation 2409/92* on fares and rates for air services;
- *Council Regulation 2410/92* amending Council Regulation 3875/87 laying down the procedure for the application of the rules on competition to undertakings in the air transport sector;
- *Council Regulation 2411/92* amending Council Regulation 3976/87 on the application of Article 85(3) of the Treaty to certain categories of agreements and concerted practices in the air transport sector.

4. Studies and reports on Community air transport

This chapter, and indeed this book, would not be complete without reference to   2.37
several selected studies and reports produced by various institutions involved in
Community air transport.

Memorandum of Understanding: ECAC and USA

The Memorandum of Understanding (MoU) was signed between the ECAC and   2.38
the Government of the USA in May 1982, principally to liberate the system of
setting trans-Atlantic scheduled air fares for passengers. The significance of the
MoU was the introduction of a "fares zones" concept within which no governmental approval was necessary if the fares in question were within the respective
zones. Those which fell outside the zones would still be subject to bilateral agreements. There were separate zones for first class, business class and economy class
fares. Because the setting of fares has traditionally been the subject of bilateral
agreements between the countries concerned, the MoU represented an important
departure from that practice precisely because the airlines involved had the
freedom to set fares that they felt were justified in the marketplace, albeit within
the relevant zone. Furthermore, this flexibility enabled the airlines to avoid the
IATA machinery for setting fares.

The Compas Report

In response to the First Memorandum of the Commission, the ECAC produced a   2.39
report in 1982 on *Competition on Intra-European Air Services*, otherwise known as the
Compas Report. The Report underlined the importance of the "zones" concept
as an instrument for achieving greater competition in European air transport. The
ECAC would act as a forum for governments of member countries to agree bilaterally on the acceptable zones for fares, capacity and routes. Although much
emphasis was placed on multilateralism, there was a clear lack of consensus which
subsequently led to a bilateral approach on the zones concept. The principal
reasons identified for this failure were the marked disparity in the economic
strength between certain airlines, which could not ensure fair competition even
within the boundaries of the zones; and further, and possibly the epitome of all
of the difficulties, the supreme reluctance of Member countries to expose their
national airlines and air transport industries to active competition.

Not all concerned were in favour of the bilateral approach, however. Among   2.40
the criticisms which emanated mainly from the stronger carriers were the
inevitable complexities and distortions that went with the diversity of bilateral
agreements. Furthermore, to agree on the acceptable zones within the setting of
an institution comprised of officials from the respective national aeronautical
authorities would only immerse the process in unnecessary delay, and hence

hinder freedom of action on the part of the airlines to introduce market-justified fares, capacity or routes.

Although the Report paled into insignificance on the multilateral aspect that carried the potential for far-reaching competition, it was nevertheless useful in two ways. First, it promoted further the zonal concept, and secondly, it subsequently became the basis for the liberalisation measures on air fares and capacity in Community air transport.

Comité des Sages: Expanding Horizons

2.41   The most recent study into the competitiveness of European air transport was carried out by a Committee of "Wise Men" as requested by the Commission "to reflect on the future of aviation in Europe as an essential tool for economic and social development". Its report, *Expanding Horizons*, was published in 1994, which made a number of observations and recommendations worthy of note here.

The study undertook an analysis of the prevailing conditions for European air transport and referred to a number of measures which could be adopted to take the industry forward. The most notable observation was the finding that the air transport industry was at a crossroad. In particular, it pointed to the "heritage" of State protection for the industry and the numerous implications arising from that practice.

2.42   The study began on the premise of a unified Europe, clearly taking full account of the preamble to the EC Treaty. The Report suggested that unless greater harmonisation was achieved without much delay, the fragmented national systems were likely to result in even higher costs. This would affect not only the profitability of the airlines, but would also impede the ability of those airlines to compete effectively inside and outside the Community. The report also referred to the excessive protection given to State-owned airlines which, it argued, was often the underlying basis for the productivity gaps between airlines of the Community. The Committee found that there was an urgent need to abandon the national flag-carrier mentality to achieve greater competitiveness, and this should be done by turning to a market-oriented approach so that services, routes, capacity and tariffs could be decided on a commercial basis by the airlines; decisions based on a nationalistic approach should therefore be as marginalised as possible. While forceful, the observation must be set alongside the point that dismantling a long-standing tradition of State protection cemented to overall governmental policy is never a simple task because considerations related to the air transport industry are always complicated by social and economic issues that cannot be easily divorced from other national policies of significance.

2.43   The Committee also advocated a strong anti-trust framework if liberalisation was to lead to a healthy and competitive industry. Practices including predatory behaviour, state aids and abuse of airport slots which distort or are likely to distort competition should be prohibited, subject to exemptions which take into account the overall economic situation of the airline and the industry. Equally, interventions could only be justified in extreme cases and, one would add, on bases other than nationality. Distinction should also be drawn, for example, between consultation and cartel, especially in relation to tariffs.

One of the most pressing issues relating to harmonisation which affected the competitiveness of the industry, according to the Committee, was the problem of infrastructural support. In particular, it pointed to the lack of a unified air traffic control (ATC) system, again suggesting that the promise of a closer "union among the peoples of Europe" in the EC Treaty should be pursued seriously. The economic rationale for a unified ATC system revolves around the need to eliminate air traffic congestion to the maximum extent possible and to avoid the duplication of infrastructure costs. Airport congestion is costly to the airlines and so are high air traffic charges, estimated at around 13.5 per cent of total operating costs of an airline. Such burdens are a major obstacle to competitiveness. Prompt examination of other areas ripe for harmonisation were also urged by the Committee, in particular aircraft certification and mutual recognition of employee qualifications to conform with a central principle of the Community on free movement of workers.

The keyword to the study was *harmonisation*. It is a means by which resources   **2.44** can be allocated more effectively, and through which lower operating costs can therefore be achieved. Together, they impact considerably on the ability of the industry to become more competitive. Absent harmonisation, absent competition.

5. Conclusion

The report of the Comité des Sages has been given substantial emphasis by the   **2.45** Council and the Commission as a preparatory document for future programmes in air transport. In particular, the Commission has issued a Communication to the Council on *The Way Forward for European Civil Aviation*.[45] This Communication analyses the difficulties facing European air transport such as persistent market barriers and inadequate infrastructure, and proposes an action programme to eliminate these difficulties. The main features of the programme are to sustain the efforts for implementing the liberalisation programme and harmonising air transport standards, improving the air traffic management system, and developing new initiatives for an external relations policy in air transport. This Communication has since received the blessing of the Council[46] which took the view that it would contribute significantly to the overall competitiveness of European civil aviation.

---

[45] COM(94) 218.
[46] [1994] OJ C309/2.

Part II

THE ANTITRUST FRAMEWORK

Chapter 3

AIR TRANSPORT COMPETITION UNDER THE EC TREATY

The regulation of competition within the Community is governed principally by the provisions of Article 85 and Article 86 of the EC Treaty. Article 85 applies in essence to agreements, decisions or practices with anti-competitive effects, while Article 86 is concerned with abuses of a dominant market position. Collectively, they set out the general principles of competition law in the Community which aim to prevent the distortion of competition within the common market. They seek to foster the realisation of Treaty principles on the free movement of services, goods, persons, and capital, and to remove significant barriers to trade within the Community. Their relevance to air transport is significant given the vast number of multilateral and bilateral air transport agreements which exist, some of which may prescribe the level of fares, capacity or inter-lining conditions and thereby produce anti-competitive effects. The application of these provisions to air transport has not been without difficulties and has in fact required the intervention of the European Court of Justice to determine their proper scope *vis-à-vis* air transport, given the special position of air transport envisaged by the EC Treaty.

3.1

Article 85 and Article 86 are regarded as general rules of the Treaty and thus apply to all sectors including transport unless they have been rendered inapplicable by an express provision in the Treaty, as for example in the case of agriculture. This has been stated by the European Court of Justice in the *French Merchant Seamen's* Case in which it remarked that "far from involving a departure from these fundamental rules, therefore, the object of the rules relating to the common transport policy is to implement and complement them by means of common action. Consequently the said general rules must be applied insofar as they can achieve these objectives [of Articles 2 and 3]".[1] Accordingly, Article 85 and Article 86 apply to the air transport sector in spite of its special treatment envisaged by the EC Treaty. This special position can be upheld only in respect of the remaining provisions of the Transport Title of the Treaty. Hence, it is subject to the same principles of the general rules of the Treaty as any other sector. The European Court of Justice stated explicitly in *Ministère Public v Asjes* that:

3.2

"the rules in the Treaty on competition, in particular Articles 85 to 90, are applicable to transport. As regards air transport in particular, it should be noted that, as is clear

---

[1] Case 167/73, *Commission v French Republic* [1974] ECR 359, at 370. See also Case 45/85, *Verband der Sachversichere EV v Commission (Fire Insurance)* [1987] ECR 405.

from the actual wording of Article 84 and its position in the Treaty, that Article is intended merely to define the scope of Article 74 *et seq.* as regards different modes of transport, by distinguishing between transport by rail, road, inland waterway, covered by paragraph (1), and sea and air transport, covered by paragraph (2) . . . It follows that air transport remains, on the same basis as the other modes of transport, subject to the general rules of the Treaty, including the competition rules."[2]

3.3   This case was particularly significant because it was decided in the absence of specific measures implementing Articles 85 and 86 in respect of air transport. The position has now changed with the adoption of Council Regulation 3975/87 and Council Regulation 3976/87 in 1987.[3] These measures are examined in the following chapter. This chapter will examine the provisions of Articles 85 and 86, in particular as they apply to air transport.

1. Article 85: the prohibitions

3.4   Article 85(1) prescribes those agreements between undertakings which are prohibited as incompatible with the common market:

"all agreements between undertakings, decisions by associations of undertakings and concerted practices which may affect trade between Member States and which have as their object or effect the prevention, restriction or distortion of competition within the common market, and in particular those which –
(a) directly or indirectly fix purchase or selling prices or any other trading conditions;
(b) limit or control production, markets, technical development, or investment;
(c) share markets or sources of supply;
(d) apply dissimilar conditions to equivalent transactions with other trading parties, thereby placing them at a competitive disadvantage;
(e) make the conclusion of contracts subject to acceptance by other parties of supplementary obligations which, by their nature or according to commercial usage, have no connection with the subject of such contracts."

3.5   A number of important elements within Article 85(1) require further consideration: agreements between undertakings; decisions by associations of undertakings; concerted practices; trade between Member States; object or effect of preventing, restricting and distorting competition.

Agreements between undertakings

3.6   An undertaking is an independent entity performing some economic or commercial activity. It will often have the characteristics of a profit-driven organisation. In *Bodson*, it was held that the applicability of Article 85 does not extend to "contracts for concessions between communes acting in their capacity as public

---

[2] Cases 209–213/84, [1986] ECR 1425 at 1466.
[3] [1987] OJ L374/1 and [1987] OJ L374/9 respectively.

authorities and undertakings entrusted with the operation of a public service".[4] This would seem to exclude undertakings which are exercising powers of a public law character, rather than an action in consequence of a commercial activity, regardless of the well-stated jurisprudence of the European Court that the competition rules nevertheless apply to public undertakings.[5] The broader view has been stated by the Commission that:

> "the term 'undertaking' must be viewed in the broadest sense covering any entity engaged in economic or commercial activities such as production, distribution or the supply of services and ranging from small shops run by one individual to large industrial companies."[6]

The notion of independence of undertakings is also significant. It implies that an undertaking within a holding or group company will fall outside the scope of Article 85(1) since a subsidiary will often be deprived of the freedom of action if dictated to act in a certain manner by the parent company.[7]   **3.7**

An agreement between undertakings needs to be distinguished between a "co-operative" agreement and a "concentration". It is characteristic of the latter to bring about a permanent and lasting change to the structure of the undertakings concerned.[8] In 1995, Lufthansa and SAS submitted to the Commission a notice seeking an exemption from the competition rules of the EC Treaty in relation to their agreement to create a joint venture that would be owned jointly and equally by them. However, the joint venture would only cover the services between Germany and Scandinavia. In its assessment, the Commission noted that "the joint venture would not have the necessary resources to carry on its economic activity on a lasting basis".[9] On the contrary, it would remain fully dependent on Lufthansa and SAS, both of which would continue to provide the services in their own name and retain their commercial independence. Since the agreement was intended to coordinate the competitive behaviour of Lufthansa and SAS, the Commission concluded that the agreement amounted to a co-operative joint venture.   **3.8**

Earlier in 1990, a notice for exemption was submitted by Sabena, KLM and BA to create Sabena World Airlines (SWA).[10] Sabena would hold 60 per cent of SWA's capital, while KLM and BA would each hold 20 per cent. The principal objective of the agreement was to improve air transport services by creating a "Eurohub" at Brussels (Zaventem) airport and by developing Sabena's intercontinental network. The Commission's initial reaction was that the proposal would reduce competition between the parties particularly since there was little scope for new airlines to compete from Brussels (Zaventem). This was especially acute on   **3.9**

---

[4] Case 30/87, *Bodson* v *Pompes Funèbres des Régions Libérées SA* [1988] ECR 2479 at 2512.
[5] Case 127/73, *BRT* v *SABAM* [1974] ECR 51; Case 41/83, *Italy* v *Commission* [1985] ECR 873.
[6] *EEC Competition Rules – Guide for Small and Medium-sized Enterprises* (1983), p.17. See Commission Decision 85/206, *Aluminium Imports from Eastern Europe* [1985] OJ L92/1 in which state-controlled trade enterprises were regarded as "undertakings" for the purposes of Art. 85.
[7] Case 15/74, *Centrafarm* v *Sterling Drug* [1974] ECR 1147.
[8] See Ch. 5 *infra*.
[9] Commission Decision 96/180, Case IV/35.545, [1996] OJ L54/28.
[10] *Twentieth Report on Competition Policy* (1990), p.84.

the London–Brussels route. Moreover, the Commission observed that a number of markets operated by Sabena and KLM overlapped. The proposal was subsequently abandoned when the parties failed to find a solution that would eliminate the competition concerns of the Commission without destroying the rationale of the agreement.

Decisions of associations of undertakings

3.10   It is apparent from the findings of the Commission that decisions of associations of undertakings would seem to include rules of the associations. The most prominent association in this respect is the IATA. As has already been mentioned, IATA is the trade organisation for *inter alia* the setting of air fares multilaterally through its traffic conferences. While it may be argued that IATA is no more than a facilitative forum which does not itself have the power to set fares nor fix prices, its very existence depends on the continued participation of the airlines, without which it would lose its *raison d'être*. Since, therefore, its activities and decisions assume all the characteristics of an anti-competitive practice, they are *prima facie* a violation of Article 85. Whether the provisions of Article 85(3) will apply to exempt these is a matter on which opinions differ.[11]

Concerted practices

3.11   A concerted practice has been held by the European Court of Justice to exist if there was:

> "a form of co-ordination between undertakings which, without going so far as to amount to an agreement properly so called, knowingly substitutes a practical co-operation between them for the risk of competition."[12]

This statement is indicative of the approach of the Court in looking at the substance of the agreement or the collusion to act in a concerted manner rather than to be solely concerned with the outward form of the alleged practice. Accordingly, the wider scope given to concerted practice would include both formal and informal (*e.g.* "gentlemen's") agreements.[13]

3.12   Further, as the European Court of Justice accepted in *Suiker Unie* v *Commission* (*Sugar Cartel* case), the existence of an actual and identifiable plan to collude need not be necessary. It would be sufficient if there was a:

---

[11] See *e.g.* A.E. Salzman, "IATA, Airline Rate-Fixing and the EEC Competition Rules" [1977] *European Law Review* 409, who takes the view that: "Rather than contributing to improved production of air transport services or progress in the economic or technical field, price-fixing precludes economic rationalisation of the market and may prevent economic progress by stifling innovation . . . It is doubtful that many consumers would agree that the existing price-fixing has afforded them their fair share of the benefits . . . The present pricing system imposes restrictions which are not only dispensable, but which are impediments to the objectives listed in Article 85(3)" (at 420–421).
[12] Case 48/69, *ICI* v *Commission (Dyestuffs)* [1972] ECR 619, at 657–658, [1972] CMLR 557 at 622.
[13] See Case 41/69, *Chemiefarma* v *Commission (Quinine)* [1970] ECR 661.

"direct or indirect contact between such operators, the object or effect whereof is either to influence the conduct on the market of an actual or potential competitor or to disclose to such a competitor the course of conduct which they themselves have decided to adopt or contemplate adopting on the market."[14]

It must seem from the opinions of the Court that the constitution of a concerted   3.13
practice need not be represented by an explicit agreement, nor indeed verbal communication, to collude. So long as there was a meeting of minds, it would suffice to be prohibited as an infringement of Article 85(1). Logic would often dictate against the making of such explicit agreements since they would *per se* run the clear risk of infringing Article 85(1). As the Commission remarked in the *Soda-ash/Solvay* case:

"There are many forms and degrees of collusion and it does not require the making of a formal agreement. An infringement of Article 85 may well exist where the parties have not even spelled out an agreement in terms but each infers commitment from the other on the basis of conduct."[15]

Trade between Member States

Perhaps one of the difficult provisions of Article 85(1) is the stipulation that   3.14
agreements, decisions and practices must be such that they "affect trade between Member States". The extent to which trade between Member States may be affected does not lend itself to ready quantification. The factual existence of cross-border or *inter*-Member State agreements, decisions or concerted practices does not *per se* affect trade between Member States. By contrast, it is possible for *intra*-Member State or *extra*-Member State agreements, decisions or concerted practices to affect trade between Member States such that they would be prohibited as an infraction of Article 85(1). Indeed, the functional importance of such a stipulation lies in "the boundary between the areas respectively covered by Community law and the law of the member States". This means that:

"Community Law covers any agreement or any practice which is capable of constituting a threat to freedom of trade between Member States in a manner which might harm the attainment of the objectives of a single market between the Member States, in particular by partitioning the national markets or by affecting the structure of competition within the common market. On the other hand conduct the effects of which are confined to the territory of a single Member State is governed by the national legal order."[16]

---

[14] Cases 40–48/73, [1975] ECR 1663 at 1942. See also Commission Decision 86/398, *Polypropylene* [1986] OJ L230/1; Commission Decision 89/190, *PVC* [1989] OJ L74/1; Commission Decision 89/191, *LdPE* [1990] OJ L74/21.
[15] Commission Decision 91/297, [1991] OJ L152/1 at pp.12–13.
[16] Case 22/78, *Hugin Kassaregister AB* v *Commission* [1979] ECR 1869 at 1899.

3.15   The leading test in the context of Article 85 was laid down in the decision of the European Court of Justice in *Société Technique Minière* v *Maschinenbau Ulm GmbH*.[17] It stated that to affect trade between Member States:

> "it must be possible to foresee with a sufficient degree of probability on the basis of a set of objective factors of law and of fact that the agreement in question may have an influence, direct or indirect, actual or potential, on the pattern of trade between Member States."[18]

3.16   Where therefore the agreement affects the flow of trade that existed *ex ante* or artificially alters the structure of competition, it is likely to be deemed to have an effect on trade between Member States. Since this formulation, there has been no shortage of cases requiring the interpretation of this provision, in some of which a broad meaning has been attached to it.

A direct or indirect effect on the pattern of trade between Member States may arise if the provision of certain goods or services is subject to some territorial discrimination. In *Re Zanussi SpA Guarantee*, for instance, the Commission decided that the limiting of guarantees by Zanussi to goods purchased and used only in that Member State had the effect of discouraging the importation of Zanussi goods from other Member States since these would not have the benefit of the guarantees.[19]

3.17   The broad interpretation which has been given to the provision is most evident in the consideration of the actual or potential effects of an agreement on inter-State trade. In 1983, the European Court of Justice held in *AEG-Telefunken* v *Commission*[20] that the absence of any actual effect on inter-State trade for the time being did not preclude an infringement of Article 85(1) on the basis of some future effect that might affect the pattern of inter-State trade. In deciding this, the Court gave its express approval to the decision of the Commission in *Re Vacuum Interrupters*[21] in which the Commission held that in the absence of a joint venture agreement between the two UK manufacturers, it could reasonably be expected that independent decisions would have been taken to develop and market the equipment in other Member States. The joint venture agreement therefore affected potential competition and the future pattern of inter-State trade. The possibility of prohibiting an agreement with potential effects thus entails a much wider scope in the enforcement of Article 85(1).

3.18   A number of decisions handed down by the European Court of Justice have also indicated that an agreement restricted to trade within a particular Member State may affect inter-State trade. This significant step was taken in the case of *Vereeniging van Cementhandelaren* v *Commission* in which the Court held that a price-fixing agreement that limited the sale of cement to the Dutch market was not compatible with Article 85(1). According to the Court, an agreement:

---

[17] Case 56/65, [1966] ECR 227.
[18] *Ibid.*, at 249.
[19] Commission Decision 78/922, OJ [1978] L322/36.
[20] Case 107/82, [1983] ECR 3151.
[21] Commission Decision 77/160, [1977] OJ L48/32. See also Commission Decision 91/329, *Scottish Nuclear–Nuclear Energy Agreement* [1991] OJ L178/31.

"extending over the whole of the territory of a Member State by its very nature has the effect of reinforcing the compartmentalization of markets on a national basis, thereby holding up the economic interpenetration which the Treaty is designed to bring about and protecting domestic production."[22]

It took a similar view in *Salonia v Poidomani*[23] and *Belasco v Commission*,[24] as did the   3.19
Commission in *MELDOC*.[25]

This principle is also applicable to agreements between undertakings in the same Member State. As the Court of First Instance held in *Publishers Association v Commission (No 2)*, an agreement between undertakings in the same Member State even if only producing "anti-competitive conduct confined to the territory of a single member-State is capable of having repercussions on patterns of trade and competition in the Common Market".[26] This decision followed the approach taken by the European Court of Justice in *Pronuptia de Paris v Schillgalis* where the Court ruled that franchise agreements which had the effect of partitioning markets even if concluded between undertakings in the same Member State may affect inter-State trade on the ground that they might prevent the franchisees concerned from establishing themselves elsewhere in the Community.[27]

In much the same way, an agreement concluded for international trade beyond   3.20
the Community or an agreement concluded between undertakings of a Member State and a non-Member State, may also affect trade between Member States so as to be prohibited by Article 85(1). This was the decision of the Commission in its first application of the competition rules to maritime transport involving France, West Africa and Central Africa on cargo shipping. In its final assessment, the Commission found that the agreements between shipowners of these countries on cargo-sharing affected trade between Member States on three grounds. First, French shipowners enjoyed a significant competitive edge in world shipping trade over other shipowners in the Community owing to their privilege of access to the profitable routes. Secondly, there was a distortion of competition between French importers and exporters and others in the Community since the former had ready access to the French and African shipowners. Thirdly, the Commission reasoned that the agreements restricted trade to a particular Member State which, in their absence, could otherwise be deflected elsewhere in the Community.[28]

In addition, for an agreement to fall within the prohibition of Article 85(1), the   3.21
European Court of Justice has stated in various judgments that the agreement must affect trade between Member States to *an appreciable extent* in order to constitute an Article 85(1) infraction. The *de minimis* rule is seen as important so as to ensure that agreements which do not have repercussions with a Community dimension will not fall foul of the provision. This was first enunciated by the

[22] Case 8/72, [1972] ECR 977 at 991.
[23] Case 126/80, [1981] ECR 1563.
[24] Case 246/86, [1991] 4 CMLR 96.
[25] Commission Decision 86/596, [1986] OJ L348/50. See also Commission Decision 87/13, *Belgische Vereniging der Banken/Association Belge des Banques*, [1987] OJ L7/27.
[26] Case T-66/89, [1992] 5 CMLR 120 at 136.
[27] Case 161/84, [1986] ECR 353.
[28] Commission Decision 92/262, *French–West African Shipowners' Committees*, [1992] OJ L134/1.

Court in *Volk* v *Vervaecke*. In that case, the Court took the line that an agreement which purportedly restricted competition would nevertheless fall outside the scope of Article 85(1):

> "when it only affects the market insignificantly account being taken of the weak position held by the parties on the market in the products in question."[29]

3.22   Whether an agreement would have significant, or otherwise insignificant, effects must remain a matter of value judgement according to the facts of each individual case. It would include the consideration of factors such as the existence of other similar agreements in that market and the possibility of market penetration by competitors.[30]

Since the adoption of the third package of measures on liberalisation, all agreements, decisions and concerted practices in air transport must necessarily bear the potential of affecting trade between Member States. Except in highly limited circumstances, the concept of trade between Member States is effectively obsolete. At any rate, the international characteristic of most air transport services increases the probability of trade between Member States being affected.

Object or effect of preventing, restricting or distorting competition

3.23   Another requisite for an agreement, decision or practice to fall foul of the Article 85(1) prohibition is that its object or effect prevents, restricts or distorts competition. In a series of cases, the European Court of Justice has read into this provision a two-fold approach. In *Société Technique Minière* v *Maschinenbau Ulm GmbH*, the Court said that the first task was to determine the *object or purpose* of the agreement. In a case where the object of the agreement is neither clear nor readily extracted from the agreement, it was then necessary to determine whether it had the *effect* of preventing, restricting or distorting competition.[31] The implication of this approach therefore was that if it could be established that the object of the agreement was to prevent, restrict or distort competition, it was then not necessary to determine whether it had such an effect.[32] This may be straightforward in some cases, but not necessarily in others, since the anti-competitive object may be apparent in the agreement itself on the basis of an objective rather than subjective assessment. This was stated in *Compagnie Royale Asturienne des Mines SA and Rheinzink GmbH* v *Commission*:

> "In order to determine whether an agreement has as its object the restriction of competition, it is not necessary to inquire which of the two contracting parties took the initiative in inserting any particular clause or to verify that the parties had a

---

[29] Case 5/69, [1969] ECR 295, at 302, [1969] CMLR 273 at 282.
[30] Case 27/87, *Erauw-Jacquery Sprl* v *La Hesbignonne Société Co-Opérative* [1988] ECR 1919.
[31] Case 56/65, [1966] ECR 227 at 249.
[32] Case 45/85, *VdS* v *Commission* [1987] ECR 405. See also Case C-234/89, *Delimitis* v *Henninger Bräu* [1991] ECR I-935.

common intent at the time when the agreement was concluded. It is rather a question of examining the aims pursued by the agreement as such, in the light of the economic context in which the agreement is to be applied."[33]

If the case is such that it becomes necessary to determine the effect rather than the object of the agreement, that analysis must inevitably require a consideration of the market context in which the agreement is expected to apply and hence to affect competition in that market. As the European Court of Justice has said: 3.24

"it would be pointless to consider an agreement, decision or practice by reason of its effect if those effects were to be taken distinct from the market in which they are seen to operate, and could only be examined apart from the body of effects, whether convergent or not, surrounding their implementation. Thus in order to examine whether it is caught by Article 85(1) an agreement cannot be examined in isolation from the above context, that is, from the factual or legal circumstances causing it to prevent, restrict or distort competition."[34]

Of course, the fact that an agreement, decision or practice prevents, restricts or distorts competition does not on its own carry any legal consequences under Community law. It must also affect trade between Member States, and do so to an appreciable extent.

Lufthansa–SAS[35]

In 1995, Lufthansa and SAS submitted to the Commission a co-operation agreement to create an integrated air transport system between the two airlines. The agreement would cover their commercial, marketing and operational relationships and at the same time integrate their world-wide networks. The objectives of the agreement would be achieved by creating a joint venture for services between Germany and Scandinavia. The joint venture, however, would not enjoy any commercial autonomy. In addition, Lufthansa and SAS would conduct joint network planning, a joint pricing policy and joint budgeting. Both would operate a hub system from five airports: Copenhagen, Stockholm, Oslo, Frankfurt and Munich. There would also be reciprocal arrangements in respect of frequent-flyer credits, code-sharing, maintenance and ground-handling and data processing. A single marketing strategy would organise the marketing of services offered by both carriers.   3.25

Relevant market
Having received comments from interested third parties, the Commission made an analysis of the agreement which began with a definition of the relevant market. This consisted of scheduled passenger and goods services for each route between Germany and Scandinavia. In the case of passenger services, the Commission took   3.26

---

[33] Cases 29 and 30/83, [1984] ECR 1679 at 1703.
[34] Cases 23/67, *Brasserie de Haecht* v *Wilkin* [1967] ECR 407 at 415.
[35] Commission Decision 96/180, [1996] OJ L54/28.

the view that the travellers were primarily business travellers in which case it was appropriate to rule out the chartered air transport market for passengers since the inconvenience of charter flights would not normally be accepted by business travellers. On this fact too, indirect services were omitted from the definition. The Commission was also not convinced that other modes of transport offered a significant alternative.

Restrictions on competition

3.27   The Commission found that there were 25 routes linking Germany and Scandinavia. Of these, 12 had a traffic density with some degree of significance. Lufthansa and SAS were each operating daily frequencies on eight of these busiest routes at the time of the agreement, accounting for about 66 per cent of the total traffic between Germany and Scandinavia.

Table 1: *Routes Linking Germany and Scandinavia: Traffic Density*

Route	Passengers	Airline
Frankfurt–Copenhagen	291,266	LH/SAS
Frankfurt–Stockholm	192,361	LH/SAS
Dusseldorf–Copenhagen	150,955	LH/SAS
Munich–Copenhagen	112,344	LH/SAS
Hamburg–Copenhagen	97,470	
Frankfurt–Oslo	87,750	LH/SAS
Berlin–Copenhagen	84,360	
Dusseldorf–Stockholm	71,140	LH/SAS
Hamburg–Stockholm	65,755	
Hanover–Copenhagen	50,381	
Hamburg–Oslo	50,235	LH/SAS
Frankfurt–Gothenburg	47,658	LH/SAS

3.28   The Commission concluded that these considerations point to a substantial restriction of actual and potential competition between Lufthansa and SAS on the routes between Germany and Scandinavia. The agreement would increase their economic power and create high entry barriers for new entrants. The co-operation would also mean that the parties would have access to considerable resources, including one of the largest fleets in Europe, as well as inter-lining opportunities. In addition, the co-ordination of their frequent-flyer programmes would attract the loyalty of business passengers at the expense of other operators without the benefit of similar programmes. More importantly, the Commission noted that Lufthansa and SAS was already in control of a substantial proportion of slots at the principal German and Scandinavian airports. The nature of the services involved, including cargo transport on which the Commission was in no doubt that competition between both parties would be restricted appreciably, inevitably meant that trade between Member States would be affected. Consequently, the co-operation agreement was incompatible with Article 85(1) of the Treaty.

2. Article 85: the exemptions

Not every agreement, decision nor practice which falls to be prohibited under   3.29
Article 85(1) will be automatically declared void. Its validity will be upheld if it is
the subject of an exemption granted pursuant to Article 85(3). An agreement may
be granted an exemption on an individual basis, or it may be exempted under a
block exemption issued by the Commission. In order to qualify for an individual
exemption, an application has to be made to the Commission. However, an
agreement drawn up in a manner to comply with the requirements of a block
exemption may similarly qualify to be exempted from Article 85(1).

The pre-requisites of an exemption are four-fold, two denoted by their positive   3.30
characteristics and the remaining two by their negative characteristics.

A qualifying agreement must contribute:

- to improving the production or distribution of goods or to promoting technical or economic progress;
- while allowing consumers a fair share of the resulting benefit;

and must not:

- impose indispensable restrictions for the attainment of such objectives;
- nor afford the possibility of substantially eliminating competition in the
  relevant market.

Improving production or distribution of goods and promoting technical or economic progress

Although the production or distribution of goods may not strictly extend to the   3.31
provision of services, the interdependence of distribution of goods and the
provision of adequate transport services to facilitate their distribution often makes
it rather more difficult to restrict the application of this requirement solely to
goods. Indeed, a number of Commission decisions have pointed in that direction.
Of course, it would often be more readily acknowledged that such facilitation is
indicative of technical or economic progress. In this regard, a certain degree of
overlap will be inevitable in some cases, while in others, the applicability of one
requirement or the other is more appropriate. IATA agreements on fares, for
instance, are not only illustrative of the benefits which accrue to passengers and
the distribution of goods, but are of importance also to economic progress of the
Community as a whole, and indeed internationally. Exemption of its activities
from the competition rules of the Treaty is evident in the measures adopted, and
also from the anti-trust laws of the USA following a show-cause letter presented
to IATA by the then Civil Aeronautics Board in 1978.[36] In 1991, the Commission
exempted the IATA Passenger and Cargo Agency Programmes under Article

---

[36] CAB Order 76–6–78, 12 June 1978.

85(3) and duly declared the inapplicability of Article 85(1).[37] The Commission had earlier expressed concerns relating to certain of IATA's resolutions (Resolutions 800, 802, 808 on passenger agency and Resolutions 801, 803 on cargo agency), that they were potentially incompatible with Article 85(1). These Resolutions were subsequently replaced by Resolution 814 series and Resolution 805 series on passenger and cargo agency respectively so that a different regime applies to agents whose business is located within the Community. *Inter alia*, the Commission accepted that the resolutions enabled airlines to reduce their costs through a system of central administration. It provided airlines with opportunities of market access which would otherwise be difficult and expensive.

Consumer benefits

3.32   The positive contributions that these agreements are to make must relate to the wider benefits which are supposed to accrue. Benefits restricted only to the parties of the agreements are not likely to suffice. In *Costen and Grundig* v *Commission*, the European Court of Justice took the view that the proper approach was to "evaluate whether the benefit resulting therefrom would suffice for a consideration that the correlative limitations on the competition were indispensable".[38] Although there is a considerable measure of discretion in the interpretation of the beneficial effects of an agreement, a pragmatic application is often pursued to achieve contextual sense. Thus, for instance, "consumers" need not mean the public in general for that may be too remote, but may instead relate to less remote, albeit limited, sections of the public.[39]

Indispensable conditions

3.33   One of the negative provisions of Article 85(3) requires that the agreements do not impose indispensable conditions for the attainment of the objectives of the agreements. In *Publishers Association* v *Commission*, the Commission had held that the Net Book Agreement in the United Kingdom and Ireland which restricted competition by virtue of its resale price maintenance system was not an indispensable feature of the agreement, contrary to the argument that it was necessary to promote the importance of books as a cultural medium.[40] The decision was subsequently overturned by the European Court of Justice.[41]

It is also common to see certain impositions which are indispensable, such as for instance a condition for the exclusivity of distribution or patenting licences in order to give a degree of assurance for the investment made or to be made. In these cases, the Commission will usually be concerned to ensure that the

---

[37] Commission Decision 91/480, [1991] OJ L258/18 and Commission Decision 91/481, [1991] OJ L258/29.
[38] Cases 56 and 58/64, [1966] ECR 429, at 503, [1966] CMLR 418 at 479.
[39] On which see, for instance, Commission Decision 68/319, *Re ACE/Berliet Agreements*, [1968] OJ L201/7.
[40] Commission Decision 89/44, [1989] OJ L22/12.
[41] Case C-360/92, [1995] 5 CMLR 33.

imposition of such conditions does not outweigh the benefits envisaged by the agreement and may, in addition, grant the exemption subject to other conditions.

Substantially eliminate competition

An agreement which is deemed to substantially eliminate competition in the   3.34
products in question will not attract an exemption. The logic for this proposition
is obvious. Since competition underlies the whole basis of Article 85 and indeed
the concept of a common market without internal barriers, an economic activity
which eliminates competition beyond the acceptable threshold cannot be compatible with the aims of the EC Treaty. An agreement which, for instance, affects
competition across 80 per cent of the market would not be granted an exemption.[42]

However, the Commission may be prepared to grant an exemption if it could
be demonstrated that the agreement was designed to secure long-term benefits. In
1991, for example, the Commission adopted a measure to respond to the impact
of the Gulf War against any adverse consequences on the policies of liberalisation
and harmonisation. In particular, it stated that it was inclined to authorise
arrangements between airlines on capacity reduction, joint operations and airport
slot exchanges.[43]

Lufthansa–SAS

As a condition for exempting the co-operation agreement between Lufthansa and   3.35
SAS, the Commission had to assess whether the agreement satisfied the four
requirements.[44]

Contribution to economic progress
First of all, the Commission examined the differences in configuration between   3.36
both airlines. In the case of Lufthansa, the Commission found that its route struc-
ture·focused substantially on intra-European routes with a correspondingly weaker
extra-Community presence. On the other hand, SAS operated primarily on
national and European routes with a large number of these routes being "intra-
Scandinivian". Extra-Community routes were virtually non-existent. On the basis
of this, the Commission was satisfied that the agreement would complement the
route networks of Lufthansa and SAS and therefore would make it possible "to
improve the services rendered to consumers, particularly on intra-European routes
and especially on those to and from Scandinavia". There would be better quality
and choice of services in terms of direct and indirect flights, as well as a larger
number of potential connections.

The Commission also examined whether the agreement would lead to the
reduction of costs because it regarded this issue as important to the competitiveness of Community airlines. In accordance with the cost-cutting plan drawn up

---

[42] See Case 209/78, *Van Landewyck* v *Commission* [1980] ECR 3125.
[43] COM(91) 59.
[44] Commission Decision 96/180, [1996] OJ L54/28.

by the two airlines, the Commission accepted that the co-ordination in traffic management, marketing, ground-handling services and data exchange would not only reduce costs, but may also lead to an appreciable increase in traffic throughout the network.

Benefit to consumers

3.37   The Commission accepted the arguments that the pooling of the networks would offer air transport users a wider range of services that were geographically more extensive. It also expected that lower fares should accrue to users as a result of the reduction in costs.

Indispensable restrictions

3.38   For Lufthansa to operate independently on the Scandinavian routes, it would have to strike an agreement with a Scandinavian carrier because its fleet structure would not permit direct operations without incurring substantial increases in costs. The Commission concluded accordingly that the restrictions of competition were necessary given the nature of the market which included a large number of regional services in Scandinavia.

Elimination of competition

3.39   The Commission noted that there were already several airlines operating on certain routes between Germany and Scandinavia. It expected that the liberalisation of air transport within the Community would enable competitors to enter the markets operated by Lufthansa and SAS, although it also noted that there were some routes which continued to present problems of competition.

Conditions of exemption

3.40   It is now axiomatic that an exemption is normally accompanied by conditions which seek to eliminate any residual concerns on the anti-competitive effects of an agreement. The Commission conceded in its analysis of the Lufthansa–SAS agreement that, despite the freedom of market access promised by the liberalisation programme, there needed to be safeguards for new entrants and to lower the entry barriers. Accordingly, conditions were imposed in several areas: routes and frequencies, interlining, alliances and airport slots.

3.41   First, as regards routes, the Commission required Lufthansa and SAS to freeze their frequency levels in respect of those routes between Germany and Scandinavia on which they were previously competing and where the capacity exceeded 30,000 seats per year. These routes were Dusseldorf–Copenhagen, Dusseldorf–Stockholm, Frankfurt–Copenhagen, Frankfurt–Gothenburg, Frankfurt–Oslo, Frankfurt–Stockholm, Munich–Copenhagen and Hamburg–Stockholm. In respect of these routes, both airlines would be required to freeze the number of daily frequencies they operated on a route which a new entrant has decided to serve. According to the Commission:

"This condition is designed to prevent the airlines already present from increasing substantially their number of frequencies with a view to squeezing the new entrant from the market. This freezing of the number of frequencies shall remain in force until such time as the new entrant actually operates services on the route."

Once the new entrant commences its services, Lufthansa and SAS will be permitted to increase their number of daily frequencies on the route in question by one. In a case where the new entrant operates with more frequencies than Lufthansa and SAS, the latter will be permitted to match but not exceed that number. This condition will be effective for a period of seven years so that other airlines can "establish a lasting foothold on the routes in question".

3.42

Since the Commission had accepted that the co-ordination of Lufthansa's and SAS' frequent-flyer programmes would erect considerable barriers to market entry, it required both airlines to afford the opportunity of participating in their joint programme to any other airline which provides or wishes to provide services on the routes in question but which does not have an equivalent programme. On the issue of interlining, the Commission was concerned that several existing alliances to which Lufthansa and SAS belonged would lead to further restrictions on competition in the German–Scandinavian markets. For instance, SAS was a member of the European Quality Alliance between Swissair, Austrian Airlines and itself which aimed to co-ordinate traffic between the airlines. SAS was required to terminate its agreements to safeguard effective competition. Lufthansa, on the other hand, had existing agreements with Transwede and Finnair, which the Commission required to be terminated. However, the Commission did not require Lufthansa to terminate its co-operation agreement with Lauda Air on the ground that none of the routes operated by Lauda Air fell within the relevant market defined in the case.

Access to the markets by new competitors is conditional upon the availability of the necessary airport slots which in the case of Frankfurt, Dusseldorf, Stockholm and Oslo are extremely scarce. Consequently, the Commission required Lufthansa and SAS to surrender, in appropriate circumstances, a sufficient number of their slots at these airports to ensure that effective competition can be maintained. This surrender would come into play "where the new entrant has been unable to obtain slots by the normal allocation procedure in force at each airport". These slots can only be used to ensure continued competition on the routes between Germany and Scandinavia, and must not be allocated to a carrier which has links with either of the two airlines.

3.43

Judicial review

This decision is now the subject of an application for judicial review by the Danish Air Transport Staff Association, Luftfartsfunktionærerne.[45] The applicant had earlier submitted its observations to the Commission that the Lufthansa–SAS

3.44

---

[45] Case T-37/96, *Luftfartsfunktionærerne* v *Commission* [1996] OJ C145/11.

co-operation agreement must be subject to the condition that staff levels in the two undertakings would not be reduced by more than one per cent over a period of two years. Subsequent to the Commission's decision, the Association learnt that the agreement had been approved without the employment condition being imposed. It submits that the Commission was under an obligation, when applying Article 85(3), to take into account the objectives of the Community which, *inter alia*, include the promotion of a high level of employment. Accordingly, the Commission's decision must acknowledge that the right to work constitutes a general fundamental right.

3. Article 85: the consequence

3.45   An agreement between undertakings, or a decision of an association of undertakings, or a concerted practice which is prohibited by Article 85(1), will be considered as automatically void and therefore unlawful by virtue of Article 85(2), unless it has been duly exempted under Article 85(3).

4. Article 86: abuse of dominant position

3.46   The general prohibition in Article 86 provides that:

> "Any abuse by one or more undertakings of a dominant position within the common market or in a substantial part of it shall be prohibited as incompatible with the common market in so far as it may affect trade between Member States."

It provides further the following non-exhaustive list of circumstances which may in particular constitute a prohibited abuse:

- direct or indirect imposition of unfair purchase or selling prices or unfair trading conditions;
- limitation of production, markets or technical development to the prejudice of consumers;
- application of dissimilar conditions to equivalent transactions with other trading parties, thereby placing them at a competitive disadvantage;
- conclusion of contracts subject to acceptance by the other parties of supplementary obligations which, by their nature or according to commercial usage, have no connection with the subject of such contracts.

3.47   The application of Article 86 to the air transport sector has arisen in a number of instances, and will continue to be applied to those cases falling outside the scope of the Council Regulation 3975/87 and Council Regulation 3976/87[46]

---

[46] [1987] OJ L374/1 and [1987] OJ L374/9 respectively.

which implemented Articles 85 and 86 in respect of intra-Community air transport. Before examining the specific cases in which Article 86 has been applied to air transport, its provisions need to be considered in greater detail.

Dominant position in the relevant market or substantial part of it

The task of establishing whether an undertaking, or undertakings collectively, has a dominant position is indisputably one of the most arduous. It is complex and requires a technical and economic assessment beyond the boundaries of law. Most importantly, it needs to be considered in the context of a particular market, of which the case law of the European Court of Justice and the Commission suggests that there are two different types.[47]

3.48

Product market

The relevant product market includes the provision of both goods and services. The leading cases in determining the relevant product market are *Europemballage Corporation & Continental Can Co Inc* v *Commission* and *United Brands* v *Commission*. In *Continental Can*, the European Court of Justice emphasised that the identification of the relevant product market was important for the purpose of deciding whether a dominant position exists, and in particular for deciding the degree of substitutability of the goods or services in question. The Court stated that the Commission had to ascertain the "characteristics of the products in question by virtue of which they are particularly apt to satisfy an inelastic need and are only to a limited extent interchangeable with other products".[48] The issue of relevant product market also arose in *United Brands* v *Commission* in the context of whether bananas might be considered as having the same market as other fruits so as to allow ready interchangeability. This, according to the Court, must depend on whether a banana had:

3.49

"such special features distinguishing it from other fruits that it is only to a limited extent interchangeable with them and is only exposed to their competition in a way that is hardly perceptible."[49]

This approach was later adopted in the important case of *Ahmed Saeed*, in which the Court stated that the test to be employed for determining the relevant product market was:

3.50

"whether the scheduled flight on a particular route can be distinguished from the possible alternatives by virtue of specific characteristics as a result of which it is not

---

[47] R. Whish, *Competition Law*, 3rd edn. (1993), suggests that there might be a third perspective of the relevant market: the temporal or seasonal market (see p.259).
[48] Case 6/72, [1973] ECR 215 at 247.
[49] Case 27/76, [1978] ECR 207 at 272.

interchangeable with those alternatives and is affected only to an insignificant degree by competition from them."[50]

In that case, the Court had in mind the alternative possibilities of charter flights, rail and road transport as well as scheduled flights on other routes capable of serving as a substitute.

3.51   Undoubtedly, measuring the degree of interchangeability of products is never an easy task. Much will depend on value judgement taking into account other variables. In *United Brands* v *Commission*, for instance, the physical characteristics of a banana such as its softness and seedlessness became an important determinant of whether it might be readily substituted by other fruits. Another variable is the substitutability of the product from the demand perspective, that is to say, whether the consumer will react to price changes in that product. The European Court of Justice, for instance, upheld the finding of the Commission in *Nederlandsche Banden-Industrie Michelin* v *Commission* that the market of replacement tyres for heavy vehicles was significantly different from the market of tyres for new vehicles, given the circumstances in which they were fitted, despite the fact that the product was essentially the same.[51] Elasticity of demand for the goods or services was, therefore, important. Similarly, in *Tetra Pak Rausing SA* v *Commission*, the Court of First Instance approved the finding of the Commission that substitutability on the supply side was an equally relevant consideration since competition in the relevant market depended also on the adaptability of plant and machinery by competitors to provide an alternative product.[52]

3.52   The jurisprudence on substitutability was also reflected in the Commission's assessment of the *London European Airways* v *Sabena* case on access to a computerised reservation system. It began by stating that the definition of the relevant market refers to:

"all substitute products existing in a given geographic area in which the conditions of competition are sufficiently uniform to enable the economic power of the undertakings in question to be judged."[53]

3.53   In that particular case, the Commission came to the conclusion that the relevant product market consisted of two facets. First, the reservation system was an interface between the system operator and air transport undertakings, and secondly, it was also the interface between the system operator and travel agencies who receive reservation requests. The relevant product market must therefore be assessed according to these two market interfaces. On that basis, determining whether Sabena enjoyed a position of market dominance in the provision of computerised reservation services through its system, "Saphir", required the consideration of:

---

[50] Case 66/86, *Ahmed Saeed Flugreisen & Silver Line Reisebüro* v *Zentrale Zur Bekämpfung Unlauteren Wettbewerbs* [1989] ECR 803, at 849.
[51] Case 322/81, [1983] ECR 3461.
[52] Case T-51/89, [1990] ECR II-309.
[53] Commission Decision 88/589, [1988] OJ L317/47, para. 13.

"both the market share of the Saphir system in relation to other computerised reservation systems and that share in relation to the supply of the system to travel agencies."[54]

The concept of demand and supply substitutability was further developed by the Commission in its consideration of the dispute between *British Midland* v *Aer Lingus* on the refusal of the latter to interline with British Midland. In that case, its assessment of the relevant product market took on a contextual analysis where it stated that the particular route in question, that is London (Heathrow)–Dublin, was a market with "considerable specific demand for fast, flexible and convenient travel between the two cities which can only be met by air transport" particularly in respect of business travellers. Hence, the conclusion must be that: 3.54

"The characteristics of surface transport on this route are sufficiently different to preclude substitutability of demand by most travellers."[55]

Furthermore, the Commission argued that services utilising Heathrow airport had unique characteristics which services into other London airports might not possess. It noted that: 3.55

"Even though air travel between Dublin and other London airports than Heathrow could sometimes be substituted to travel to Heathrow, that is not so for a large number of travellers [business travellers]."[56]

Business travellers have a traditional preference for Heathrow, given its wide range of connecting services for onward travel which other London airports may not offer. At any rate, the Commission concluded that, even if the relevant product market included services to other London airports, Aer Lingus continued to possess a dominant market share.   3.56

On supply substitutability, the Commission had little difficulty in drawing the conclusion on two counts that Aer Lingus had a dominant position on the London (Heathrow)–Dublin route. First, in the relevant period the bilateral agreement between the United Kingdom and Irish Governments provided for no other airlines to operate services on that route. Secondly, the congestion at Heathrow simultaneously restricted the availability of slots and increased the opportunity costs of "slot swapping" for London (Heathrow)–Dublin services.[57]

Geographic market

The geographic market to which the product relates is also a significant prerequisite of whether the undertaking in question enjoys a dominant position. This will often turn on the width or narrowness of the market in which the goods or services are provided. Its importance has been stated by the European Court of   3.57

---

[54] *Ibid.*, para. 15.
[55] Commission Decision 92/213, [1992] OJ L96/34, para. 14.
[56] *Ibid.*
[57] *Ibid.*

Justice in *United Brands* v *Commission*, where it stated that Article 86 has to be analysed according to:

> "a clearly defined geographic area in which [the goods or services] are marketed and where the conditions are sufficiently homogeneous for the effect of the economic power of the undertaking concerned to be able to be evaluated."[58]

3.58   Thus, for instance, in *British Telecommunications*, the Commission stated the obvious that the (then) nationalised industry had a statutory monopoly for which the relevant geographic market must be the United Kingdom, rather than the Community as a whole.[59] This principle was also amplified by the European Court of Justice in *Alsatel* v *Novasam SA*.[60]

Likewise, in *London European Airways* v *Sabena*, the Commission faced little difficulty in identifying the geographic market as Belgium since reservations were made by customers residing in Belgium, and transactions were made in the Belgian currency with travel agents who operated principally in the Belgian national market.[61] A conclusion otherwise would seem conspicuously out of order with the requirement of substantiality. In *British Midland* v *Aer Lingus*, the geographic market was defined to include both the United Kingdom and Ireland given the differences in the ways in which the provision of the services depended on arrangements at the national level.[62]

Dominant position

3.59   The determination of a relevant market is no more than a pre-condition for deciding whether Article 86 has been infringed. It needs also to be established that within that relevant market or a substantial part of it, the undertaking enjoys a dominant position. Whether or not a dominant position exists is not readily quantifiable, but:

> "it relates to a position of economic strength enjoyed by an undertaking which enables it to prevent effective competition being maintained in the relevant market by affording it the power to behave to an appreciable extent independently of its competitors, customers and ultimately of its consumers."[63]

In the case of air transport, therefore, the Court of Justice explained in *Ahmed Saeed* that this economic strength must depend in large measure on "the competitive position of other carriers operating on the same route or on a route capable of serving as a substitute".[64]

---

[58] Case 2/76, [1978] ECR 207 at 270.
[59] Commission Decision 82/361, [1982] OJ L360/36.
[60] Case 247/86, [1988] ECR 5987.
[61] Commission Decision 88/589, [1988] OJ L317/47, para. 16.
[62] Commission Decision 92/213, [1992] OJ L96/34, para. 15.
[63] Case 27/76, *United Brands* v *Commission* [1978] ECR 207 at 277.
[64] Case 66/86, *Ahmed Saeed Flugreisen & Silver Line Reisebüro* v *Zentrale Zur Bekämpfung Unlauteren Wettbewerbs* [1989] ECR 803, at 850.

A useful determinant of market power is whether the undertaking in question is   3.60
a monopoly by virtue of a statutory enactment.[65] But where a statutory monopoly
does not exist, the Court and the Commission will focus on the market shares of
the undertaking. Unless it is a statutory monopoly, to have a market share of 100
per cent is highly improbable. The difficulty then is to draw the line where a
certain market share gives rise to a dominant position.

"Furthermore although the importance of the market shares may vary from one
market to another the view may legitimately be taken that very large shares are in
themselves, and save in exceptional circumstances, evidence of the existence of a
dominant position."[66]

The case law of both the Court and the Commission does not, however, place   3.61
an absolute emphasis on market share as a determinant of dominance; it recognises
the fluidity of market share. Although a large market share will create a strong presumption of dominance, it is by no means conclusive evidence of such dominance.
On the provision of computerised reservation services by Sabena, for instance the
Commission concluded that the market share held by the "Saphir" system of
between 40 per cent and 50 per cent did not automatically mean market dominance, but that it must be assessed in proportion to the number and competitive
strength of other providers. In that case, the Commission found that, in the system
operator–airline interface, all the airlines operating at Brussels used "Saphir"
which indicated the importance of having access to the system. In the system
operator–travel agents interface, the Commission found the existence of five other
systems which were used by no more than 20 agencies, contrasting markedly with
the 118 agencies which subscribed to "Saphir".[67]

Other factors indicating dominance need to be taken into account. These must   3.62
inevitably vary according to the circumstances of each case; for instance, barriers
to entry or exit in particular those imposed by government or enacted by statutory
provisions as illustrated in *Hugin* v *Commission*,[68] or opportunity costs arising from
airport congestion as was the case in *British Midland* v *Aer Lingus*. In that case too,
the Commission had regard to the bilateral restrictions between the United
Kingdom and Irish Governments, but more importantly to the share of passengers
carried by Aer Lingus (mainly Irish nationals), in the order of 75 per cent which
were also reflected in the share of ticket sales.[69] A combination of a market share
as low as 40 per cent and these factors may therefore constitute dominance for
the purposes of Article 86.[70]

An undertaking which has a dominant position in "a substantial part of the   3.63
common market" may infringe Article 86 if it abuses that position. What

---

[65] See *e.g.* Case 41/83, *Italy* v *Commission* [1985] ECR 873.
[66] Case 85/76, *Hoffman-La Roche* v *Commission* [1979] ECR 461.
[67] Commission Decision 88/589, [1988] OJ L317/47, paras. 24–26.
[68] Case 22/78, [1979] ECR 1869.
[69] Commission Decision 92/213, [1992] OJ L96/34, paras. 18–20.
[70] See *e.g.* Case 2/76, *United Brands* v *Commission* [1978] ECR 207 at 282–285; cf. Case 85/76, *Hoffman-La Roche* v *Commission* [1979] ECR 461; Case 322/81, *Nederlandsche Banden-Industrie Michelin* v *Commission* [1983] ECR 3461.

constitutes a substantial part is again not open to ready quantification. The catalogue of circumstances relevant to each individual case needs to inform the extent of the market affected. In *British Midland* v *Aer Lingus*, the Commission referred to the annual number of passengers on the London (Heathrow)–Dublin route which approximated 1.7 million, thus being one of the busiest routes in the Community. In addition, the sales turnover for the route was in the region of ECU 50 to 100 million.[71] While it may be possible to claim that dominance throughout the Community, or indeed throughout one Member State, presupposes dominance also in a substantial part of the common market,[72] it will be less so if the case was such that the dominant position related to a more localized market, say, a part of one Member State. As the European Court of Justice put it in *Suiker Unie* v *Commission*, it is relevant to consider "the pattern and volume of the production and consumption of the said product as well as the habits and economic opportunities of vendors and purchasers".[73] In short, the consideration of market share alone will not suffice to ascertain whether a dominant position exists, or does not exist, in a substantial part of the common market.

Abuse

3.64   Once it has been established that a dominant position exists within a relevant market, it then needs to be ascertained whether there has been an abuse of that position; for a dominant position *per se* is not an infraction of the EC Treaty competition rules. Article 86 sets out a non-exhaustive list of conduct which could constitute an abuse of dominant position, namely, pricing, market restrictions and unfair or irrelevant conditions. It is, however, possible to infer from the fact of dominance that market abuse exists since an undertaking with such a characteristic "has a special responsibility not to allow its conduct to impair undistorted competition on the common market".[74] The consequence of this remark has particular relevance to the air transport sector since the market is often dominated by a monopolistic or oligopolistic structure, including such ancillary areas as computer reservation systems and ground-handling.

3.65   The prohibitions set out in Article 86 were considered in turn by the Commission in the *London European Airways* v *Sabena* case. First, it examined the conduct of Sabena in refusing London European access to its "Saphir" system on the ground that the costs structure and strategy of the latter would trigger a price competition with Sabena, and held that such conduct was incompatible with the system of free competition provided under the Treaty because it "aimed to produce an artificial increase in fares". Secondly, the conduct also had the characteristics of limiting production, markets or technical development to the prejudice of consumers given that the service intended by London European between Brussels and Luton may consequently be abandoned.

---

[71] Commission Decision 92/213, [1992] OJ L96/34, para. 17.
[72] See *e.g.* Case C-41/90, *Hofner & Elser* v *Macrotron* [1991] ECR 1.
[73] Case 40/73, [1975] ECR 1663.
[74] Case 322/81, *Michelin* v *Commission* [1983] ECR 3461 at 3511.

Thirdly, the Commission concluded that Sabena had abused its dominant position in that it required London European to give the ground-handling contract to Sabena as a condition of access to "Saphir". According to the Commission, a handling contract had no relevance to a computer reservation contract, which was intended to obtain air transport services for passengers speedily and efficiently.[75]

The line of case law of both the Commission and the European Court of Justice   3.66
has demonstrated that the concept of abuse in Article 86 is capable of having, and has indeed had, a wide interpretation. In particular, it must be considered in the light of the EC Treaty as a whole, not least the provisions of Articles 2 and 3. For example, the Court rejected the argument in *Continental Can* that Article 86 could not have a bearing on changes to market structure such as mergers.[76] Further, the Court has, for instance, accepted that abuse need not exist in the market in which the undertaking has a dominant position, but may instead relate to an ancillary or neighbouring market.[77]

In *Michelin* v *Commission*, the European Court expanded the meaning of abusive conduct for the purposes of Article 86 to cover:

"practices which are likely to affect the structure of a market where, as a direct result of the presence of the undertaking in question, competition has already been weakened and which, through recourse to methods different from those governing normal competition in products or services based on traders' performance, have the effect of hindering the maintenance or development of the level of competition still existing on the market."[78]

This line of reasoning was again in consideration when the Commission was   3.67
asked to rule on the case of *British Midland* v *Aer Lingus* on interlining.[79] The Commission began with its observation that a refusal to interline was not a method of normal competition on the merits. Interlining was a practice adopted on a world-wide basis, generating acknowledged benefits to both airlines and passengers. In the eyes of the EC Treaty, interlining was a matter of duty if:

"the refusal or withdrawal of interline facilities by a dominant airline is objectively likely to have a significant impact on the other airline's ability to start a new service or sustain an existing service on account of its effects on the other airline's costs and revenue in respect of the service in question, and when the dominant airline cannot give any objective commercial reason for its refusal."

The reference to this idea of proportionality was particularly relevant in the case   3.68
since Aer Lingus continued to maintain interline facilities with BA and Dan Air, but refused to continue with BMA when it started to provide competing services.

---

[75] Commission Decision 88/589, [1988] OJ L317/47, paras. 29–31.
[76] Case 6/72, *Europemballage & Continental Can* v *Commission* [1973] ECR 215.
[77] See Case 311/84, *Centre Belge d'Etudes de Marché Télé-marketing* v *CLT* [1985] ECR 3261 and *B&I* v *Sealink – Holyhead* Twenty-Second Report on Competition Policy (1990).
[78] Case 322/81, *Michelin* v *Commission* [1983] ECR 3461 at 3514.
[79] Commission Decision 92/213, [1992] OJ L96/34.

The consequences of such an action could be severe as it would affect "the well-informed business travellers who require fully flexible tickets and who make a disproportionately large contribution to the revenue of the new entrant; significantly reducing this revenue will have a serious effect on the economics of the new entrant's operations". Aer Lingus claimed, and the Commission rejected, that interlining with BMA would not make commercial sense if the result was a loss of revenue to itself. Since it could not objectively justify its conduct on the ground of efficiency nor some other legitimate commercial reasons such as creditworthiness, the Commission concluded that the conduct "was intended and was likely to hinder the development of competition". It did not matter that at the time of the infraction, it could not be determined conclusively whether BMA "was later willing and able to remain on the route in spite of the disadvantages imposed on it".[80]

Trade between Member States

3.69   Any abuse of dominant position would only infringe Article 86 if it affects trade between Member States to an appreciable extent. An interpretation similar to Article 85(1) is adopted here. Where two or more airlines from different Member States are involved, or where a particular service involves destinations beyond a Member State, it would be difficult to avoid the conclusion that trade between Member States has not been affected. While the Commission did not refer to this issue in the *Olympic Airways* case,[81] it held in *London European Airways* v *Sabena* that the refusal of access to the "Saphir" computer reservation system affected an airline of another Member State in as much as it affected a service between two Member States.[82] A similar view was taken in *British Midland* v *Aer Lingus* which concerned interlining facilities between two airlines and a route between two Member States.[83]

5. Relationship between Article 85(3) and Article 86

3.70   A few observations need to be made on the relationship between an exemption granted under Article 85(3) and Article 86, in particular the effect of an exemption on Article 86. Unlike Article 85, where individual or block exemptions may be issued by the Commission, no provision for doing so has been made in the case of Article 86. Thus, the prohibition against an abuse of dominant position cannot be waived by the Commission. The absence of a mechanism for exemptions to be granted under Article 86 has already attracted several decisions of the Court

---

[80] *Ibid.*, paras. 25–30.
[81] Commission Decision 85/121, [1985] OJ L46/51.
[82] Commission Decision 88/589, [1988] OJ L317/47, para. 32.
[83] Commission Decision 92/213, [1992] OJ L96/34, para. 31.

of Justice, most significantly in the case of *Ahmed Saeed* which examined in detail the applicability of Articles 85 and 86 in the air transport sector.[84] Moreover, the Commission has also discounted the absence of a mechanism to grant an exemption under Article 86 as a limitation. In *British Midland* v *Aer Lingus*, for instance, the Commission alluded to the possibility of an alleged abusive conduct being subject to objective commercial justifications such as perhaps the lack of creditworthiness.[85]

Where a dominant undertaking has been deemed to have abused its position in accordance with Article 86, and has entered into an agreement or practice to which Article 85(1) is applicable, it is unlikely that the Commission will grant an individual exemption to the undertaking under Article 85(3). The basis for this observation lies in the supposition that anti-competitiveness inheres in the activities of a dominant undertaking, which position must inevitably be reinforced if it enters into an agreement further restricting competition.[86] In that respect, the agreement must fail the requirement that it will not substantially eliminate competition.   3.71

Greater difficulties, however, rest with the issue of block exemptions. The thorny question is whether a dominant undertaking deemed to have abused its market position under Article 86 may be permitted to enjoy the benefits of a block exemption. If it is so permitted, a central tenet of the EC Treaty would have been defeated; if it is not permitted, the only solution available to the Commission seems to be the termination of the block exemption at the expense of destroying the benefits enjoyed by other agreements under the block exemption. This latter solution would seem to be disproportionate to the aim of eliminating the anti-competitive effects of the abuse. That was the view taken by the Court of First Instance in *Tetra Pak Rausing SA* v *Commission*. It upheld the decision of the Commission that the acquisition by Tetra Pak of a patent licence was an abuse of its dominant position, even though the licence benefited from a block exemption: 3.72

"[I]n the scheme for the protection of competition established by the Treaty the grant of exemption, whether individual or block exemption, under Article 85(3) cannot be such as to render inapplicable the prohibition set out in Article 86 . . . If the Commission were required in every case to take a decision withdrawing exemption before applying Article 86, this would be tantamount, in view of the non-retroactive nature of the withdrawal of exemption, to accepting that an exemption under Article 85(3) operates in reality as a concurrent exemption for the prohibition of abuse of a dominant position."[87]

---

[84] Case 66/86, *Ahmed Saeed Flugreisen & Silver Line Reisebüro* v *Zentrale Zur Bekämpfung Unlauteren Wettbewerbs* [1989] ECR 803.
[85] Commission Decision 92/213, [1992] OJ L96/34. See further, Case 311/84, *Centre Belge d'Etudes de Marché Télé-marketing* v *CLT* [1985] ECR 3261 and Commission Decision 88/138, *Eurofix-Bauco* v *Hilt*, [1988] OJ L65/19.
[86] See *e.g.* Case 43/85, *ANCIDES* v *Commission* [1987] ECR 3131.
[87] Case T-51/89, [1990] ECR II-309, at 358-359.

Chapter 4

THE ANTITRUST REGULATIONS

Until 1987, competition in the air transport sector was regulated by means of the   4.1
transitional Articles 88 and 89. The limitations were many, and a number of
European Court of Justice decisions pointed to the unsatisfactory nature of applying the competition rules of Articles 85 and 86 in the absence of specific implementing measures. This difficulty was eventually resolved with the adoption of the
first of three liberalisation packages by the Council in 1987. It comprised four
legislative measures on procedures, block exemptions, fares on scheduled services,
as well as capacity sharing and route access. Prior to considering the application
of these measures, Articles 88 and 89 need to be examined, at least in so far as
they remain applicable to air transport matters which are not covered by any
implementing measure.

1. The transitional Articles

In the first place, measures on air transport fall to be dealt with under Article   4.2
84(2) of the Treaty which authorises the Council to "decide whether, and to what
extent and by what procedure". As Chapter 2 has already revealed, little was done
by the Council until 1987. This meant that the enforcement of the competition
rules of the EC Treaty had to be undertaken pursuant to Articles 88 and 89. The
decisions of the Court of Justice in the two leading cases of *Ministère Public* v *Asjes*
and *Ahmed Saeed* referred to and explicitly approved this manner of approach to
ensure that the objectives of the Treaty were not prejudiced even in the absence
of specific implementing legislation.[1] Article 88 provides:

> "Until the entry into force of the provisions adopted in pursuance of Article 87, the
> authorities in Member States, shall rule on the admissibility of agreements, decisions
> and concerted practices and on abuse of a dominant position in the common market
> in accordance with the law of their country and with the provisions of Article 85, in
> particular paragraph 3, and of Article 86."

Article 89, on the other hand provides: 4.3

---

[1] Cases 209-213/84, *Ministère Public v Asjes* [1986] ECR 1425 and Case 66/86, *Ahmed Saeed Flugreisen
& Silver Line Reisebüro v Zentrale Zur Bekämpfung Unlauteren Wettbewerbs* [1989] ECR 803.

"Without prejudice to Article 88, the Commission shall, as soon as it takes up its duties ensure the application of the principles laid down in Articles 85 and 86. On application by a Member State or on its own initiative, and in co-operation with the competent authorities in the Member States, who shall give their assistance, the Commission shall investigate cases of suspected infringement of these principles. If it finds there has been an infringement, it shall propose appropriate measures to bring it to an end."

Both, Articles 88 and 89 are known as the "transitional Articles" on the assumption that, at some point in time, specific implementing measures would be adopted to apply the provisions of Articles 85 and 86. Indeed, it is provided in Article 87 that:

"within three years of the entry into force of this Treaty, the Council shall, acting unanimously on a proposal from the Commission and after consulting the Assembly, adopt any appropriate regulations or directives to give effect to the principles set out in Articles 85 and 86."

If this has not been achieved within that period, the Council is authorised to act by a "qualified majority".

4.4   Thus, for example, Council Regulation 17/62 was adopted to apply the competition principles generally across all sectors, as qualified by subsequent measures in the form of Council Regulation 141/62 and Council Regulation 1017/68.[2] Likewise, Council Regulation 4056/86 was adopted in respect of the maritime sector.[3] In 1987, the Council adopted the first set of liberalisation measures which comprised, *inter alia*, Council Regulation 3975/87 and Council Regulation 3976/87 to implement Articles 85 and 86 in respect of air transport.[4] In spite of this, Articles 88 and 89 remain of considerable relevance. For instance, the growing use of code-sharing agreements, some of which will inevitably restrict competition, has prompted the Commission to begin an investigation into the use of such agreements. Code-sharing deals do not amount to mergers so as to bring about a lasting change in the structure of the undertakings, which would normally lose their independence. Hence, Council Regulation 4064/89 on the control of concentrations or mergers does not apply.[5] The Commission's action to investigate these agreements was a specific response to the proposed code-sharing deal between BA and American Airlines. Other code-sharing agreements which will come under its scrutiny concern trans-Atlantic services principally: Lufthansa–United Airlines; KLM–NorthWest Airlines; Austrian Airlines–Swissair–Sabena–Delta Airlines; SAS–United Airlines; and BA–USAir.[6] The power of investigation in these cases will be derived from Article 89 which empowers the Commission to "propose appropriate measures".

---

[2] [1959–1962] OJ (Sp. edn.) 204; [1959–1962] OJ (Sp. edn.) 291; [1968] OJ (Sp. edn.) 302 respectively.
[3] [1986] OJ L378/14.
[4] [1987] OJ L374/1 and [1987] OJ L374/9 respectively.
[5] [1989] OJ L395/1. See Ch. 5 *infra*.
[6] *Financial Times*, 2 July 1996.

Council Regulation 17/62

Council Regulation 17/62 was adopted in 1962 in accordance with the EC 4.5
Treaty requirement to "establish a system ensuring that competition shall not be
distorted in the common market".[7] In effect, Regulation 17/62 confers on the
Commission the necessary powers to apply the competition rules of the Treaty.
National authorities of Member States, however, remain competent in cases
where the Commission has not initiated proceedings under the Regulation or has
been requested by the Commission to investigate a suspected infringement of
Articles 85 or 86. Sole power "to declare Article 85(1) inapplicable pursuant to
Article 85(3)" has also been conferred on the Commission.[8] Regulation 17/62
remains relevant in so far as the sectors which are not classified as "air transport"
have implications for competition. "Ancillary" sectors of air transport such as for
example computer reservation systems and ground-handling services will come
within the scope of this Regulation.

Council Regulation 141/62

Council Regulation 17/62, however, was unlimited in its scope of application. 4.6
This meant that the transport sector was also subject to the competition rules
pursuant to the Regulation, notwithstanding the special treatment envisaged by
the EC Treaty. This became apparent when the Commission proposed the
adoption of a Council Regulation to amend the scope of Regulation 17/62. The
preamble to Council Regulation 141/62 expressly recognises that given "the distinctive features of the transport sector, it may prove necessary to lay down rules
governing competition different from those laid down or to be laid down for other
sectors of the economy".[9] Accordingly, the transport sector was excluded from the
scope of Regulation 17/62.

The meaning of transport in this context has been given a narrow inter- 4.7
pretation. This was evident in the decision of the Commission involving a
complaint against the ground-handling services provided by Olympic Airways at
Greek airports, for which service it enjoys a monopoly. The Association des
Compagnies Aériennes de la Communauté had complained that the decision of
Olympic Airways to increase by approximately 50 per cent the charges for
ground-handling services was an abuse of a dominant position. Central to the
investigation was the provision of adequate information by Olympic Airways to
the Commission. The refusal to supply the information was justified on the basis
that Articles 85 and 86 did not at that time apply to the air transport sector, and
hence, the powers of investigation under Council Regulation 17/62 were
inapplicable. On the first issue, the Commission adopted the line of argument
postulated by the European Court of Justice in the *French Merchant Seamen* case in
which it stated that Articles 85 and 86 were general rules of the Treaty applicable

---

[7] [1959–1962] OJ (Sp. edn.) 204, preamble.
[8] Art. 9.
[9] [1959–1962] OJ (Sp. edn.) 291.

also to the transport sector. The special position of air transport was only in respect of the Transport Title.[10] On the second and more important issue, the Commission reasoned that, contrary to Olympic Airways' view, Regulation 17/62 was applicable to ground-handling services:

> "since they do not form part of the transport market within the meaning of Council Regulation 141/62 . . . Handling services are not as such a transport service."[11]

4.8 A similar position was taken by the Commission in *London European Airways* v *Sabena* in which it held that ancillary activities to the transport sector such as the provision of services for access to computer reservation systems were not exempted under Regulation 141/62, but continued to be subject to Regulation 17/62 instead. It reasoned that:

> "The sole purpose of a reservation is to ensure that a traveller leaves when he wishes, but it can certainly be separated from the transport service proper. As in many other sectors, the selling of tickets is separate from the service attached to the ticket."[12]

Council Regulation 1017/68

4.9 As the recital of Regulation 141/62 recognised, it was possible "to envisage the introduction within a foreseeable period of rules of competition" for application to rail, road and inland waterways. On that basis, in 1968, the Commission proposed for adoption Council Regulation 1017/68 to bring rail, road and inland waterways within the ambit of Council Regulation 17/62.[13] By implication, therefore, sea and air transport continued to be excluded from that Regulation, but were nevertheless subject to the competition rules by virtue of Articles 88 and 89.[14] This exclusion has now been superseded by Council Regulation 3975/87 and Council Regulation 3976/87 as part of the common policy to liberalise Community air transport.

2. The procedural rules

4.10 Council Regulation 3975/87 sets out the procedures by which complaints of anti-competitive practices may be investigated by vesting the appropriate powers in the Commission while at the same time preserving the residual functions of competent authorities of Member States.

---

[10] Case 167/73, *Commission* v *French Republic* [1974] ECR 359.
[11] Commission Decision 85/121, [1985] OJ L46/51, para. 5.
[12] Commission Decision 88/589, [1988] OJ L317/47, para. 20.
[13] [1968] OJ (Sp. edn.) 302.
[14] See Cases 209-213/84, *Ministère Public* v *Asjes* [1986] ECR 1425 and Case 66/86, *Ahmed Saeed Flugreisen & Silver Line Reisebüro* v *Zentrale Zur Bekämpfung Unlauteren Wettbewerbs* [1989] ECR 803.

Scope

The scope of Regulation 3975/87 as originally stipulated was restricted to   4.11
"international air transport between Community airports".[15] It was applicable to
both Community airlines and non-Community airlines flying between
Community airports, but not applicable to air transport where the originating or
destination point involved a non-Community airport, nor to domestic air transport. This was the subject of an observation by the European Court of Justice in
Ahmed Saeed, stating that:

> "It must be inferred . . . that domestic air transport and air transport to and from
> airports in non-member countries continue to be subject to the transitional provision
> laid down in Articles 88 and 89."[16]

An amending Council Regulation 2410/92 was subsequently adopted in 1992
to delete the "international" scope of the Regulation, thereby expanding the scope
of Council Regulation 3975/87 to include domestic air transport within a single
Member State.[17] Air transport involving a non-Community airport continues to
be outside the scope of any specific regulatory measure.

Non-application of Article 85(1)

At the time of drafting, considerable discussion went into the issue of whether, and   4.12
to what extent, the scope of Council Regulation 3975/87 should be restricted
from application to certain technical agreements. It was therefore agreed that the
prohibition in Article 85(1) should not extend to agreements, decisions and concerted practices whose "sole object and effect is to achieve technical improvements
or co-operation".[18] Thus, for instance, an interlining agreement in air transport is
regarded as a technical or co-operation agreement. The Commission has stated
that although there was no obligation on airlines to share interline facilities, in
certain cases it was important to ensure that new or smaller airlines could establish
themselves. This condition would usually be imposed for a period of two years to
enable the competitor to develop itself on the route in question.[19] Indeed, the
Commission has intervened on numerous occasions to ensure that interlining
facilities were offered to smaller competitors. In 1990, for example, it required
Lufthansa to offer its facilities to Air Europe on the London–Munich and
London–Dusseldorf routes.[20] On the other hand, an agreement, decision or practice which also includes an object or has an effect not intended to achieve
technical improvements or co-operation is not likely to benefit from the non-
application of Article 85(1).

---

[15] Art. 1(2).
[16] Case 66/86, *Ahmed Saeed Flugreisen & Silver Line Reisebüro* v *Zentrale Zur Bekämpfung Unlauteren Wettbewerbs* [1989] ECR 803, at 845
[17] Council Regulation 2410/92, [1992] OJ L240/18.
[18] Art. 2(1).
[19] Twentieth Report on Competition Policy (1990), p.61.
[20] Twentieth Report on Competition Policy (1990). See also *British Midland* v *Aer Lingus* [1992] OJ L96/34.

4.13   A non-exhaustive list of such agreements, decisions and practices is annexed to the Regulation. They include:

- technical standards for aircraft, aircraft parts, equipment and aircraft supplies where they are set by an internationally recognised organisation (*e.g.* ICAO), or by an aircraft or equipment manufacturer;
- technical standards for fixed installations for aircraft where they are set by an internationally recognised organisation;
- a non-discriminatory exchange, leasing, pooling or maintenance of aircraft parts, equipment or fixed installations for the purpose of operating air services and joint purchase of aircraft parts;
- a non-discriminatory introduction, operation or maintenance of technical communications network;
- exchange, pooling or training of personnel for technical or operational purposes;
- organisation or execution of emergency transport in the event of breakdown or delay;
- organisation or execution of "successive or supplementary air transport operations", and the fixing of rates and conditions for such operations;
- consolidation of individual consignments;
- establishment or application of uniform rules on tariffs, provided they do not directly or indirectly fix fares or conditions;
- sale, endorsement and acceptance of tickets between air carriers including refunds;
- clearing and settling of accounts between air carriers.

4.14   The catalogue of arrangements which have been exempted from the prohibitions of Article 85(1), although so-called "technical agreements", are by no means free from commercial connotations.

Complaints and investigations

4.15   An investigation into a suspected infringement of either Article 85(1) or Article 86 may be triggered by means of a written complaint submitted by a Member State or by a natural or legal person who is able to establish a legitimate interest. Alternatively, an investigation may be initiated by the Commission itself.[21]

Where the Commission has made the finding that there has been an infringement, it does not, however, have to issue a decision requiring the infringement to be brought to an end. Article 4(1) confers on the Commission a discretion whether to do so. Instead, it may in the first instance issue a recommendation to the undertakings in question to terminate the infringement before issuing a decision. By

---

[21] Art. 3(1). See also the detailed procedures spelt out in Commission Regulation 4261/88, [1988] OJ L376/10.

contrast, it is under a duty to issue a decision rejecting the complaint if its investigation concludes that there has not been an infringement.

Likewise, in a case involving Article 85 in which the Commission has found that the agreement, decision or concerted practice in question satisfies the prohibitions in Article 85(1) and the provisions in Article 85(3), it must issue a decision applying Article 85(3). The exemption under Article 85(3) may be retrospective in effect.[22]

Expedited procedure

In 1991, on a proposal from the Commission, the Council adopted Regulation 1284/91 to confer interim enforcement powers on the Commission: **4.16**

> "to take prompt action in cases where air carriers engage in practices which are contrary to the competition rules and which may threaten the viability of services operated by a competitor or even the existence of an airline company and thus cause irreversible damage to the competitive structure."[23]

Specifically, the Regulation empowers the Commission to issue a decision temporarily preventing the implementation of a practice or requiring the cessation of a practice which the Commission believes to be infringing Article 85 or 86 until such time as it has taken a permanent decision according to Article 4 of Council Regulation 3975/87. The exercise of this power, however, is subject to three conditions: **4.17**

- that the Commission has "clear *prima facie* evidence" that the practice is contrary to the provisions of Article 85 or 86;
- that the object or effect of the practice is directly to jeopardise the existence of an air service; and,
- that recourse to normal procedures may be insufficient to protect either the air service or the airline concerned.[24]

The nature of an interim measure is such that it is temporary, and cannot therefore exceed six months, although it may be renewed for a period not exceeding three months.[25]

Exemptions

Quite apart from the non-application of Article 85(1) to certain technical agreements, provision has also been made under Council Regulation 3975/87 for the Commission to issue exemptions; in this case, however, individual exemptions. Block exemptions are considered below. Individual exemptions under this Regulation may be granted in two ways. First, where the Commission finds, in the course of its investigation following a complaint or on its own initiative, that   **4.18**

---

[22] Art. 4(3).
[23] Recital (2), [1991] OJ L122/2.
[24] Art. 1(1).
[25] Art. 1(2).

the agreement, decision or practice in question satisfies the provisions of both Article 85(1) and (3), it is under an obligation to apply the exemption.

Secondly, an application for an individual exemption, which has to be made in Form AER, may be submitted by one or more undertakings to the agreement, decision or practice, as in the case of the agreement between Lufthansa and SAS.[26] If such an application is not already subject to an investigation by the Commission, the latter is required to publish a summary of the application in the *Official Journal of the European Communities*, having regard to the need to protect business secrets. The intention is to invite third party comments relating to the application. Should the Commission find that the proposed agreement is indeed prohibited by Article 85(1) and cannot benefit from the application of Article 85(3) and, therefore, take a decision condemning it, the parties are nevertheless protected, from the date of application.[27]

4.19   However, the Commission is required to grant an exemption, as applied for, if the requirements of Article 85(3) have been satisfied notwithstanding that the agreement, decision or concerted practice falls within the scope of Article 85(1). If the Commission does not notify the applicants that there are serious doubts about the applicability of Article 85(3) following 90 days after the publication of the application, then the agreement, decision or concerted practice will be deemed exempt under Article 5(3) of Regulation 3975/87. In 1995, for example, the Commission took no action in respect of an agreement between Scandinavian Leisure Group (SLG) and Simon Spies Holding (Spies) to establish a new airline, Premiair, to supply air transport services for tour operators owned by SLG and Spies.[28] These services had previously been provided by two separate airlines, Scanair for SLG and Conair for Spies. The Commission concluded that there were no serious doubts about the exemptability of the agreement within the terms of Article 5(3) of the Regulation, and it should therefore be exempted for six years from the date of publication, 7 October 1995.

Duration

4.20   An exemption granted under Council Regulation 3975/87, whether as a result of a Commission investigation under Article 4 or as a result of an application under Article 5, has a maximum duration of six years. In the former case, the date from which the exemption is to take effect will be indicated by the decision, while in the latter case, from the date of publication of the application in the *Official Journal*. An exemption may, however, be renewed for a longer period provided the conditions attached to the exemption continue to be satisfied.[29] However, the Commission is empowered to declare the applicability of the prohibition in Article 85(1) to an agreement, decision or concerted practice in a case where 90 days have elapsed since the publication of an application under Article 5, but before

---

[26] Commission Decision 96/180, Case IV/35.545, [1996] OJ L54/28. See Ch. 3 *supra*.

[27] Commission Regulation 4261/88, [1988] OJ L376/10. See J.Goh, "Air Transport Competition in the EEC: The Antitrust Procedures" (1992) 21 *Transportation Law Journal* 91 for a more detailed consideration of the Regulation.

[28] *Twenty-Fifth Report on Competition Policy* (1995), p.69.

[29] Art. 6(1) and (2).

the expiry of of the six year period. The decision to intervene may be issued on the basis of inaccurate information being supplied, an abuse of the exemption, or a contravention of Article 86, and in these cases the decision may be retroactive in effect.[30]

Revocation

An exemption which has been granted under Council Regulation 3975/87 may be revoked or amended in accordance with the circumstances laid down in Article 6(3). These circumstances are that:

- there has been a change in the material facts pertaining to the exemption;
- there has been a breach of an obligation attached to the exemption by the parties;
- the exemption had been granted according to incorrect information, or induced by deceit;
- there has been an abuse of the exemption.

It is not clear, however, whether the exemption will be revoked or amended if a   4.21
breach of its conditions or its abuse were to be committed by one, but not all, of the parties to the agreement, decision or concerted practice. Practical considerations suggest that it should not matter whether the breach or abuse was committed by one or more parties since the exemption was granted to the agreement, decision or practice as a whole rather than the individual parties to such an arrangement. A decision of the Commission to revoke an exemption in all cases, except the first, may be retroactive in effect.

Negative clearance

The procedure of negative clearance is unique, but its aim is obvious. In many   4.22
respects, this form of advance advice is "the great virtue of administrative regulation".[31] While litigation is formal and elaborate, negative clearance is unburdened by rigid rules; while litigation looks to the past and towards punitive measures, negative clearance looks to the future and seeks to be preventive; and while litigation occurs spasmodically, negative clearance takes place continuously. Hence, it provides a useful means for an undertaking or undertakings to an agreement to seek the opinion of the Commission on whether the agreement in question or the practice of the arrangement falls within the scope of Article 85(1) or 86. It is, however, not an exemption, for Article 86 in particular, does not make provision for exemptions.

In an application to the Commission, the applicant will be required to provide reasons as to why Article 85(1) or 86 is inapplicable, that is to say, why the agreement does not have the object or effect of preventing, restricting or distorting competition within the Community to an appreciable extent, or that the decision concerned does not entail an abuse of a dominant position. If the Commission is minded to give the clearance sought, it will certify accordingly by taking a decision *on the basis of the facts in its possession*.[32] Clearly then, where incomplete information

---

[30] See Art. 5(3).
[31] T.K. McCraw, *Prophets of Regulation* (1984), p.129.
[32] Art. 3(2).

has been given to the Commission, the clearance will lack the necessary validity. An application for negative clearance does not, however, require the consent of the other parties to the agreement, although it is expected that they should have knowledge of such an application.

4.23   It is noteworthy that in an application, the Commission is often engaged in a process of negotiation with the applicant. This is true in cases where the Commission feels that the agreement would fall foul of the competition rules but that a negotiated settlement could be achieved by extracting assurances from the undertakings concerned. In most cases, obtaining those assurances is unlikely to be difficult since a disagreement will probably lead to the Commission applying its formal authority under the Regulation. A helpful illustration can be found in the merger between BA and British Caledonian in which the Commission took the view that the assurances given to the Monopolies and Mergers Commission by BA were inadequate and must therefore be supplemented with further commitments from BA to ensure that the merger would not operate against the competition rules of the EC Treaty.[33]

The Commission also adopts a policy of discouraging applications for negative clearances in cases where the agreements *clearly* do not come within the scope of either Article 85(1) or 86. In addition to simplifying the procedure further, this has the benefit of expediency. At any rate, where an application has been submitted, and the agreement is one which is clearly not within the prohibitions of the competition rules, the Commission does not usually issue a negative clearance.

Hearings

4.24   Article 16 of Council Regulation 3975/87 sets out the requirements relating to hearings. Hearings must be given to the parties concerned if the Commission takes or has taken objection to the agreement in question in one of the following instances:

- refusing a negative clearance certificate (Article 3(2));
- taking a decision resulting from an investigation (Article 4);
- taking a decision to issue interim measures (Article 4a);
- granting an exemption (Article 5(4));
- revoking an exemption granted by default (Article 5(3));
- revoking an exemption granted expressly (Article 6(3));
- taking a decision to impose fines (Articles 12 and 13).

Hearings are *ex parte* and "shall not be public".[34]

4.25   Article 8 of Commission Regulation 4261/88 places a mandatory obligation on the Commission to afford third parties the opportunity to put forward their views provided they can demonstrate a sufficient interest. Except in cases where the parties have so requested to put their arguments orally or in cases where the Commission has proposed to impose a fine, these representations may only be

---

[33] See Ch. 5 *infra*.
[34] Commission Regulation 4261/88, Art. 12(3).

made in writing. The Commission is also empowered to afford to any other person the opportunity to comment orally.

Information

It is axiomatic to the consideration of any competition case that adequate   4.26
information be supplied to enable a full and thorough analysis. It is therefore
natural that the Commission should place a considerable emphasis on the need
to provide complete and accurate information. A decision to issue a negative
clearance or to declare the application of Article 85(3) is usually based on the facts
that the Commission possesses. The effect of providing incomplete or false information would render the negative clearance ineffective, or in the case of a decision to apply Article 85(3) to the agreement, voidable. In order to carry out
functions in respect of air transport competition, the Commission may obtain all
necessary information from Member States and their competent authorities and
of course from the undertakings concerned as well as other undertakings. Where
a request for information has been made, the undertakings in question "shall be
bound to supply the information requested". A failure to comply with such a
request, or to comply fully, is liable to attract a decision from the Commission.[35]

Article 12(1)(a) and (b) of Council Regulation 3975/87 further empowers the   4.27
Commission to impose fines from 100 ECU to 5,000 ECU for the provision of
incorrect or misleading information regardless of whether it had been so provided
intentionally or negligently; or periodic fines from 50 ECU to 1,000 ECU per
each day of non-compliance.[36] The enforcement authority of the Commission in
this respect carries with it considerable significance not least because it encourages
an applicant to be vigilant in providing adequate information.

Clearly though, an intentional and negligent supply of incomplete or incorrect
information may be interpreted very widely. And the Commission is mindful of
the extensive scope that it entails. But it has indicated that the powers of enforcement will be exercised only in circumstances where false or grossly inaccurate
information has been supplied by the applicant, or in cases where there has been
a suppression of information, or a deliberate supply of false opinions.[37]

Jurisdiction

The division of responsibility for investigating competition matters in air transport   4.28
reflects, to some extent, the separation set out in Articles 88 and 89 of the EC
Treaty. Article 7 of Council Regulation 3975/87 expressly stipulates that the competent authorities of Member States:

> "shall retain the power to decide whether any case falls under the provisions of Article
> 85(1) or Article 86 of the Treaty, *until such time* as the Commission has initiated a

---

[35] Art. 9.
[36] Art. 13(1)(c).
[37] See J.Goh, n. 27 *supra*.

procedure with a view to formulating a decision in the case in question or has sent notification . . ." (emphasis added)

The competent authorities of Member States, however, do not have the power to grant exemptions pursuant to Article 85(3). That is the sole power of the Commission.

4.29   Where the Commission has assumed jurisdiction to investigate, it is, however, obliged by the Regulation to perform its investigatory functions "in close and constant liaison with the competent authorities of the Member States".[38] Its powers of investigation include:

- examination of books and other business records;
- copying extracts from books and business records;
- asking oral explanations on the spot;
- entering premises and vehicles used by the undertakings.

4.30   Where the procedure to investigate has been invoked, the undertakings concerned are under a legal requirement to submit to the investigation, which presumably implies co-operating to meet all reasonable requests of the Commission. Failure to do so may be liable to fines from ECU 100 to ECU 5,000.[39] Periodic fines from ECU 50 to ECU 1,000 per day may also be imposed for the period of non-submission.

Penalties

4.31   The powers of the Commission to impose fines on undertakings for infringing Regulation 3975/87 are considerable. In addition to "technical fines" for the supply of incorrect or misleading information, or refusal to submit to an investigation, it may also impose "substantive fines" where the undertakings have either intentionally or negligently infringed Article 85(1) or 86 of the EC Treaty, or committed a breach of any obligation imposed pursuant to an Article 85(3) exemption. These range from ECU 1,000 to ECU 1m, or "a sum in excess thereof but not exceeding 10% of the turnover on the preceding business year" of the undertakings participating in the infringement. In considering the amount of the penalty, however, the Commission is required to have regard to both the gravity and duration of the infringement. For instance, in *British Midland* v *Aer Lingus*, the Commission referred to the length of the refusal to interline and the conduct of Aer Lingus which was "intended to affect the structure of competition by penalizing a competitor entering an important market and therefore is particularly serious".[40]

---

[38] Art. 8(1). For competent authorities, see Cases 209-213/84, *Ministère Public* v *Asjes* [1986] ECR 1425 and Case 66/86, *Ahmed Saeed Flugreisen & Silver Line Reisebüro* v *Zentrale Zur Bekämpfung Unlauteren Wettbewerbs* [1989] ECR 803. See also J.Basedow, "National Authorities in European Airline Competition Law" (1988) *ECLRev.* 342.

[39] Art. 12(1)(c).

[40] Commission Decision 92/213, [1992] OJ L96/34, para. 42.

Its powers to impose fines include also periodic fines from ECU 50 to ECU   **4.32**
1,000 per day until the termination of an Article 85(1) or 86 infringement, or
compliance as regards obligations of an exemption or supply of information. This
power to impose periodic fines is subject to a wider discretion of the Commission
to "fix the total amount of the periodic penalty payment at a lower figure than
that which would result from the original decision".[41]

3. The block exemptions

Block exemptions are provided for in Council Regulation 3976/87. It authorises   **4.33**
the Commission to adopt detailed measures for exempting certain air transport
agreements, decisions and practices. The principal aim of issuing block exemptions is to enable air carriers, within a limited time period, to "adapt to a more
competitive environment".[42] Subsequent amendments in 1990 and 1992 were
adopted to alter the scope of the enabling legislation.

Scope

Like Council Regulation 3975/87, the scope of Council Regulation 3976/87 was   **4.34**
initially restricted to "international air transport between Community airports".
This was amended in 1992 when the Council adopted Regulation 2411/92 to
remove the provision "international" thus expanding the scope of the enabling
legislation to include air transport between airports in a single Member State.[43]

Enabling provisions

Article 2 of Council Regulation 3976/87 sets out the matters in respect of which   **4.35**
the Commission may adopt specific regulations for granting block exemptions.
The most recent of such measures is Commission Regulation 1617/93 which must
expire on 30 June 1998.[44]

Joint planning and co-ordination

Agreements, decisions of undertakings or concerted practices intended to plan and   **4.36**
co-ordinate the schedule of an air service may be exempt from Article 85(3) by
virtue of Commission Regulation 1617/93.[45] The applicability of the exemption,
however, is subject to a number of conditions. The scope of the exemption is
restricted to scheduled air services, although under the third package of liberalisation measures adopted in 1992, the distinction between scheduled and charter

---

[41] Art. 13(2).
[42] [1987] OJ L374/9.
[43] [1992] OJ L240/19.
[44] [1993] OJ L155/18, as amended by [1994] OJ L15/20.
[45] *Ibid.*, Art. 2.

air services has effectively been abolished. The conditions for the applicability of the exemption are as follows:

- The arrangements aim to ensure a satisfactory supply of service during less busy times, periods, or on less busy routes. Whether a particular time or period, or indeed route, is more or less busy than another will be a matter of value judgement. A useful consideration will be the distinction between peak and off-peak times or the total number of passengers carried by reference to the previous season or year. These must be non-binding so that the parties are not held to the arrangements as a legal obligation such as to provide the same level of capacity or maintain the same schedule when traffic forecasts have been over- or under-estimated.

- The arrangements are intended to establish schedules which will facilitate interline connections for passengers and freight, and the minimum capacity to be provided for such schedules.

- The arrangements do not limit directly or indirectly the capacity to be provided by the parties, or require the sharing of capacity.

- The arrangements must not prevent the parties from changing their plans, either relating to additional capacity or schedules, and must not impose penalties nor require the prior consent of other parties for the change.

- The arrangements must not prevent the parties withdrawing from the planning or co-ordination for future seasons, and must not impose penalties except that a notice of not more than three months may be required.

- The arrangements must not seek to influence the capacity or schedules of other non-participating carriers.

Revenue sharing from joint operations

4.38 Article 3 of Commission Regulation 1617/93 specifies the conditions which an agreement relating to the joint operation of an air service has to satisfy so as to enjoy the benefit of the exemption.

- The joint operation is concerned with the sharing of costs and revenues of one airline with another in respect of a scheduled air service which the former is operating.

- There was no direct service between the two airports in question during all the four seasons preceding the joint operation. Alternatively, the capacity under the joint operation does not exceed 30,000 seats per year, although this allowance may be doubled on routes of over 750 kilometres and on which there is a maximum of a twice-daily direct service.

- The airline operating the service in question does not offer more than 90,000 seats per year at one of the airports involved, including the capacity resulting from the joint operation.

- The revenues from air transport within the markets defined by the Regulation for the air carrier operating the service do not exceed ECU 400m per year.

This includes revenues from any other airline which directly or indirectly has a controlling shareholding in the former.

- The agreement must not restrict the parties from providing additional capacity, nor from independently determining the fares, capacity and schedules of the air services concerned.
- The agreement must enable either party to terminate the joint operation on giving three months' notice, provided that it expires at the end of a traffic season.
- The maximum duration of the joint operation is three years.

Tariff consultations

Agreements to fix tariffs are ostensibly an infringement of Article 85(1) since their main effect is to exclude price competition. The benefits of tariff co-ordination have, however, been greatly manifested by the conveniences created under the IATA system for both airlines and users, and cannot therefore be ignored. But an outright exemption for such agreements, on the other hand, may constitute a blatant infringement of the Treaty competition rules. Therefore, a compromise between the need for an exemption on the one hand, and for a competitive environment on the other hand, had to be struck when the Council considered the enabling Regulation 3976/87. Pursuant to the enabling provision, the Commission laid down in Article 4 of Commission Regulation 1617/93 the conditions which have to be satisfied for the block exemption to apply to consultations on passenger and cargo tariffs.   **4.39**

- The arrangements must not be more than a consultative machinery to discuss air fares and cargo rates, and must be entirely voluntary and open to any carrier.
- The consultations must result in interlining facilities between the participating carriers except when objective and non-discriminatory reasons of a technical or commercial nature can be established.
- The consultations must relate only to tariffs, and not capacity, nor entail an agreement on agents' remuneration.
- Tariffs under consultation must not be applied discriminatorily on the basis of the nationality of passengers nor their place of residence in the Community.
- Where the filing of tariffs is required, each individual airline will be required to file the tariffs which were not the subject of the consultations with their respective aeronautical authorities responsible for tariff approval.
- In respect of all consultations, the Commission and the Member States concerned must be notified so as to enable them to participate as observers.

In 1996, the Commission adopted Regulation 1523/96 to abolish the block exemption in respect of cargo rates.[46] Its reasonings were two-fold. First, when the block exemption was granted, there was a perceived need to allow airlines the   **4.40**

---

[46] [1996] OJ L190/11.

time to adjust to a new competitive environment. However, that was no longer necessary. Secondly, the block exemption had been granted on the ground that it would facilitate the interlining of freight transport by air. In the Commission's view, cargo rates resulting from consultations were in actual fact 70 per cent higher than market prices. Moreover, airlines which were not involved in the consultations were nevertheless engaged in interlining agreements. Consequently, the tariff consultations no longer contributed to, nor were they essential for, interlining.

Slot allocation and scheduling

4.41   Slot allocation at airports is now subject to Council Regulation 95/93 adopted in 1993, which is considered further in Chapter 10. The present system of slot allocation according to the IATA model has all the characteristics of an anti-competitive practice which would infringe Article 85(1). Like tariff consultation, however, it has produced important benefits, though more importantly, there does not appear to be a better alternative way of allocating slots at airports. Accordingly, the block exemption under Article 5 of Regulation 1617/93 would only apply if certain conditions are met.

- The process of consultation on slot allocation must be open to all carriers who have expressed an interest in the slots.

- Rules of priority on slot allocation must not be discriminatory either on grounds of nationality or carrier identity. They may, however, take into account airport constraints and traffic distribution rules as well as rights acquired by carriers through the historical use of slots in the corresponding seasons.

- The rules of priority must be available to any interested party.

- New entrants must be allocated at least 50 per cent of newly created, unused and surrendered slots, to the extent that they have outstanding slot requests.

- Information relating to allocation criteria, slots held, allocated and requested must be readily available.

- The Commission and the Member States concerned must be entitled to participate as observers.

Computer reservation systems

4.42   One of the most significant developments in air transport since the advent of deregulation and liberalisation has been the introduction of computerised reservations. This is a particularly powerful means of securing market share for those carriers which have a large network providing for convenient interlining services for users. Those airlines which have been able to develop and exploit their extensive network through the use of computer reservation systems (CRSs) have been able to make important in-roads into the market of their competitors. Since the adoption of the enabling legislation and the block exemption for CRSs, the most recent being Commission Regulation 1618/93,[47] the Council has adopted

---

[47] [1993] OJ L155/23.

Regulation 2299/89 setting out a Code of Conduct on CRSs,[48] as subsequently amended by Council Regulation 3089/93.[49] The conditions for exemption are fundamentally similar to the provisions of the Code of Conduct. Hence, the incorporation of the Code of Conduct in a CRS agreement will most probably enjoy the benefits of the block exemption. The issues are considered in more detail in Chapter 11.

Ground-handling services

The block exemption in respect of ground-handling services was adopted on the basis that certain agreements could produce economic benefits particularly in ensuring that services of a high standard are provided with continuity and at a reasonable cost. Commission Regulation 82/91 was adopted by the Commission[50] pursuant to its powers in the enabling Regulation 3976/87 for block exemptions. This exemption expired on 31 December 1992. When Regulation 3976/87 was amended by Council Regulation 2411/92, the provision for exempting certain ground-handling services was omitted to prepare for its eventual liberalisation.[51] Thus, the Commission was no longer able to adopt an implementing Regulation in respect of such services.   **4.43**

The Commission has now initiated a consultation procedure to consider the option of opening up the ground-handling markets at Community airports as part of its wider programme of liberalisation.[52] This will be achieved over three years from 1998 to 2001. A common position has also been agreed by the Council.[53]

Withdrawal of exemption

Council Regulation 3976/87 empowers the Commission to withdraw the benefit of an exemption if in a particular case the Commission finds that either the parties to the agreement have breached a condition of the exemption or the agreement is no longer compatible with the provisions of Article 85(3), or has infringed Article 86.   **4.44**

Article 7(1) provides that in the case of a condition being breached, the Commission has a number of options in the way in which the breach can be dealt with. First, it can address recommendations to the parties concerned. Secondly, and in the event of failure to adopt the recommendations, the Commission may then take a decision prohibiting the actions, requiring the performance of certain acts, withdrawing the entire block exemption but granting individual exemptions instead, or withdrawing the entire block exemption without the compensation of individual exemptions.

However, Article 7(2) which deals with an agreement that satisfies the requirements of Article 85(3) but nevertheless infringes Article 86, is less straightforward. The   **4.45**

---

[48] [1989] OJ L220/1.
[49] [1993] OJ L278/1.
[50] [1991] OJ L10/7.
[51] [1992] OJ L240/19.
[52] COM(96) 75.
[53] [1996] OJ C134/30.

Commission is empowered to "withdraw the benefit of the block exemption from those agreements, decisions or concerted practices" if it finds in "any particular case" the effects of the agreement, decision or practice are incompatible with Article 85(3) or prohibited by Article 86. The difference between singularity and plurality is therefore crucial. It is less clear because, on one interpretation, the Commission is empowered only to withdraw the block exemption *in toto*, and on another interpretation, the Commission appears to be empowered to withdraw merely the benefit of the exemption in respect of the infringing party. Nevertheless, on the strength of *Tetra Pak Rausing SA* v *Commission*,[54] it is possible to submit that in such cases, the Commission should not be expected to withdraw the entire block exemption so as to deprive other agreements of the benefits it is intended to provide. The cost of doing this may be highly disproportionate to the end objective of removing the ills of the anti-competitive practice. However, this is not to deny the claim that all the parties to the agreement are collectively bound and must collectively assume the responsibilities and consequences of the agreement accordingly; nor is this to deny the possibility of individual exemptions being granted by the Commission in accordance with Council Regulation 3975/87.

---

[54] Case T-51/89, [1990] ECR II-309.

Chapter 5

AIRLINE MERGERS

1. Introduction

Mergers in air transport are not uncommon. Given invariably the high capital costs of operating an airline business, there is always scope for mergers, or concentrations as they are otherwise known. To achieve the objectives of competition and choice to the benefit of users, the control of airline mergers becomes a crucial issue if such mergers are not to lead to any substantial reduction in competition. Not every merger, however, will produce effects detrimental to effective competition. Mergers in the air transport sector have often been justified on the basis of efficiency gains such as cost reductions and consolidation of resources. Thus, in limited circumstances, the threat of takeovers, for example, can provide an important stimulus to efficiency and greater competitiveness.

Nevertheless, there is a certain inevitability that the Community air transport industry will have to restructure itself as fifteen national markets become one. The industry has already witnessed a series of mergers, both prior to and following the introduction of the liberalisation programme. More recently, a number of mergers have been authorised by the Commission, some with conditions attached. In particular, in the Air France–Sabena and BA–TAT decisions, the Commission required assurances that competition would not be unduly reduced by those mergers. In other cases, such as Delta–Pan Am and BA–Dan Air, the Commission cleared the mergers as being compatible with the common market.

These cases were examined under Council Regulation 4064/89. on merger control which was adopted by the Council 16 years after it was first proposed (Merger Regulation).[1] One of the principal reasons for the delay was the difficulties perceived by several Member States regarding the operation of the Regulation, for example the absence of a sophisticated merger law framework in those Member States which may not be able to deal with certain types of mergers not covered by the Regulation. Hence, the insertion of Article 22(3) into the Regulation which allows for such mergers to be referred to the Commission by national authorities.[2]

The Merger Regulation is a generic measure which applies to all sectors envisaged by the EC Treaty, rather than being air transport specific. Be that as it may, a body of case law on air transport mergers has evolved over time. Prior to the Merger Regulation, the control of mergers fell within the scope of Articles

5.1

5.2

5.3

---

[1] [1989] OJ L395/1 as corrected by [1990] OJ L257/14.
[2] See *infra*.

85 and 86 as implemented by Council Regulation 3975/87.[3] A number of cases were investigated by the Commission under the competition rules including the takeover of B.Cal by BA in 1988 and of UTA by Air France in 1990. However, the application of Articles 85 and 86 to certain mergers was deemed to be insufficient to control "all operations which may prove to be incompatible with the system of un-distorted competition envisaged in the Treaty".[4] Thus, mergers are today examined in accordance with the Merger Regulation although to the extent that it is not applicable, Articles 85 and 86 will remain relevant. Indeed, the Commission has developed a case law that, *inter alia*, distinguishes between "concentrative" and "co-operative" arrangements.[5] In the case of the former, it is likely to fall within the scope of the Merger Regulation while Articles 85 and 86 will probably apply to co-operative agreements such as that between Lufthansa and SAS.[6] Such a simple distinction is of course not sufficient to determine the actual arrangements concluded in what is a highly complex industry and in which the extent and nature of ownership is considerably diverse.

5.4   Where mergers have not resulted, other forms of airline alliance have been established. More recent developments have taken the form of code-sharing and franchising of airline brand both of which fall short of a merger or takeover, but sufficiently significant to raise implications for the competitive state of air transport. Code-sharing is the use by one airline of its flight code on a service operated by an aircraft of another airline. This development is often explained by the need to gain access to a market which otherwise can only be achieved inefficiently, or prevented by the laws of ownership in airlines although the latter will be held as a contravention of Community law. The well publicised proposal announced by BA and American Airlines recently on a code-sharing agreement is an obvious case[6a]. Significantly, this has prompted the Commission to launch an investigation into the major code-sharing agreements including those between Lufthansa–United Airlines, Swissair–Austrian Airlines–Sabena–Delta Airlines, KLM–NorthWest Airlines, SAS–United Airlines and BA–USAir. Franchising, on the other hand, has existed in a variety of forms previously. In a franchise agreement, the franchisee typically pays the franchiser a fee for access to its brand or name. This implies that the franchisee is expected to meet the service and other standards of the franchiser although in some cases the franchisee will continue to retain independence over fares, scheduling and other matters. Where franchising differs from code-sharing is in the service characteristics of the airline which are adopted. Code-sharing is usually restricted to the flight code. Franchising has proved popular with an airline with a world-wide network and market and a comprehensive loyalty programme or other frequent flyer benefits. Franchising will allow it to increase its feed-traffic at no capital cost by securing access to markets which it would not have entered for reasons of efficiency associated with high costs and fleet configuration. In return, the franchisee would continue the

---

[3] [1987] OJ 374/1.
[4] Recital 6 of Merger Regulation.
[5] See Commission Notice on the distinction between concentrative and co-operative joint ventures, [1994] OJ C385/1.
[6] Commission Decision 96/180, [1996] OJ L54/28.
[6a] [1996] OJ C289/4.

viability of the services on a thin route through the support and marketing strength of the franchiser. A useful illustration is the BA–Loganair franchise which has allowed the Scottish-based airline to rationalise its routes and ensure the continuity of services on those routes.

This chapter on mergers will take the following approach. First, it will examine the residual application of Articles 85 and 86 and the leading cases in air transport which have been considered by the Commission. Secondly, it will provide an examination of the Merger Regulation as it applies to air transport, and this will comprise an analysis of its scope of application and its substantive relevance to airline mergers. The Merger Regulation also provides for a number of derogations from certain provisions which will be considered accordingly. **5.5**

2. Application of Articles 85 and 86

As has been noted, prior to the adoption of the Merger Regulation in 1989, an emerging body of case law on airline mergers could already be detected. This was represented by the decisions of the Commission in BA–B.Cal, Air France–UTA and KLM–Transavia. These mergers were examined in accordance with the provisions of Articles 85 and 86. **5.6**

A merger that is constituted of "undertakings, decisions by associations of undertakings and concerted practices which may affect trade between Member States and which have their object or effect the prevention, restriction or distortion of competition within the common market", will be prohibited by Article 85(1) as incompatible with the common market. An exemption, however, can be obtained if the requirements in Article 85(3) can be satisfied.

Article 86, on the other hand, prohibits as incompatible with the common market an "abuse by one or more undertakings of a dominant position within the common market or in a substantial part of it . . . in so far as it may affect trade between Member States". The Court of Justice has already given this provision a wide interpretation and has, in particular, ruled that mergers could be considered as an abuse of a dominant position.[7] **5.7**

Although to a large extent the Merger Regulation has removed mergers from the scope of Articles 85 and 86, their continuing application is explicitly recognised by recital 23 of the Regulation:

"whereas it is therefore necessary to exclude from the scope of this Regulation those operations which have as their object or effect the co-ordination of the competitive behaviour of undertakings which remain independent, since such operations fall to be examined under the appropriate provisions of the Regulations implementing Articles 85 and 86 of the Treaty."

---

[7] See Ch. 3 *supra* and Case 6/72, *Europemballage & Continental Can* v *Commission* [1973] ECR 215.

It is also significant that for those mergers which fall within the scope of the Merger Regulation, the directly effective prohibition of abuse of a dominant position in Article 86, as recognised by the Court in *BRT* v *SABAM*,[8] will no longer apply.[9]

British Airways–British Caledonian[10]

5.8   B.Cal was created as a "second force" airline in 1976 as a result of a comprehensive review of British air transport policy. Although it was given a measure of preference to foster its growth, B.Cal proved less than successful. The takeover proposal by BA was, however, referred to the Monopolies and Mergers Commission (MMC) not simply on the basis of the competition implications that may arise from the takeover, but more significantly the unprecedented nature of the case in British air transport history. The MMC subsequently approved the takeover subject to a host of conditions including the surrender of several B.Cal route licences for which BA was not permitted to re-apply.[11] The Commission took up the case because it was concerned that the merger would substantially reduce airline competition within the common market. As a condition of its approval, BA was required to give additional undertakings to the Commission that would improve the prospects of competition substantially.

5.9   In brief, the following undertakings were given by BA:

- it will not appeal to the Minister against a decision of the Civil Aviation Authority (CAA) declining to license BA to operate on domestic routes in the United Kingdom and routes between London (Gatwick) and Paris, Brussels and Nice previously operated by B.Cal.;

- it will not use more than 25 per cent of the slots at Gatwick for the summer seasons of 1989–1992;

- it will not operate services under B.Cal's licences between Gatwick and Athens, Copenhagen, Hamburg and Stuttgart;

- it will withdraw its application for licences to operate between Gatwick and Hamburg, Stuttgart and Rome, and not re-apply until April 1991;

- it will not object to an appeal by Air Europe against a decision of the CAA for a licence to operate between Gatwick and Rome;

- it will accept that priority on capacity of up to 4,000 seats weekly will be given to another airline licensed by the CAA to operate on the Heathrow–Milan and Gatwick–Milan routes;

- it will not object to an application by another airline to operate in competition with it on any route within the Community;

---

[8] Case 127/73, [1974] ECR 51.
[9] See Case 66/86, *Ahmed Saeed Flugreisen and Silver Line Reisebüro* v *Zentrale zur Bekämpfung Unlauteren Wettbewerbs* [1989] ECR 803.
[10] Eighteenth Report on Competition Policy (1988).
[11] *British Airways–British Caledonian Group*, (CM.247, 1987).

- it will not effect any transfer of services between Gatwick and Heathrow in a way that would be detrimental to the interests of users or competition.

The BA-B.Cal merger was the first airline merger investigated by the Commission.   5.10
There was therefore little in the way of specific guidance which it could reflect on in examining the case. Nevertheless, the use of undertakings has emerged as an important tool in securing a balance between the need to authorise mergers in appropriate cases and to ensure the mergers do not affect competition adversely.

Air France–UTA–Air Inter[12]

The merger between Air France, UTA and Air Inter was part of the restructuring   5.11
programme undertaken by Air France. Although the Commission expressed initial doubts as to the compatibility of the merger with the common market, it subsequently authorised the merger on the grounds that the assurances given by Air France would ensure greater market access for new airlines to allow genuine competition to take place.

As a condition of approving the Contrat de Plan, Air France gave the undertaking that an independent sector separate from the merged group would be set up to provide services in competition with it. The new sector would be comprised of the airlines already operating. Accordingly, Air France would withdraw its participation from TAT, a French scheduled airline. To foster the entry and growth of new airlines, Air France would also be required to freeze its capacity levels on Nice/Marseilles–Bastia/Ajaccio routes and to relinquish its dominance over the Paris (Orly)–Nice route so that airlines outside the group could benefit from operating on that route.

The French authorities also gave the undertaking that it would license at least   5.12
one other French airline outside the merged group to operate on eight routes which account for more than half the domestic traffic in France. In addition, other French airlines requesting to operate to and from the overseas departments would be duly licensed. Since UTA was previously an independent, long-haul airline, the Commission required an undertaking from the French authorities that at least one other airline outside the group would be licensed to operate both intra- and extra-Community routes.

KLM–Transavia[13]

Transavia operated primarily in the charter market with limited scheduled   5.13
services. In 1988, KLM purchased 40 per cent of equity in Transavia with an option to increase it to 80 per cent which it duly exercised in 1991. Under the agreement, KLM was also entitled to appoint two of the five directors in Transavia, in addition to which KLM was able to influence the development of

---

[12] *Twentieth Report on Competition Policy* (1990), p.91.
[13] *Twentieth-First Report on Competition Policy* (1991), p.72.

scheduled services by Transavia including the condition that it would not compete with KLM in its scheduled services.

KLM already had an interest in Martinair which operated in the charter market. Together, Transavia and Martinair dominated about 75 per cent of the Dutch charter market. Even though both airlines were operating in competition, the Commission was concerned that the acquisition by KLM in Transavia created a potential for commercial co-operation contrary to Article 85(1), thereby strengthening the dominance of KLM in the Dutch air transport market.

5.14   Although the Commission eventually authorised the concentration, KLM and the Dutch authorities were required to provide a number of undertakings. First, the Dutch authorities agreed to secure a substantial increase in competition by liberalising 13 major and 22 secondary scheduled routes out of Amsterdam. It also agreed to adopt a liberal licensing policy for charter services. In addition, KLM undertook to refrain from acquiring any further interest in other Dutch airlines outside the group.

3. Application of the Merger Regulation: the scope

5.15   For the Merger Regulation to apply, two conditions must exist:

- there must be a concentration under the terms of the Regulation, and
- the concentration must have a Community dimension as defined in the Regulation.

Once these conditions have been established, the Commission must examine the compatibility of the concentration with the common market by reference to the strength and dominance of the newly formed operation in the applicable market. In cases where the concentration may be declared incompatible with the common market, it may nevertheless be authorised if the Commission deems the undertakings which have been offered are sufficient to ensure that competition will not be prejudicially affected, or in the words of the Regulation, "significantly impeded".

4. Requirement of a concentration

5.16   The question of whether an operation is classified as a concentration, or alternatively a co-operation, is crucial because in the case of the latter the operation will fall outside the scope of the Merger Regulation but will instead come within the scope of Council Regulation 17/62[14] generally and Council Regulation 3975/87 in the case of air transport. The Commission has already acknowledged that the task of classifying such operations "has proved to be one of the most

---

[14] [1959–1962] OJ (Sp. edn.) p.204.

delicate matters the Commission has had to resolve".[15] A series of notices has been issued by the Commission in 1994 to shed some light on various complex concepts such as a "concentration", "undertakings concerned" and "turnover".[16]

Article 3(1) of the Merger Regulation defines a concentration as comprising:

"(a) two or more previously independent undertakings merging, or
(b) one or more persons already controlling at least one undertaking, or one or more undertakings, acquiring, whether by purchase of securities or assets, by contract or by any other means, direct or indirect control of the whole or parts of one or more other undertakings."

Undertakings

According to Commission Notice on the notion of undertakings, an "undertaking" implies "the actors in the transaction in so far as they are the merging, or acquiring and acquired parties".[17] Ascertaining the undertakings concerned in the transaction is important because it will provide the basis for calculating the turnover so as to decide whether the concentration falls to be examined under the Regulation. A typical problem, for example, is the case of a joint venture acquiring another undertaking. The question arises as to whether the joint venture should be regarded as a single undertaking concerned, or whether each of its parent companies should be separately considered as undertakings concerned. In such cases, the Commission will have to examine "the economic reality of the operation to determine which are the undertakings concerned" by taking into account such factors as the financial and other resources of the joint venture.   5.17

Concentration

A concentration can be distinguished between the formation of a new undertaking from two previously independent undertakings, and the acquisition of control in an undertaking by one or more other undertakings. In addition, a *de facto* merger may also occur where two previously independent undertakings combine their activities to create a single economic unit with common economic management.[18]   5.18

Article 3(2) further provides that a concentration shall consist of:

"a joint venture performing on a lasting basis all the functions of an autonomous economic entity, which does not give rise to co-ordination of the competitive behaviour of the parties amongst themselves or between them and the joint venture."

In the case of an operation, including a joint venture, which "has as its object or effect the co-ordination of the competitive behaviour of undertakings which remain independent", the Merger Regulation will not be applicable.

---

[15] *Twenty-First Report on Competition Policy* (1991), p.85.
[16] Commission Notices, [1994] OJ C385/1; C385/5; C385/12; C385/21.
[17] Commission Notice on the notion of undertakings concerned, [1994] OJ C385/12.
[18] Commission Notice on the notion of a concentration, [1994] OJ C385/5.

Control

5.19 Control can arise in the context of sole or joint control, and in the case of joint control there is typically an agreement which may combine the competitive behaviour of the undertakings or lead to the formation of a subsidiary undertaking in which the two parent undertakings exercise joint control. According to Article 3(3), control is constituted:

> "by rights, contracts or any other means which, either separately or in combination and having regard to the considerations of fact or law involved, confer the possibility of exercising decisive influence on an undertaking."

This can take the form of ownership or the right to use all or part of the assets of an undertaking, or rights or contracts which confer decisive influence on the composition, voting or decisions of the organs of an undertaking. Control may be acquired by persons or undertakings holding the rights or being entitled to rights under the contract, or alternatively having the power to exercise such rights other than being holders of or contractually entitled to the rights.

Sole control

5.20 Sole control usually exists where the acquiring undertaking has the ability to decide on its own the activities of the undertaking acquired through a capital shareholding of 50 per cent or more in the latter. This can be seen in the first air transport concentration falling within the scope of the Merger Regulation between Delta Airlines and Pan Am in 1991.[19] The merger arose as a result of Pan Am's decision to withdraw from the trans-Atlantic market following its financial difficulties. An agreement was accordingly entered into with Delta for the latter to acquire the trans-Atlantic air transport business. Specifically, the agreement related to the acquisition of Pan Am's route authorisations to operate between the USA, namely New York, and Europe as well as the routes of Miami–London, Detroit–London and Washington–Frankfurt. Delta was also to acquire the Frankfurt hub operations of Pan Am. In the USA, Delta would acquire the Boston–New York–Washington operations. These transactions were a direct acquisition of control by Delta of Pan Am's assets, and thus qualified as a concentration within the meaning of Article 3(1) of the Merger Regulation.

5.21 However, the fact of capital holding is not necessarily a conclusive determinant, particularly in a case where there is no majority holding. Where for instance the remaining shareholders are fragmented or unable to exercise collective influence, then a minority shareholding may nevertheless confer on the acquiring undertaking a relative or *de facto* "majority" and the possibility to control the undertaking in question.[20]

---

[19] Commission Decision 91/C289, [1992] 5 CMLR 56.
[20] Commission Notice on the notion of a concentration, [1994] OJ C385/5.

Joint control and concentrative joint venture

Joint control is a more complicated issue simply by virtue of the fact that it calls **5.22**
for a value judgement to be made of the requirement of "decisive influence"
stipulated in Article 3(3). In a joint venture where the parent companies have
equal capital shareholding, so that decisions concerning the joint venture must
have a common agreement between them, the fact of joint control is apparent.
Where, however, the capital participation is not equal, the assessment turns on
the issue of whether the minority shareholder is capable of exercising a decisive
influence which goes beyond the traditional protection afforded to a minority
investor. As Article 3(3) has provided, control can be created by contract, rights
or other means. Thus, it is possible for a minority shareholder to have joint
control of a venture if, for example, it has equal board representation, weighted
voting rights or the right of veto on strategic business decisions.

It is, however, a requirement of Article 3(2) that the joint venture is of a **5.23**
concentrative nature, as opposed to a co-operative joint venture which would fall
within the scope of Article 85. For a concentrative joint venture to arise, it will
need to have a permanent character which does not give rise to a co-ordination
of competitive behaviour. The case law of the Commission evinces two categories
of approach to the question of co-ordination which in all cases are underlined by
the consideration of entry into the relevant market. First, in the case where the
parent companies remain active in the same product and geographic market as
the joint venture, there is likely to be a co-ordination of behaviour, and it will
therefore fall outside the scope of the Merger Regulation. Secondly, where both
parents withdraw completely or permanently from the market or enter an entirely
new market, with the prospects of re-entry highly unlikely, this would be regarded
as a concentrative joint venture within the Merger Regulation. The same reasoning would seem to apply to a case where only one of the parent companies with-
draws from the market.[21]

(a) *Air France–Sabena.*[22] The issue of joint control in air transport concentrations **5.24**
was the subject of a comprehensive consideration by the Commission in its investigation into the merger between Air France, the Belgian State and Sabena.
Sabena had given an undertaking as a condition of the Bfrs 30.2b State aid in
1991, that it would seek an industrial partner as part of its restructuring programme.[23] Air France eventually emerged as the preferred partner. Under the
agreement, Air France would hold 37.5 per cent of the capital and voting rights
in Sabena through Finacta, a company in which Air France would have majority
control. The Belgian State, on the other hand, would hold 62.5 per cent of the
capital and voting rights of Sabena. In addition, Finacta would have the right to:

- approve the appointments of Sabena's chairman and its deputy;
- appoint five of 12 additional board members, within which strategic,
  business, investment and industrial-plan decisions would require 75 per cent
  of the votes;

[21] Commission Notice, [1994] OJ C385/1, which details the pertinent considerations in differentiating
between a concentration and co-ordination of competitive behaviour.
[22] Commission Decision 92/C272, [1994] 5 CMLR 1.
[23] Commission Decision 91/555, [1991] OJ L300/48. See Ch. 13 *infra*.

- appoint half of the members of the executive committee designed to act on behalf of the board of directors particularly in respect of business strategies, budget planning, organisational structure, investment and implementation of the industrial plan.

5.25   In addition, the agreement provided for the chairmen of Air France and Sabena to consult with each other in the event of a major difficulty in the functioning of the bodies or implementation of the business and investment plans.

On the basis of these provisions, the Commission concluded that the transaction gave rise to a joint venture. In particular, it had regard to the influence of Air France in the day-to-day management of Sabena by virtue of its right of veto on the appointments of the chairman and its deputy. Moreover, notwithstanding the majority holding held by Sabena, there was no specific machinery for resolving disputes "which would give it predominance in the event of major difficulties". Indeed, Air France enjoyed rights which went beyond those normally vested in minority shareholders. By contrast, when Air France (Finacta) divested its holding in Sabena, the subsequent acquisition by Swissair of 49.5 per cent of the capital of Sabena was regarded by the Commission as a minority shareholding which did not confer on it the power of influence over strategic decisions in the joint venture.[24]

5.26   In the Air France–Sabena merger, the Commission also concluded that the joint venture was concentrative in nature such that it fell within the scope of the Merger Regulation. First, it considered that the joint venture would perform on a long-term basis all the functions of an independent economic entity with particular reference to the 30-year term of the agreement which was subject to further extension for 10-year periods.

5.27   Secondly, given the sole ownership of the Belgian State in Sabena prior to the agreement, the joint venture meant that its air transport activities would be completely subsumed into the venture. Given that it owned no other airline company, nor was it likely that a new airline would be formed, it could not be considered as an actual or potential competitor. There was also a lack of co-ordination of the competitive behaviour of Air France and the joint venture, Sabena. The Commission pointed to the unequal expertise in the air transport sector between Air France and Sabena. The fact of Sabena having to find an industrial partner underlined its relative lack of expertise and the need to benefit from the route synergy and experience of a new partner. Furthermore, the influence by Air France in strategic decisions and the fact that the appointment of Sabena's chairman required the express consent of Air France established "a certain preponderance" in the management of the joint venture. Thus, under those circumstances the acquisition by Air France of joint control of Sabena did not have the object or effect of co-ordinating the competitive behaviour of enterprises which remained independent.

5.28   (b) British Airways–TAT.[25] The concentration between BA and TAT concerned the acquisition by BA of 49.9 per cent of the capital of TAT European Airlines, under

---

[24] Commission Decision 96/180, [1996] OJ L54/28. See Ch. 7 infra.
[25] Case T-2/93, Air France v Commission [1994] ECR II-323.

a joint venture agreement in which the French-registered carrier TAT SA would hold the remaining 50.1 per cent of the shareholding. The agreement also provided an option for BA to acquire the 50.1 per cent shareholding at any time until 1 April 1997.[26] In addition, the agreement provided that:

- TAT SA would nominate five of the nine board members with the rest being nominated by BA;
- the President and Director-General of TAT would be appointed with the consent of BA;
- major decisions could only be taken by the board if at least one TAT SA nominated and one BA nominated member voted in favour;
- the deputy Director-General for commercial affairs was to be nominated by BA.

On these considerations, the Commission decided that TAT was a joint venture that was controlled by BA and TAT SA jointly.   5.29

The Commission also concluded that the anticipated duration of six and a half years of the agreement was sufficiently long to effect a lasting change in the structure of BA and TAT SA, given in particular that air transport is a sector constantly exposed to rapid legal and economic changes. It also found that the transaction lacked the object or effect of co-ordinating the competitive behaviour of BA, TAT SA and TAT on the grounds that the agreement required TAT SA to cease operating on certain routes on which the joint venture would be operating and that the relationship between BA and the joint venture was characterised by the substantial and growing influence by BA on the way in which the joint venture was to be run and developed, and the leading role it would play in the management of the joint venture.

This decision became the subject of a judicial review application by Air France   5.30
on the ground, *inter alia*, that the Commission was wrong to have concluded that the transaction amounted to a joint venture instead of finding that BA had assumed the sole control of TAT.[27] Air France had alleged that the question of whether sole or joint control had been assumed was a question of fact to be assessed "in the light of the economic objectives pursued by the acquiring undertaking". It submitted that in this case, the real object of the concentration was to integrate the domestic and international operations of TAT into the organisation and structure of BA. The legal and financial aspects of the transaction were inadequate considerations on their own.

The Court of First Instance rejected the submissions of Air France and upheld the argument of the Commission that the joint control of TAT stemmed from the 50.1 per cent shareholding of TAT SA and the need for at least one TAT SA nominee to vote in favour of a strategic decision prior to its approval. It added that the business plan underpinning the transaction was agreed jointly by TAT SA and BA, which BA had no unilateral power to amend.

---

[26] This option was exercised in 1996 and approved by the Commission, thus enabling BA to have sole control of TAT: [1996] OJ C316/11.
[27] Case T-2/93, *Air France* v *Commission* [1994] ECR II-323.

5. The Community dimension

5.31   The formation of a concentration does not on its own qualify to be investigated under the Merger Regulation. In addition to its existence, that concentration must have a "Community dimension" subject to the derogations provided in Article 1 of the Regulation. A Community dimension will exist where:

- the combined aggregate world-wide turnover of all the undertakings concerned is more than ECU 5,000 million; and

- the aggregate Community-wide turnover of each of at least two of the undertakings concerned is more than ECU 250 million,

unless each of the undertakings concerned achieves more than two-thirds of its aggregate Community-wide turnover within one and the same Member State.[28]

5.32   Whether or not a concentration has a Community dimension is a question which the Commission has sole responsibility to decide unless the Commission chooses to refer the concentration to the national competent authorities under Article 9, or a Member State opts to exercise its default powers "to protect legitimate interests other than those taken into consideration by this Regulation" under Article 21. For mergers which are deemed not to have a Community dimension, the principle of subsidiarity will be invoked and these cases will qualify to be investigated by the national authorities.[29] This does not, however, prejudice the jurisdiction of the Commission to investigate the concentration under Articles 85 and 86 since these provisions continue to be applicable in appropriate cases as previously.

Calculation of turnover

5.33   Article 5 of the Merger Regulation sets out the general methodology for calculating the aggregate turnover for the purpose of determining whether a concentration has a Community dimension. Article 5(1) stipulates that the aggregate turnover:

"shall comprise the amounts derived by the undertakings concerned in the preceding financial year from the sale of products and the provision of services falling within the undertakings' ordinary activities"

In calculating the amounts achieved by the undertakings concerned, Article 5(4) requires the respective turnovers of its parent companies, subsidiaries, and other subsidiaries of the parent companies to be added together.[30] However, turnover

---

[28] These thresholds are now the subject of a consultation exercise to consider the possible reduction to ECU 2,000m and ECU 100m respectively: (1996) 1/2 *EU Bulletin*, para. 1.3.39.

[29] See Case T-3/93, *Air France* v *Commission* [1994] ECR II-121.

[30] The relevant turnovers specified in Article 5(4) are those of: (i) the undertaking concerned; (ii) those undertakings in which the undertaking concerned, directly or indirectly (a) owns more than half the capital or business assets, or (b) has the power to exercise more than half the voting rights, or (c) has the power to appoint more than half the members of the supervisory board or (d) has the right to manage the undertakings' affairs; (iii) those undertakings which have the above right or powers over the undertaking concerned; (iv) those undertakings in which undertakings of (iii) have the above rights or powers; (v) those undertakings in which two or more undertakings in (i) to (iv) jointly have the above rights or powers.

derived from transactions *between* such undertakings must not be taken into account, nor should rebates and taxes "directly related to turnover" because they refer to "indirect taxation". Nonetheless, in the Commission Notice on the calculation of turnover, the Commission stated that this must include "turnover derived from, and thus resources devoted to, all areas of activity of the parties, and not just those directly involved in the concentration".[31]

Partial acquisition: British Airways–Dan Air [32]

In 1992, the Commission was confronted with the take-over by BA of Dan Air,   5.34
a subsidiary of the Davies and Newman Holdings group. Dan Air operated primarily charter services, although it had also begun limited scheduled services. An important condition of the agreement was that Dan Air was required to effect the "discontinuation or disposal of the charter operations . . . the transfer, repudiation or termination of all contracts for charter flights" prior to the agreed completion date.

In the preliminary inquiry, the Merger Task Force had reached the conclusion that the Commission had no jurisdiction in the matter on the ground that the aggregate turnover of Dan Air was below the thresholds established by the Regulation, and thus, had no Community dimension. In particular, it found that the aggregate Community-wide turnover of Dan Air without taking into account the charter activities amounted to ECU 232.9 million. The ECU 250 million threshold would have been exceeded if these activities were taken into account. The refusal to assume jurisdiction to investigate was subsequently challenged by way of judicial review in the Court of First Instance by Air France.

Although one of the major issues concerned the existence of an "act" in the   5.35
form of a Commission decision for the purposes of Article 173, Air France alleged that the Commission had been wrong to disregard the turnover derived from Dan Air's charter operations. In particular, it alleged that the Commission was obliged to take account of the turnover achieved by an undertaking which is a party to a concentration in respect of its ordinary activities during the preceding year as laid down in Article 5(1).

However, Article 5(2) provides for a derogation such that "only the turnover relating to the parts which are the subject of the transaction shall be taken into account". Relying upon this provision, the Commission argued that the calculation of turnovers and its methodology must reflect the real economic significance of the operation in relation to the structure of the bid. A calculation would be meaningless unless it applied to undertakings in the form in which they existed at the time of the transaction or concentration. The Commission added:

> "Even though the reference to the turnover for the preceding financial year is intended to provide a clear and indisputable basis, it cannot result in the structural changes arising after that date being ignored . . . The provision is not in any way concerned with what happens to those parts of the undertaking which are not transferred."

---

[31] Commission Notice on the calculation of turnover, [1994] OJ C385/21.
[32] Case T-3/93, *Air France* v *Commission* [1994] ECR II-121.

5.36   On the facts, the Court of First Instance concluded that the submission of the Commission was a correct interpretation to give to Article 5(1) and (2). According to the Court of First Instance, the objective of Article 5(2) was:

> "to determine the real dimension of the concentration for the purposes of examining whether, having regard to the parts of the undertaking which are actually acquired, whether or not constituted as legal entities, the proposed operation has a 'Community dimension' . . . and despite the fact that the article contains no express reference to the discontinuance of activities, the Court considers that the concepts of the partial transfer and the partial discontinuance of activities are comparable, inasmuch as they both allow a precise appraisal to be made of the exact subject-matter, composition and extent of the proposed concentration."

5.37   Since the Commission had decided that it had no jurisdiction over the concentration for its lack of a "Community dimension", the responsibility for investigating the merger fell upon the national authorities in accordance with the principle of subsidiarity. In this case, it was the Secretary of State, and on a reference by him, the Monopolies and Mergers Commission (MMC). The Secretary of State, in agreement with the Office of Fair Trading, declined to refer the matter to the MMC on the ground that "the public interest would be better served by not referring".[33] This decision provoked a response from independent airlines such as Virgin Atlantic Airways, British Midland, Air UK and Britannia Airways who sought to challenge the decision by way of judicial review asserting that the Secretary of State had acted unlawfully by not referring the matter.

5.38   In the High Court, Schiemann J. refused to grant the leave sought. An appeal to the Court of Appeal was subsequently dismissed on the footing that the Secretary of State was not required to consider Article 86 of the Treaty in deciding whether or not to refer the case to the MMC, and if this was so, then the question becomes a matter solely for him in the exercise of his discretion under domestic competition law.[34] There is a certain oddity in the reasoning of the Court of Appeal. Article 86, in contrast to Article 85, has been declared as directly effective.[35] That being the case, the Secretary of State's discretion should have been limited by the direct effects of the provision. It is precisely because the merger did not fall within the scope of the Merger Regulation that Article 86 and its directly effective nature must continue to apply. It would also be a misconceived argument to state that the Merger Regulation provided an exception to this since EC Treaty provisions can only be derogated from expressly by the Treaty itself. Consequently, the Merger Regulation could only have disapplied equivalent implementing measures such as Regulation 17/62, and Regulation 3975/87 in respect of concentrations, but not Article 86.

---

[33] *The Times*, 3 November 1992.
[34] *R* v *Secretary of State for Trade and Industry ex parte Airlines of Britain & Virgin Atlantic Airways, The Independent*, 8 December 1992.
[35] Case 66/86, *Ahmed Saeed Flugreisen and Silver Line Reisebüro* v *Zentrale zur Bekämpfung Unlauteren Wettbewerbs* [1989] ECR 803.

Territorial turnovers

Air transport is essentially an international operation and thus makes it difficult to   5.39
achieve an accurate calculation of the aggregate Community-wide turnover.
Whilst the determination of the aggregate world-wide turnover is sufficiently
straightforward, highly detailed information and data need to be available to
distinguish between turnover resulting from non-Community and Community
operations, and indeed to determine whether more than two-thirds of that
turnover was achieved within one Member State. Accordingly, the second subparagraph of Article 5(1) specifies that:

> "Turnover, in the Community or in a Member State, shall comprise products sold and
> services provided to undertakings or consumers, in the Community or in that Member
> State as the case may be."

(a) *Delta–Pan Am.*[36] In 1991, the Commission examined the merger between   5.40
Delta–Pan Am insofar as it affected Community routes. Three possibilities of
determining the aggregate turnover were suggested:

- *country of destination*: this method of calculation would be to attribute the
  operating revenues derived from trans-Atlantic services to the country of
  destination, that is to say, the Community destination outside the home
  country of the airline;
- *equal division*: this method would entail the allocation of revenues on a 50:50
  basis between the country of origin and country of destination, which would
  consequently allow the cross-border characteristic of the service to
  be considered;
- *point of sale*: the revenues under this method would simply be attributed to
  the Member State in which the ticket was sold.

Unfortunately, the Commission failed to indicate the preferred method of
calculation, leaving the question open for future cases. This was justified on the
basis that "in each of the three alternatives Delta and the part of Pan Am that is
being purchased achieve a Community-wide turnover that exceeds 250m ECUs".

(b) *Air France–Sabena.*[37] The issue arose again in the Commission's consideration   5.41
of the participation by Air France in Sabena. Although the Commission concluded that the aggregate world-wide turnover of both Air France and Sabena
exceeded the ECU 5,000m threshold, it acknowledged the difficulty inherent in
choosing a criterion for calculating the Community turnover and the possibility
of different results. In its decision, the Commission re-stated the three possible
methods of calculation first enunciated in Delta–Pan Am without making a
conclusive choice, although on this occasion it expressed a preference for the
second method. Attributing the revenues equally "seems to be closer to the spirit
of Article 5(1) because it refers to the two places between which the air transport
service was actually supplied, thus incorporating the transfrontier nature thereof".

---

[36] Commission Decision 91/C289, [1992] 5 CMLR 56.
[37] Commission Decision 92/C272, [1994] 5 CMLR 1.

In the event, it concluded that each of three methods produced a Community turnover that exceeded the threshold laid down in Article 1(2).

6. Application of the Merger Regulation: market analysis

Compatibility with the common market

5.42   Once a concentration is deemed to have a Community dimension, the Commission must then consider whether the concentration is compatible with the common market by reference to the criteria of whether it creates or strengthens a dominant position. Article 2(2) states specifically that a concentration which "does not create or strengthen a dominant position as a result of which effective competition would be significantly impeded in the common market or a substantial part of it" must be declared as compatible.

5.43   For its assessment of the compatibility of a concentration with the common market, the Commission is required to take into account the "appraisal criteria" provided in Article 2(1) of the Regulation. These criteria are:

- the need to maintain and develop effective competition within the common market in view of, among other things, the structure of all the markets concerned and the actual or potential competition from undertakings located either within or without the Community;

- the market position of the undertakings concerned and their economic and financial power, the alternatives available to suppliers and users, their access to supplies or markets, any legal or other barriers to entry, supply and demand trends for the relevant goods and services, the interests of the intermediate and ultimate consumers, and the development of technical and economic progress provided that it is to consumers' advantage and does not form an obstacle to competition.

5.44   In the statement issued by the Commission on the interpretation of the Regulation in 1990, it also confirmed that the criteria of "the structure of all the markets concerned" included markets which are within and outside of the Community, and "technical and economic progress" would be construed in the light of the principles developed under Article 85(3).[38]

In addition, recital 13 of the Regulation states that the Commission "must place its appraisal within the general framework of the achievement of the fundamental objectives referred to in Article 2 of the Treaty, including that of strengthening the Community's economic and social cohesion, referred to in Article 130a". This has been construed by the Commission as requiring it to have regard to "the competitiveness of undertakings located in regions which are greatly in need of

---

[38] [1990] 4 CMLR 314.

restructuring owing *inter alia* to slow development".[39] The point was made in the introductory section that certain mergers may have a neutral effect on competition, and may accordingly be authorised. In particular, recital 4 of the Regulation calls for the Commission to recognise that certain mergers may be in line with:

"the requirements of dynamic competition and capable of increasing the competitiveness of European industry, improving conditions of growth and raising the standard of living in the Community."

According to the Commission in its *Twenty-First Report on Competition Policy*, the appraisal of concentrations generally involves three stages: the determination of the relevant product, of the geographic market, and the assessment of their compatibility with the common market.

Relevant product market
In essence, a relevant product market will consist of all those products which are regarded as interchangeable or substitutable by the consumer, by reason of the products' characteristics, their prices and the intended use.[40] An implied requisite of this test is that the products must compete to a sufficient degree so that effective competition is regarded to exist between them.   5.45

Relevant geographic market
The issue of relevant geographic market has already been considered in Chapter 3. Suffice it to say that its basic definition is the area in which the undertakings concerned operate and where the conditions of competition are sufficiently homogeneous and may be distinguished from adjacent areas because the conditions of competition between them are appreciably different.[41] The definition of the relevant geographic market can take a narrow or wide meaning, depending on the factors deemed applicable. In the airline merger cases, the Commission has identified two definitions: 5.46

- individual routes: where each route connecting the relevant gateways are regarded as a distinct market;
- bundle of routes: where there is a degree of substitutability between the gateways.[42]

A dominant position significantly impeding effective competition
Dominant position is not defined in the Regulation. The Commission has had to develop an approach towards dominant positions and has explicitly adopted the meaning given by the European Court of Justice in relation to Article 86 of the   5.47

---

[39] *Ibid.*
[40] Commission Decision 91/619, *Aérospatiale-Alenia-De Havilland* [1991] OJ L334/42. See also Case 66/86, *Ahmed Saeed Flugreisen and Silver Line Reisebüro* v *Zentrale zur Bekämpfung Unlauteren Wettbewerbs* [1989] ECR 803.
[41] Commission Decision 90/C327, *Cargill-Unilever* [1990] OJ C327/14.
[42] See the concentrations of Delta-Pan Am, Air France-Sabena and BA-TAT, *infra.*

Treaty,[43] that is, a position of economic strength enjoyed by an undertaking which enables it to prevent effective competition being maintained in the relevant market by affording it the power to behave to an appreciable extent independently of its competitors, its customers and ultimately of consumers.[44] In the context of air transport, the Court stated in *Ahmed Saeed* that the test for dominant position was whether the service on a particular route could be distinguished from the possible alternatives by reference to its specific characteristics, as a result of which it was not interchangeable with those alternatives and was affected only to an insignificant extent by competition from them.[45]

5.48   The difficulty with the test in the context of Article 86 is that it seeks to prohibit the abuse of a dominant position that has been created, while the control of mergers implies the prohibition of future dominant positions which impede effective competition before they come into being. This necessarily involves a complex value judgement of the prospective strength of the new entity. *Inter alia*, this would include questions of whether the dominant position is temporary or whether the barriers of entry are sufficiently low.

Four criteria have been adopted by the Commission for determining the likely market strength of the new entity resulting from a horizontal merger and the degree to which effective competition can still be possible or otherwise impeded.[46]

5.49   (a)   Market share. In general, a concentration which results only in a low market share will be declared compatible with the common market. Indeed, in recognising that certain mergers may have a neutral effect on competition, recital 15 of the Regulation explains the need for a *de minimis* approach.

> "Whereas concentrations which, by reason of the limited market share of the undertakings concerned, are not liable to impede effective competition may be presumed to be compatible with the common market; whereas, without prejudice to Articles 85 and 86 of the Treaty, an indication to this effect exists, in particular, where the market share of the undertakings concerned does not exceed 25% either in the common market or in a substantial part of it."

Conversely then, a new entity with high market share will usually suggest the existence of a dominant position; 40 per cent has been suggested as reasonable to characterise a high market share.[47] However, high market shares are not always conclusive of the fact of a dominant position since it may be possible for active and actual competition to exist in parallel, or for the market shares to be temporary particularly in a newly developed market. The significance of market shares must therefore be assessed in the light of trends in market shares, duration of those market shares and the market context.

---

[43] Case 27/76, *United Brands v Commission* [1978] ECR 207.
[44] *Twenty-First Report on Competition Policy* (1991), p.362.
[45] Case 66/86, *Ahmed Saeed Flugreisen and Silver Line Reisebüro* v *Zentrale zur Bekämpfung Unlauteren Wettbewerbs* [1989] ECR 803, at 849.
[46] *Twenty-First Report on Competition Policy* (1991), p.363.
[47] D.Ridyard, "Economic Analysis of Single Firms and Oligopolistic Dominance under the European Merger Regulation" (1994) 5 *ECLRev* 255.

(b)   Structure of demand. The structure of demand is characterised by the buying   5.50
power of the consumers. Where, for example, there is substantial recourse to alternative supply, the flexibility of demand will usually ensure competition between
the undertakings in the relevant market.

(c)   Structure of supply. This is usually defined as the strength of the remaining
competitors in the relevant market so that their continued participation results in
a competitive pressure in the new entity. This must depend, *inter alia*, on the
number of actual competitors left, their strength, and the gap between them and
the new entity.

(d)   Potential of competition. This can come either from established competitors
through the expansion of capacity or alternatively from new entrants into the
market. The consideration of barriers to entry is therefore crucial. These will
include restrictions arising from bilateral agreements and the lack of take-off and
landing slots at congested airports.

These criteria for appraising the market strength of newly formed undertakings   5.51
have been applied by the Commission in its decisions on airline mergers. In
particular, they have been considered at length in the mergers of Delta–Pan Am,
Air France–Sabena and BA–TAT, which are now examined further. In passing,
it should be noted that the first occasion on which the Commission prohibited a
merger under the Merger Regulation was in relation to the Aérospatiale/Alenia-
-De Havilland case. Amongst other things, the Commission found that the
merger would strengthen the position of Avions de Transport Régional (ATR),
which is jointly controlled by Aérospatiale and Alenia, as much as it would
increase its share of the market substantially. Moreover, de Havilland's elimination from the market would effectively mean that competition in the market
was significantly reduced; neither was there a "realistic significant potential
competition". Consequently, the merger was judged as incompatible with the
common market.[48]

7. Application of the substantive principles

Delta–Pan Am[49]

This merger involved the acquisition by Delta of Pan Am's trans-Atlantic   5.52
operations. The Commission had already found that the transaction gave rise to
a concentration which assumed a Community dimension. The question which
followed was whether the concentration could be declared as compatible with the
common market.

---

[48] Commission Decision 91/619, [1991] OJ L334/42. The only other block to a merger was
Commission Decision 94/922 *MSG Media Service*, [1994] OJ L364/1.
[49] Commission Decision 91/C289, [1992] 5 CMLR 56.

In terms of the relevant geographic market, the Commission chose eventually to leave the question of a narrower or wider market definition open because on the two market definitions adopted in the decision, no dominant position would be created nor strengthened. In the first definition of the relevant geographic market, the Commission considered that each route between the USA and the Community could be regarded as a distinct market, having regard also to the regulatory restrictions stemming from the bilateral agreements. Secondly, it reasoned that the relevant market could be defined as "a bundle of routes" on the basis that there was sufficient demand-side substitutability between certain routes. For example, a New York-London service could be substituted by New York–Paris or New York–Amsterdam. Thus, for the purposes of that case, the Commission considered that services into London, Frankfurt, Paris, Amsterdam, Brussels, Zurich and Copenhagen, which accounted for 75 per cent of all trans-Atlantic scheduled services, had a certain degree of substitutability between them.

5.53   On the issue of market shares, the Commission first noted the large number of carriers operating on the trans-Atlantic market. There were some 38 carriers, the majority of whom operated a daily service. Secondly, it noted that the transaction would result in Delta acquiring 33 trans-Atlantic routes although they excluded the densest route of New York–London which was acquired earlier by United Airlines.

On the basis of the narrow market definition, that is where each route is regarded as a distinct market, the Commission concluded that there would be no overlap between the undertakings concerned on the city pairs, and consequently, there would be no addition of market shares since the trans-Atlantic routes operated by Delta originated from Atlanta, Cincinnati, Dallas (Fort Worth) and Orlando, but not New York, Detroit, Miami nor Washington. Under the wider market share test, the overall market share of Delta would be approximate 16 percent of the total scheduled trans-Atlantic traffic, and accordingly would not exceed the 25 per cent threshold.

5.54   Although the transaction would result in Delta having the highest market share in the trans-Atlantic business, the structure of the market was such that effective competition would continue to exist since Delta would be "exposed to a large number of strong competitors with significant presence in the overall transatlantic air traffic" including American Airlines, United, Trans-World Airlines, British Airways, Lufthansa, Air France and KLM. One important consideration of the concentration noted by the Commission was the ability of Delta to provide more effective competition with other American carriers by offering connecting services between domestic traffic in the USA and the Community, and *vice versa*. Notably, Pan Am could not have offered such on-line services given its corporate emphasis on international services with only limited domestic operations. Under those circumstances, the concentration was not incompatible with the common market.

Air France–Sabena[50]

5.55   In contrast to the Delta–Pan Am concentration, the Commission made the observation in this case that the relevant geographic market was between France

---

[50] Commission Decision 92/C272, [1994] 5 CMLR 1.

and Belgium. Consequently, the distances were too short for them to be considered as a bundle of routes. It added that if substitutability was to underpin the assessment of the relevant market, then factors such as length of the routes, distances between airports of each city, and frequency of services must be taken into account. Thus, for example, the greater the distance between the originating point and destination, the greater the likelihood that one route can be substituted by another. Likewise, the closer the distance between two airports serving the same city conurbation, the greater the degree of substitutability. In respect of alternative modes of transport, the Commission considered them as distinct markets in general, and thus unlikely to be a substitute, unless there is a genuine possibility of such substitution.

The analysis of this concentration was more complex given the structure of the   5.56
markets concerned, both the intra- and extra-Community markets operated by Air France and Sabena. The Commission began first by looking at the market position of the undertakings in relation to the French–Belgian market. Three routes were identified as significant in the assessment principally because there was an overlap of operations between them with the following traffic distribution:

(a)   Brussels–Lyon: Air France 50 per cent; Sabena 50 per cent
(b)   Brussels–Nice: Air France 50 per cent; Sabena 50 per cent
(c)   Brussels–Paris: Air France 40 per cent; Sabena 60 per cent

As a consequence of the merger, a monopoly situation would exist in each of the different markets.

As to potential competition, the Commission was not satisfied that the   5.57
conditions were prospectively good. It pointed out that in particular the Brussels–Lyon and Brussels–Nice routes were unlikely to attract new entrants since demand would be static and thus provide little opportunity for the minimum frequency required to sustain viable services. Indeed, "freedom of access to the market created by the third package could lead to effective competition only in the long term". By contrast, although the Commission acknowledged that a monopoly situation would similarly arise on the Brussels–Paris route, it noted that this market might possibly be exposed to a certain degree of competition stemming from other modes of transport, namely rail. On balance, however, it concluded that the possibility of substitution in this market was too imperfect. For example, in the case of transit passengers, rail travel was not an adequate substitute. In the event, the Commission concluded that the transaction would not lead to the creation or strengthening of a dominant position, but only in the light of undertakings extracted from Air France and Sabena that one of them would withdraw from the relevant market in favour another operator with a guarantee of the necessary slots.

The Commission then examined the markets relating to Turkey and Hungary,   5.58
and concluded that the Paris–Ankara and Brussels–Ankara routes could be considered as a bundle under the wider market test. By implication then, the Paris–Budapest and Brussels–Budapest routes could also be regarded as a bundle. It gave the following explanation:

"For the several million people living north of the area of attraction of the Paris airports and south of the area of attraction of Brussels airport, these airports may be regarded as capable of being substituted for one another, because of their proximity, for fairly long flights such as those to Ankara and Budapest."

5.59   On the facts, the Commission found that the transaction would result in the new entity acquiring a high market share on each of the routes: Paris/Brussels–Ankara 81 per cent and Paris/Brussels–Budapest 54 per cent. In spite of these circumstances, the Commission decided that the undertaking given by the parties was adequate to ensure that no dominant position would be created nor strengthened as a result of which effective competition would be significantly impeded in the common market or a substantial part of it. The undertaking was to secure multiple designation on those markets in favour of other competitors, but it would be triggered only if the annual threshold of 100,000 passengers on each market was surpassed. This latter condition was accepted on the basis that there was a need for a minimum number of passengers to ensure viable operations.

The Commission also examined the markets in respect of the African continent. Because of the long duration of flights, limited frequency and the possibility of substitution on originating flights from the Community, the routes to Africa were treated as a bundle. Although the Commission found that Air France and Sabena enjoyed a strong presence in certain markets, it decided that the concentration would not result in the creation or strengthening of a dominant position on the basis that the parties had undertaken to withdraw from those markets for the benefit of a new entrant.

5.60   The Commission's analysis of the market strength of the parties also focused on the issue of dominance at the airports, particularly at Brussels (Zaventem) airport where the business plan of the merger had indicated that Sabena and Air France would operate a "hub and spoke" network serving 75 destinations upon completion of the expansion programme at the airport. Undoubtedly, this would require a substantial proportion of the slots available at the airport, the effect of which will be to strengthen the dominance of Air France and Sabena and equally to deny new operators the necessary slots to provide competing services. In that regard, Air France and Sabena agreed to restrict themselves for 10 years to "65% of the slots available for each rolling period of two hours" and subject to a ceiling of "75% of slots available for each rolling period of 60 minutes". The transaction was consequently not opposed by the Commission.

British Airways–TAT[51]

5.61   The Commission had decided that 49.9 per cent capital participation by BA in TAT did not raise any serious doubts as to its compatibility with the common market. In the first place the Commission had identified the London–Paris and London–Lyon routes as the relevant market given that it was only on those routes where the services of BA and TAT overlapped. However, both would be regarded

---

[51] Case T-2/93, [1994] ECR II-323.

as distinct markets although there was a possible degree of substitutability between airports on those routes.

Among the airlines which operated from the Paris (Charles de Gaulle) airport on the London–Paris route, only Dan Air, a subsidiary of BA, and TAT operated out of Gatwick. The remaining operators on the route including BA operated from either Heathrow or Stansted. While therefore the market shares of BA and TAT from Heathrow were not affected, the concentration would result in a market share of 98.6 per cent on the London (Gatwick)–Paris route, where BA through Dan Air would have 81.6 per cent and TAT would have 17 per cent. Overall, the BA–TAT concentration would give them a market share of 52.2 per cent on the London–Paris route. Air France was the nearest competitor with a 32.9 per cent market share.

As regards the London–Lyon route, the Commission had found that the only **5.62** operators were BA and Air France from Heathrow and TAT from Gatwick. The effect of the concentration was therefore to give BA–TAT a 100 per cent market share on the Gatwick–Lyon route. This, however, translated into 58.6 per cent on the London–Lyon route as a whole with Air France having a 41.4 per cent market share. It was therefore possible to conclude that there was a degree of substitutability on the routes in question. But in the final analysis, the Commission accepted that this would not always operate at an airport which lacked the necessary slots.

This part of the decision was subsequently impugned in the Court of First Instance by Air France on the ground that the Commission's analysis of the two relevant markets of London–Paris and London–Lyon was incomplete because it did not correspond to economic reality.[52] Air France submitted that, instead, the Commission should have defined the relevant market as "international air transport provided anywhere in the common market between different Member States". This would have required it to consider the entire European network of BA.

In many ways, the challenge by Air France inevitably called on the Court of **5.63** First Instance to make a judicial pronouncement on the substantive correctness of the Commission's decision because it had to review the definition of the relevant market adopted by the latter. In doing so, it upheld the formulation adopted by the Commission as being consistent with the principles developed by the Court of Justice in *Ahmed Saeed*.[53] The Court rejected as untrue the allegation that the Commission had failed to consider the wider consequences of the concentration. In any case, Air France was not able to demonstrate the extent to which the concentration would create or strengthen a dominant position in any of the markets upon which it had founded its case.

8. Powers of investigation

Although by virtue of Article 21(1), the Commission has the sole jurisdiction to **5.64** investigate mergers with a Community dimension and take the decisions provided

---

[52] *Ibid.*
[53] Case 66/86, *Ahmed Saeed Flugreisen and Silver Line Reisebüro* v *Zentrale zur Bekämpfung Unlauteren Wettbewerbs* [1989] ECR 803.

for in the Regulation, a number of exceptions are also provided in parallel which differ in nature. First of all, as seen earlier, there is an implied devolution of investigative powers to national authorities where a concentration has no Community dimension, although this does not prejudice the powers of the Commission in respect of Articles 85 and 86.

Referrals to Member States: distinct markets

5.65   Article 9(1) of the Regulation empowers the Commission to "refer a notified concentration to the competent authorities of the Member State concerned" provided that the undertakings concerned and the authorities of the other Member States are informed without delay. This provision is the product of a proposal from Germany during the gestation period of the Regulation. Such referrals, however, can only be made in the circumstances specified in Article 9(2). Within three weeks of the notification being received:

> "a Member State may inform the Commission, which shall inform the undertakings concerned, that a concentration threatens to create or to strengthen a dominant position as a result of which effective competition would be significantly impeded on a market, within that Member State, which presents all the characteristics of a distinct market, be it a substantial part of the common market or not."

5.66   A distinct market is to be defined by reference to the relevant geographical market consisting of the area in which:

* the undertakings concerned are involved in the supply and demand of products or services, and

* the conditions of competition are sufficiently homogeneous and can be distinguished from neighbouring areas given that conditions of competition in those areas are appreciably different.

In defining the geographical extent of the distinct market, regard must be had to the nature and characteristics of the products and services in question, existence of entry barriers, consumer preferences, and appreciable differences in the market shares held by the undertakings between the area concerned and the adjacent areas.

5.67   The Commission retains nevertheless a residual power to examine a case which it considers as having a distinct market "in order to maintain or restore effective competition on the market concerned" under Article 9(3)(a). Or alternatively, it may refer the case to the authorities of the Member State, though Member States are authorised only to take such measures as are "strictly necessary" to safeguard or restore competition in the market in question. Where, therefore, no distinct market or the threat of it exists, then the provisions of Article 9 become inapplicable. Indeed, the Commission has already stated in its 1990 statement of interpretation that:

"Article 9 should only be applied in exceptional cases . . . confined to cases in which the interests in respect of competition of the member-State concerned could not be adequately protected in any other way."[54]

This is simply because a concentration which either creates or strengthens a dominant position in a market which represents a substantial part of the common market should in principle be declared as incompatible with the common market. Ultimately, decisions of the Commission under Article 9 are subject to judicial review.

Protection of legitimate interests of Member States

In derogation to the provisions of Article 21(1) and (2), which confer on the Commission the exclusive jurisdiction to investigate and decide on a concentration with a Community dimension, Article 21(3) stipulates that: **5.68**

"Member States may take appropriate measures to protect legitimate interests other than those taken into consideration by this Regulation and compatible with the general principles and other provisions of Community law.
Public security, plurality of the media and prudential rules shall be regarded as legitimate interests within the meaning of the first subparagraph."

Member States may also invoke other public interest grounds provided they are first communicated to the Commission who must assess their compatibility with general principles of Community law.   **5.69**

These provisions provide a considerable width of discretion to Member States to intervene in the appraisal of a concentration. However, the Commission has indicated that they should be given a narrow interpretation.[55] In any event, they should not result in the creation of additional rights for Member States. The aim of the provision, according to the Commission, is to give recognition of the residual powers of Member States to intervene in concentrations which affect the territory of that Member State so that a concentration may be prohibited or subject to additional undertakings on the basis of the stipulated grounds. They do not abrogate the authority of the Commission, in that Member States are not empowered to authorise concentrations which the Commission has opposed.

The appropriate measures which Member States may adopt must conform to the principle of proportionality. This entails that such measures must be appropriate to the objective, and demands the minimal action necessary or imposes the least restrictive conditions to protect the legitimate interests. In addition, of course, the measures must comply with the general principles of law so that, for example, they are not arbitrary nor restrict trade between Member States.   **5.70**

---

[54] [1990] 4 CMLR 314. See Commission Decision 92/C50, *Steetley–Tarmac* [1992] OJ C50/25 and *CPC–McCormick–Rabobank–Ostmann* Twentieth Report on Competition Policy (1990), the two occasions when the Commission acceded to the request.
[55] [1990] 4 CMLR 314.

Public security

5.71   Typically, this will relate to concentrations involving national defence which would be contrary to the essential interests of security, although the Commission has said that it is capable of having a wider definition to encompass security of supplies considered vital to the essential interests of the Member State.

Plurality of media

5.72   This ground recognises the importance of maintaining diversified sources of information, opinions and views.

Prudence

5.73   This has been interpreted by the Commission as especially concerned with the financial services sector, for instance in the regulation of banks, insurance companies and the like.

Referrals by Member States

5.74   Article 22(3), which enables a Member State to request the Commission to investigate on its behalf a concentration which falls outside the Regulation, is the result of a proposal from smaller Member States, particularly The Netherlands. Their concerns were that the lack of a sophisticated national framework for merger control would lead to inequitable results. Thus, Article 22(3) specifically enables a Member State to request the Commission to appraise a concentration which has no Community dimension but nevertheless creates or strengthens a dominant position which would significantly impede effective competition within the territory of the Member State concerned, so that trade between Member States is affected.

5.75   This provision has been invoked once in respect of air transport. The Belgian government, in consequence of the absence then of national merger legislation, requested the Commission to investigate the concentration between BA and Dan Air, which the Commission had earlier declared as not having a Community dimension.[56] In the end, the Commission chose not to oppose the concentration on two grounds. The Commission reasoned that because the Belgian authorities had not provided sufficient information to enable it to proceed with an investigation, no notification was therefore lodged in accordance with Article 22(3). On the substantive issue of whether the concentration was compatible with the common market, the Commission noted that Article 22(3) provided only for intervention if trade between Member States was affected. Although the relevant market in that case was the Brussels–London route, the Commission found that the transaction did not create nor strengthen a dominant position that was incompatible with the common market.[57]

---

[56] Case T-3/93, *Air France* v *Commission* [1994] ECR II-121.
[57] Commission Decision 93/C68, [1993] OJ C68/5. See *Twenty-Third Report on Competition Policy* (1993), p.187.

Delegation of investigative powers to Member States

The Commission may delegate to the competent authorities of the Member States   5.76
the powers to investigate concentrations in accordance with Article 12 of the
Regulation. The delegation should only be authorised in circumstances when first,
the Commission considers it "necessary" for the duties under Article 13(1) to be
carried out, and secondly when a decision has been taken pursuant to Article
13(3).

Article 13(1) sets out the investigative powers of the Commission to enter any
premises of the undertakings, examine and copy their books and business records,
and to ask for spontaneous oral explanations. Article 13(3) on the other hand
enables the Commission, by a decision, to order the undertakings to submit
to investigation.

9. Notification and commencement of proceedings

Article 4 of the Regulation requires that all concentrations with a Community   5.77
dimension must be notified to the Commission within one week of the agreement
or acquisition being concluded.[58] Where, however, a concentration has been
implemented, the Commission may require divestment, cessation of joint control
"or any other action that may be appropriate in order to restore conditions of
effective competition" pursuant to Article 8(4).

On notification, the Commission has three options for its decisions, all of which   5.78
must be reached within a maximum of one month from the day of notification,
although in the case where insufficient information has been supplied, the time
period will begin from the day when complete information is received.[59] Powers
for obtaining information are contained in Article 11 of the Regulation. The three
options for the Commission are either:

- to conclude, by means of a decision, that the concentration does not fall
  within the scope of the Regulation;

- to conclude that the concentration, although falling within the scope of the
  Regulation, does not raise serious doubts as to its compatibility with the common market. Accordingly, it "shall decide not to oppose and shall declare
  that it is compatible". No formal decision appears to be necessary;

- to conclude that the concentration falls within the scope of the Regulation
  and raises serious doubts as to its compatibility with the common market. In
  this case, it "shall decide to initiate proceedings". Article 8(1) requires that
  all proceedings initiated shall be closed by means of a decision. Decisions

---

[58] See Commission Regulation 2367/90, [1990] OJ L219/5 on notification, time limits and hearings.
[59] Art. 6(1) of Merger Regulation.

which declare the compatibility of the concentration may be accompanied by conditions or undertakings, or modifications to ensure compatibility. Such decisions will also apply to restrictions ancillary to the concentration, which require that they be necessary and directly related to the implementation of the concentration.[60] In the case of a final decision where the Commission is minded to authorise the concentration subject to modifications or conditions, it must be taken "as soon as it appears" that the serious doubts have been removed. On the other hand, where the Commission is minded to declare the incompatibility of the concentration with the common market, then it must do so within a maximum of four months.

5.79   Some of these issues became pertinent in the acquisition of Dan Air by BA.[61] The proposed concentration had not been notified to the Commission since the initial view was that the concentration did not exceed the Community dimension thresholds. Nevertheless, BA informed the Merger Task Force (MTF) of the proposed concentration, which in turn advised the Commission of its opinion that the transaction fell outside the scope of the Regulation if the charter activities of Dan Air were not taken into account. Subsequent to this informal notification, the MTF informed BA that the concentration did not have a Community dimension on an initial analysis although it stated that those were the views of the MTF and were not therefore binding on the Commission. Although the Commission did issue a formal statement confirming that it had no jurisdiction over the concentration, these discrepancies were the subject of a preliminary analysis by the Court of First Instance in Air France's application for judicial review against the substantive decision of the Commission. The Court considered that the statement issued by the Commission was to all intents and purposes an "act" which was amenable to an application for judicial review. It adopted the reasoning of the Court of Justice in *IBM* v *Commission* that:

> "Any measure the legal effects of which are binding on, and capable of affecting the interests of, the applicant by bringing about a distinct change in his legal position is an act or decision which may be the subject of an action under Article 173 for a declaration that it is void."[62]

5.80   Such statements issued by the Commission on the application of the Regulation have the effect of either precluding the application of any other rules, in particular national laws on the control of mergers, or absolving the parties concerned of the obligation to notify in accordance with Article 4 of the Regulation. Furthermore, such statements have an effect on Member States whose territory is directly or indirectly affected by the transaction as regards Article 22(3).

---

[60] See the notice issued by the Commission: [1990] OJ C203/5.
[61] Case T-3/93, *Air France* v *Commission* [1994] ECR II-121.
[62] Case 60/81, [1981] ECR 2639, at 2651.

10. Conclusion

The importance of merger control in Community air transport cannot be over-   5.81
stated. The dynamism of the industry must mean that changes are inevitable, and
mergers are simply another response to the changing conditions of the market.
Consolidation in the sector is becoming increasingly common, and indeed
inevitable. This may take the form of an outright merger, or other forms of co-
operation falling short of a merger such as code-sharing agreements and franchising. Scrupulous control of both transactions which may have negative competitive
overtones is quintessential to effective competition and the enhancement of user
interests. The decision of the Commission to examine the various code-sharing
agreements represents its concern that only agreements which do not adversely
affect competition and trade between Member States should be authorised.
Specific powers for investigating such cases are still lacking, and the Commission
has had to turn to the transitional Article 89 of the EC Treaty which confers on
it a general remit to investigate competition cases.

Part III

THE REGULATORY FRAMEWORK

Chapter 6

LICENSING OF AIRLINES

The process of air transport liberalisation culminated with the third package of measures, arguably the most far-reaching. The third package introduced a system which seeks to vest automatic rights in carriers which satisfy certain criteria. An airline intending to provide air transport services for remuneration is required to have a combination of two authorisations, typically one relating to the operating fitness and the other to the routes on which services are to be provided. Thus, the possession of an operating licence does not on its own permit an airline to provide services for remuneration. It is merely a licence for "entry into the profession". In most cases also, the grant of an operating licence is dependent on the air carrier having been granted an Air Operator's Certificate (AOC).

6.1

This chapter examines Council Regulation 2407/92 which seeks to regulate the granting of an operating licence. The fundamental aim of the Regulation is, first, to secure a uniform system of licensing, and by virtue of the common rules under this system, eliminate discrimination in the licensing of Community air carriers. Thus, an air carrier which satisfies the requirements of the Regulation "shall be entitled to receive an operating licence" as provided for by Article 3(2).

6.2

1. Scope

Under the terms of Regulation 2407/92, an operating licence is defined as "an authorisation granted by the Member State responsible to an undertaking, permitting it to carry out carriage by air of passengers, mail and/or cargo . . . for remuneration and/or hire". There are essentially seven requirements in the Regulation to be satisfied for an operating licence to be issued to an applicant.

6.3

All air carriers established in the Community which are providing, or seeking to provide, services for the carriage of passengers, mail or cargo for reward are required to possess a valid operating licence. For the purposes of Regulation 2407/92, an air carrier is defined as "an air transport undertaking with a valid operating licence". Three exceptions apply:

- non-power driven aircraft;
- ultra-light power driven aircraft;
- local flights not involving carriage between two airports.

Thus, flights such as those used for surveys, personal pleasure or fun-rides do not fall within the scope of the Regulation, and are not subject to its requirements. However, the laws of Member States and Community law governing the grant of an AOC will apply.

2. An operating licence

Place of business

6.4   An operating licence cannot be granted unless the principal place of business of the applicant, and where applicable its registered office, are located in the Member State responsible for granting that operating licence.

Main occupation

6.5   An applicant for an operating licence must have as its main occupation an air transport business, or the combination of an air transport business and other commercial operation of aircraft including aircraft maintenance and repair.

Ownership of carrier: nationality and effective control

6.6   As is common in the history of air transport, Regulation 2407/92 requires an applicant for an operating licence to be an undertaking "owned and continue to be owned directly or through majority ownership by Member States and/or nationals of Member States". Accordingly, this applies to publicly-owned and privately-owned entities as well as "hybrid" entities comprising public and private ownership.

In addition to the fact of ownership, an applicant undertaking must be "effectively controlled by such States or such nationals". This latter criterion is to ensure that an applicant subject to effective control by non-Community States or nationals in spite of their minority shareholding is excluded from the entitlement to an operating licence. The Regulation defines effective control in Article 2(g) as a "relationship constituted by rights, contracts or any other means which, either separately or jointly and having regard to the considerations of fact and law involved, confer the possibility of directly or indirectly exercising a decisive influence on an undertaking". This control may result from either "the right to use all or part of the assets of an undertaking [or] rights or contracts which confer a decisive influence on the composition, voting or decisions of the bodies of an undertaking or otherwise confer a decisive influence on the running of the business of the undertaking." Thus, whether there is a decisive influence will depend on the assessment, for example, of the classes of shares and the weighting of shares, of any financial conditions arising from loans or guarantees and the like, and of the composition of the Board and management.

An exemption applies to those carriers which have been listed in the Annex of   6.7
Council Regulation 2343/90[1] and to cargo carriers listed in Council Regulation
294/91.[2] These carriers are deemed to have met these requirements if at the time
Regulation 2407/92 came into effect they satisfied the other requirements of the
Regulation and continued to be controlled by the same third country or their
nationals. This provision was necessary to ensure that air carriers with "quasi-
Community" ownership such as the Scandinavian Airlines System (SAS) are not
prejudiced. Other air carriers listed in the Annex of Council Regulation 2343/90
are Britannia Airways and Monarch Airlines.

Swissair–Sabena

In the first ever case to be considered under this provision, and indeed Regulation   6.8
2407/92, the Belgian Government requested the Commission to examine the
compatibility of an agreement providing for an equity participation by Swissair in
Sabena.[3] The agreement provided that Swissair would acquire 49.5 per cent of
Sabena's share capital. The proposed acquisition had arisen as a consequence of
the decision to terminate the structural link between Sabena and Air France. This
relationship was established in 1992, when Finacta, a subsidiary of Air France,
acquired 37.49 per cent of Sabena's share capital.[4]

The agreement would involve a series of three transactions. First, Société
Fédérale d'Investissement (SFI), which is a Belgian public holding company,
would purchase all the Sabena shares held by Finacta. This purchase would be
financed by a loan of Bfrs 4bn from Swissair. This loan would be subject to
691,666,127 warrants which would permit Swissair to purchase additional shares
in Sabena in circumstances specified in the agreement.

The second transaction would comprise an increase in the share capital of   6.9
Sabena to the value of Bfrs 9.5bn. This would be provided in part by the Belgian
Government and institutional investors (Bfrs 2bn), by SFI (Bfrs 1.5bn) and by
Swissair (Bfrs 6bn). Importantly, the agreement also provided on the one hand
that institutional investors were to act through "a single special-purpose vehicle
established in Belgium under majority ownership and effective control of Belgian
nationals". On the other hand, the Belgian Government and SFI were to enter
into a shareholders' agreement with that special-purpose vehicle in respect of
voting arrangements and rights of refusal in the Sabena shares. The effect of these
arrangements was to ensure that "the joint views of the Belgian State and SFI will
always prevail over those of the institutional investors".

In the third transaction, Swissair would provide a further Bfrs 0.5bn in return
for 223,830,770 special participation certificates in Sabena. However, these
certificates would not form part of Sabena's capital nor carry any voting rights.
Nevertheless, Swissair would be entitled to the same dividend as ordinary shareholders, with a guarantee of at least 5 per cent of their issue price. Additionally,

[1] [1990] OJ L217/8.
[2] [1991] OJ L36/1.
[3] Commission Decision 95/404, [1995] OJ L239/19.
[4] See Ch. 5 *supra* on this merger.

Swissair would be entitled to the repayment of the original issue price prior to any repayment on capital stock in the event of liquidation; there would be no entitlement to liquidation surplus, however.

6.10   Although Switzerland is not presently a member of the European Economic Area, it is also not a Community Member State. Swissair, which is established in Switzerland, is therefore not a Community carrier entitled to an operating licence issued by virtue of Regulation 2407/92. Consequently, the key question which the agreement raised was whether Sabena continued to comply with the four substantive requirements of Article 4 of the Regulation: principal place of business, main occupation, ownership, and effective control.

Principal place of business

6.11   Since under the agreement Sabena was to remain a separate legal entity with a registered office and corporate headquarters in Belgium, it complied with the requirement that the principal place of business and registered office of an operating licence holder was to be located in the licensing Member State.

Air transport as the main occupation

6.12   The fact that the articles of association of Sabena defined the company purpose as the provision of domestic and international air services as well as other ancillary activities was sufficient for the Commission to be satisfied of this requirement.

Majority ownership by Member States or nationals of Member States

6.13   According to the Commission's assessment, this requirement was intended to safeguard the interests of the air transport industry within the Community. Its application was to ensure that carriers from non-Community countries would not be allowed to take advantage of the common air transport market by way of participation in the ownership and control of Community carriers.

The view of the Commission in that case was that majority ownership would be established if at least 50 per cent plus one share of the capital of the carrier in question was owned by Member States or nationals of Member States. In addition, the nature of the capital was an important consideration in determining ownership, and ultimately the degree of control. Ownership revolves around the notion of equity capital which typically confers the right to participate in decisions affecting the management of the entity, and to be entitled to profits or residual assets in the event of liquidation. Therefore, if the capital participation did not confer upon its holders any of these two rights "to an appreciable extent", the Commission would normally disregard it in ascertaining the ownership structure of an entity. In respect of this agreement then, the Commission decided that the special participation certificates, to which Swissair was entitled in return for the additional contribution, did not constitute equity capital. Indeed, given the nature of the contribution, and the absence of certain rights, it was more akin to a loan capital.

6.14   The assessment of the extent of ownership held by Swissair in Sabena must therefore be restricted to the shares derived from the Bfrs 6bn subscription and the shares potentially accruing from the warrants granted to Swissair for its Bfrs

4bn loan. As a result of the transactions, the distribution of the voting shares in Sabena would be as follows:

(a) Swissair   2,686,969,251 (49.5 per cent)
(b) Belgium, SFI and Institutions   2,740,283,257 (50.5 per cent)

As regards the warrants, the agreement explicitly provided that they could only be converted into additional shares in the event of a change in the regulatory environment permitting Swissair to participate beyond the initial level of 49.5 per cent. In this respect, the warrants cannot affect the ownership structure of Sabena under the prevailing regulatory framework. Accordingly, more than 50 per cent of the voting shares would be held by the Belgian State, SFI and institutional investors, although the Commission accepted that the agreement appeared to be a transitional solution until the existing ownership and control restrictions were lifted on a reciprocal basis.

Effective control

The international nature of air transport business means that cross-border   6.15
ownership is not uncommon. In certain circumstances, this makes it notoriously difficult to ascertain effective control with any degree of precision. In applying the requirement of effective control to the Swissair–Sabena agreement, the Commission explained that this meant Member States or nationals of Member State must have:

> "the ultimate decision-making power in the management of the air carrier concerned. They must be able, either directly or indirectly through appointments to the decisive corporate bodies of the carrier, to have the final say on such key questions as, for example, the carrier's business plan, its annual budget or any other major investment or co-operation projects. Such ability must not be substantially dependent upon the support of natural or legal persons from third countries."

Although the distribution of the voting shares meant that Swissair was the single   6.16
largest shareholder in Sabena, the remaining shareholders were either subject to the special-purpose vehicle or shareholders' agreement which ensured that the joint views of the Belgian Government and SFI would always prevail in practice. On corporate governance, the agreement provided that the primary responsibility for the management of the carrier would rest with the board of directors. Its remit extended to strategic decisions, general policy issues, adoption of business plan and annual budget, fleet investments and changes to the route network. Of the 12 directors, six would be appointed by Sabena and five by Swissair. On this arrangement, "only the board members representing the Belgian shareholders will jointly be able to veto decisions of the board without any further support from other board members".

Special rules were provided for the appointment of the twelfth member and   6.17
chairman of the board. His appointment would be based on a joint proposal, or failing this upon a proposal by Swissair. The limitation on this latter authority was the ability of the general meeting to reject the proposal, or to dismiss the chairman

by majority vote. The Commission deduced accordingly that, since the Belgian shareholders held the majority of votes at the general meeting, they would have the ultimate say in the fate of the chairman. In addition, this majority provided the Belgian shareholders with the veto powers over the appointment of the Chief Executive Officer (CEO). At any rate, the CEO was required to operate within the limits set by the board. The veto rights of Swissair would be restricted to amendments to the articles of association, increases or decreases in Sabena's capital, liquidation, and merger or de-merger. The Commission was satisfied that these rights merely reflected the normal degree of protection given to minority shareholders, as was required by Belgian company law in any event. On these grounds, the Commission concluded that the agreement did not confer on Swissair the rights to exercise effective control over Sabena.

6.18   Finally, the agreement also provided the Belgian State with the right to acquire all the shares held by Swissair, although it was accepted that this option would be exercised only in the extreme case of irreconcilable differences between the parties. Nevertheless, it gave rise to an incentive for the parties to seek a satisfactory resolution to any differences.

Ownership of aircraft

6.19   The issue of ownership of an undertaking applying for an operating licence is distinct from the ownership of aircraft. Since the leasing of aircraft is common practice in air transport and frequently involves aircraft owned by nationals of third countries, to require ownership of aircraft as a pre-requisite for the entitlement to an operating licence would have been unduly burdensome, if not impossible for first-time applicants or smaller operators. This would defeat a prime objective of the liberalisation exercise: competition. Accordingly, to provide for leasing arrangements, Regulation 2407/92 does not require ownership of aircraft as a condition for the granting or maintaining of an operating licence so long as the carrier has one or more aircraft at its disposal under any lease agreement.

6.20   However, such aircraft used by an air carrier must be registered either in the national register of the Member State in which the operating licence is issued or within the Community as that Member State sees fit. A waiver may be granted in cases where the lease agreement is intended to meet the short-term needs of the carrier or in exceptional circumstances.

6.21   Lease agreements in air transport are typically classified into "wet leases" or "dry leases". A wet lease includes a set of crew members while a dry lease refers merely to the aircraft. All lease agreements are subject to the approval of the appropriate licensing authority of Member States to ensure that safety and liability standards are met. Any conditions attaching to the approval must be incorporated into the lease agreement between the parties. In the case of a wet lease, and notwithstanding that the air carrier leasing out the aircraft has been granted an operating licence which represents a satisfactory compliance with safety standards, the national licensing authority can withhold the approval of the lease agreement where it falls short of the safety requirements.

Financial fitness

First-time applicants

The requirement of financial fitness for first-time applicants is two-fold. An applicant   6.22
needs to be able to demonstrate at any time that it can meet, first, its actual and
potential obligations for a period of 24 months and secondly, its fixed and operational costs according to its business plan, assuming no income from its operations
for a period of three months. Both must be based on realistic assumptions.

The business plan must show projections for a minimum period of two years   6.23
and detail all financial links with any other commercial activities in which the
applicant is engaged. In particular, the business plan must provide information
and data listed in Annex A of Regulation 2407/92:

- most recent internal management accounts and audited accounts for the
  previous year;
- projected balance sheet for the following two years including a profit and loss
  account;
- basis for projected expenditure and income for items such as fuel, fares,
  salaries, maintenance, depreciation, currency fluctuations, airport charges,
  traffic and revenue forecast;
- projected cash flow and liquidity plans for first two years of operations;
- details of start-up costs, from submission of application to commencement of
  operations, including a statement explaining how these costs will be met;
- details of existing and projected sources of finance;
- details of aircraft financing, whether purchase or lease as well as the terms
  of the lease;
- Articles of Association and details of shareholders, including nationality and
  type of shares held.

In practice, those carriers already established and possessing a valid operating   6.24
authorisation will have that licence converted or deemed to have been granted by
virtue of the Regulation, provided of course the requirements of the Regulation
continue to be met.

Mandatory notice

For both new and established carriers, a notice to the appropriate licensing   6.25
authority is required in cases where plans have been made which affect their
operations or structure, and may consequently affect their financial position. The
notice can take the form of a 12 month business plan, submitted two months in
advance of the period in which the change or changes are intended to take effect.

- Operation of a new service to a continent or world region not previously
  served.

Although the Regulation does not detail whether in such cases the service in   6.26
question is one which has not been provided by *any* carrier in the past or simply

by *that* carrier, it is ascertainable by reference to the language of Article 5(3) as well as the intention of Regulation 2407/92 that this requirement is concerned with a route which has not been previously served by the carrier planning to do so, since an expansion of this scale may have considerable financial implications for the carrier.

- Changes in the type or number of aircraft used.

6.27   Likewise, changes in aircraft type or number can call for significant financial commitment, and thus affect the ability of the carrier to meet its other obligations. The intention of the Regulation appears, however, to be specifically concerned with plans for expansion, and thus a reduction in the aircraft fleet, for example, is not likely to attract the level of scrutiny which an addition would.

- Substantial change in the scale of activities.

6.28   This would appear to cover two situations. First, it is a reinforcement of the provision requiring that an undertaking's main occupation is the operation of an air transport business as a condition to the grant of an operating licence. Secondly, and more relevantly, a notice of such changes is essential to ensure that any plans for expansion do not affect the ability of the carrier to meet its obligations.

- Intended mergers or acquisitions, and any change in a single shareholding representing 10 per cent or more of the total shareholding in the carrier or its parent or ultimate holding company.

6.29   This is intended to deal with situations in which the change in shareholding affects the ownership and effective control of the carrier, and particularly cases where such a change affects the level of investment in the carrier or its value.

Where any of the proposed changes is deemed by the licensing authority to have "a significant bearing on the finances of the carrier", it will require a revised business plan to be submitted to reflect more accurately the financial effects stemming from the changes planned.[5] This business plan must show projections for a period of at least 12 months from the time when the changes are to take effect. In its revised business plan, the carrier is required to include the following information and data listed in Annex B of Regulation 2407/92:

- most recent internal management balance sheet and audited accounts for the previous year;
- details of proposed changes such as changes in type of service, share capital, shareholders or details of proposed merger or takeover;
- projected balance sheet for the current financial year including a profit and loss account and all proposed changes with a significant bearing on finances;
- past and projected expenditure and income for items such as fuel, fares, salaries, maintenance, depreciation, currency fluctuations, airport charges, traffic and revenue forecast;

---

[5] Council Regulation 2407/92, Art. 5(4).

- projected cash flow and liquidity plans for the following year taking into account the financial effects of the proposed changes;

- details of aircraft financing, whether purchase or lease as well as the terms of the lease.

In the case of mergers or takeovers, in particular, the licensing authority of the   6.30
Member State will decide whether an operating licence held by the carrier needs
to be resubmitted for approval; likewise, if any of the proposed changes results in
a change to its legal position. Article 11(3), however, allows for the carrier to "continue with operations unless the licensing authority decides that safety is at risk".

Financial reporting

Annual audited accounts must be submitted by a carrier to the licensing authority   6.31
as part of the latter's function in reviewing the financial position of Community air
carriers. This does not prejudice the ability of the licensing authority to conduct
periodic financial reviews to establish whether "financial problems exist with an air
carrier licensed by [it]".[6] It may require the production of such information and
data relevant to its review, particularly those listed in Annex C of the Regulation.

- audited accounts not later than six months after the relevant financial period and the most recent internal management balance sheet, if necessary;

- projected balance sheet for the following financial year, including a profit and loss account;

- past and projected expenditure and income for items such as fuel, fares, salaries, maintenance, depreciation, currency fluctuations, airport charges, traffic and revenue forecast;

- projected cash flow and liquidity plans for the following year.

If, upon assessment, the licensing authority deems the air carrier no longer able   6.32
to meet its actual and potential obligations for a period of 12 months, it may
suspend or revoke the operating licence. An intermediate relief may take the form
of a temporary licence pending financial reorganisation of the air carrier, provided
that safety is not at risk. An operating licence will also be revoked in cases where
the carrier is facing insolvency or similar proceedings and the licensing authority
is satisfied that "there is no realistic prospect of a satisfactory financial recon-
struction within a reasonable time".[7]

Exemptions

Air carriers which operate exclusively with aircraft of less than 10 tonnes as   6.33
maximum take-off weight, or with aircraft of less than 20 seats, will not be subject
to the requirements of business plans, mandatory notice and financial reporting.
However, such carriers are subject to a further parameter that they must be able
to demonstrate readily that their net capital is at least ECU 80,000 and be

---

[6] Art. 5(5).
[7] Art. 12.

able also to provide such information as required by the licensing authority for its financial review of carriers.

6.34   Nevertheless, for those carriers who "operate scheduled services" or whose annual turnover is in excess of ECU 3m, Member States have a residual discretion to decide whether to subject them to the financial fitness tests provided in the Regulation. It is unclear, however, why operators of scheduled services have been distinguished from, presumably, non-scheduled operators who are typically charter operators, since the measure providing for market access has effectively abolished the distinction.[8] In any event, as freedom of operation begins to take shape consequent upon the liberalisation measures, the distinction between scheduled and charter services for remuneration will gradually disappear. This has been the experience with deregulation in the USA. No doubt, a limited distinction between scheduled and non-scheduled services will continue to apply to take into account, for example, general aviation and pleasure flights.

Air carrier insurance

6.35   Article 7 of the Regulation requires every air carrier to be insured to meet its liability in case of accidents relating to the passengers, luggage, cargo, mail and third parties. The extent to which the liability is to be insured will no doubt vary according to the type and size of aircraft used, including the category of airports used, for instance, whether they are usually congested or otherwise.

Managerial competence

6.36   In addition to the comprehensive financial fitness tests, an air carrier may be required to meet the test of managerial competence. This requirement is discretionary and dependent upon the decision of Member States whether to adopt it as part of its criteria for issuing an operating licence. It is, however, reasonable to assert that most Member States and indeed most aviation nations adopt criteria for managerial competence which are broadly comparable.

Although Article 6(1) vests in Member States this discretion, it refers nevertheless to such criteria as "persons who will continuously and effectively manage the operations of the undertaking are of good repute or that they have not been declared bankrupt" for the purposes of issuing an operating licence, and persons who have been involved in "serious professional misconduct or a criminal offence" for the purposes of revoking or suspending an operating licence.

6.37   The intention of Article 6 is to ensure that those Member States which adopt such criteria "accept as sufficient evidence in respect of nationals of other Member States the production of documents issued by competent authorities in the Member State of origin or the Member State from which the foreign national comes" that those requirements have been met so as to ensure uniformity in the licensing system and to eliminate any room for discrimination on the basis of nationality.

---

[8] See Ch. 7 *infra*.

Air Operator's Certificate (AOC)

An AOC is a common feature of any air transport licensing system. It is aimed   6.38
at ensuring the highest degree of safety and airworthiness of both the carrier and
aircraft. Article 9 of Regulation 2407/92 makes the possession of a valid AOC a
condition for the grant of an operating licence. Until more recently, AOC criteria
for Community carriers were based on national laws and requirements. This
change was effected by the adoption of Council Regulation 3922/91.[9] This measure is intended to harmonise technical requirements and administrative procedures between Member States in accordance with the Joint Aviation Requirement
issued by the JAR Board.

---

[9] [1991] OJ L373/4.

Chapter 7

MARKET ACCESS AND TRAFFIC RIGHTS

1. Introduction

The liberalisation of market access for Community carriers began life with the adoption of Council Decision 87/602, as part of the first package of measures adopted in 1987. The aim of providing greater market access, according to the preamble of the Decision, was to achieve "flexibility and competition in the Community air transport system . . . stimulate the development of the Community air transport sector and give rise to improved services for users".[1] The scope of market access was further expanded in 1990 with the adoption of the second package of measures which, *inter alia*, included Council Regulation 2343/90.[2] This replaced Council Decision 87/602 as well as Directive 83/416.[3]

Limited freedom of market access was, however, introduced in 1983 when the Council adopted Directive 83/416 relating to the authorisation of scheduled inter-regional services. *Inter alia*, this provided a general right to operate inter-regional services where a Member State affected was required to authorise the carrier concerned if the Member State in which the carrier was registered had approved the application. This right was, however, subject to a range of exceptions. In particular, the scope of the Directive was highly restrictive: it applied only to inter-regional services which were over 400 kilometres in distance unless air transport allowed for a "substantial" saving of time relative to surface transport; to services which were operated with aircraft of no more than 70 seats or 30 tonnes of maximum take-off weight; and to services which were between a combination of two airports opened to international scheduled traffic listed as category 2 or 3 airports. Two subsequent amendments were introduced. The first was simply to extend the provisions of the Directive to Spain and Portugal following their accession. The second, however, was more telling. *Inter alia*, it expanded the scope of the Directive by eliminating the conditions relating to distance and capacity.[4] The effect was to allow more services to be authorised under the terms of the Directive.

7.1

7.2

---

[1] [1987] OJ L374/19.
[2] [1990] OJ L217/8.
[3] [1983] OJ L237/19.
[4] Council Directive 86/216, [1986] OJ L152/47; Council Directive 89/463, [1989] OJ L226/14.

2. Background to the liberalisation

Multiple designation

7.3   Council Decision 87/602 provided Community carriers operating scheduled services with greater freedom of access to routes between Member States which they were not already operating. The greater freedom of access took the form of a requirement on the part of Member States to accept any multiple designation by another Member State. However, the obligation to accept multiple designation was restricted to services on a "country pair" basis and excluded any obligation to accept multiple designation on "any one route". Thus, for instance, multiple designation would be accepted in respect of services between the United Kingdom and France, but would not be necessarily so on the London (Heathrow)–Nice route.

7.4   Nevertheless, the Decision established a staggered framework for the incremental development of multiple designation on a "city-pair" basis. In the first year of operation of the Decision, it required Member States to accept multiple designation of city-pair routes on which 250,000 passengers were carried the preceding year, and in the second year 200,000 passengers (or on routes with more than 1,200 return flights annually), and in the third year 180,000 passengers (or 1,000 return flights).[5] This staggered system applied to city-pairs, but not necessarily to any one route. For example, it might have applied to services between London and Paris, but not necessarily to London (Heathrow)–Paris (Orly).

7.5   Multiple designation was retained under Regulation 2343/90 for both country-pair and city-pair services with lower threshold requirements. The former was a general obligation requiring Member States to accept multiple designation, while the obligation for city-pair services would only arise, in the first year of operation of the Regulation, if 140,000 passengers were carried on the route concerned in the preceding year (or where there were more than 800 return flights annually) and 100,000 passengers (or 600 return flights) in the second year of operation.

Regional services and hubs

7.6   Subject to various restrictions, Decision 87/602 also established for Community carriers the third and fourth freedom rights for scheduled services between category 1 airports or airport systems of one Member State and regional airports in another Member State. Category 1 airports or airport systems included Amsterdam (Schipol), Paris (Charles de Gaulle and Orly) and London (Heathrow, Gatwick and Stansted).

An important provision in respect of the third and fourth freedoms is the requirement of *reciprocity*. Article 6(4) of the Decision stipulates that a Member State who has authorised a carrier to operate the third and fourth freedom services under the Decision, "shall raise no objection to an application for the introduction of a scheduled air service on the same route by an air carrier of the other State concerned".

---

[5] Art. 5(2).

Fifth freedom

Fifth freedom rights have traditionally been controversial and jealously protected.   7.7
Decision 87/602 nevertheless took the small step of introducing limited fifth
freedom rights provided that the carrier seeking to operate fifth freedom services
could also claim to operate third or fourth freedom services. For the fifth freedom
right to take effect, the carrier must have been authorised by the State of registration and the service in question would be operated "as an extension of a service from, or as a preliminary of a service to, its State of registration". In addition, the right would apply only to services between airports of which one is not
listed in category 1 and the fifth freedom capacity does not exceed 30 per cent of
the carrier's annual capacity on the routes in question.

A case arose in 1989 where Aer Lingus sought to combine the authorisations it   7.8
had to operate Dublin–Manchester and Dublin–Milan services so that they could
be provided as fifth freedom services between Dublin–Manchester–Milan. Milan,
however, was listed in Article 6(2)(ii) of the Decision as an airport system falling
outside the scope of the Decision in respect of third and fourth freedom authorisation, which the Italian authorities sought to rely on. Since the other conditions
of Article 8 which authorised fifth freedom services were met, the case hinged on
the question of whether the term "without prejudice to Article 6(2)" in Article 8
was such that fifth freedom services were also subject to the restriction excluding
Milan from the scope of the third and fourth freedom authorisation. Ironically, no
decision was taken in respect of this substantive point. Rather, the European Court
of Justice focused on the technical point of whether the interim measures sought
by the Commission as a matter of urgency were justified so that further damage
or loss could be avoided. It took the view that even if the interim measures were
granted, they did not guarantee a complete cessation of the actions which were
alleged to be violating Community law pending the full judgment. In addition, the
Court did not consider the estimated annual loss of £Ir 1.6m in revenue "as
sufficiently serious injury to justify urgency". This was because Aer Lingus was a
national airline whose business volume was such that that estimated loss of revenue
was not of sufficient magnitude so as to cause irreparable financial injury.[6]

Extension of freedoms

More importantly, Regulation 2343/90 extended the application of third and   7.9
fourth freedoms from regional-hub services to services which were between
airports or airport systems of one Member State and airports or airport systems
of another Member State. Apart from the overriding exemptions provided in the
Regulation, the only qualification for the third and fourth freedom rights was that
the airports or airport systems must already be "open for traffic between Member
States or for international services".[7] This extension was supported by a general
requirement on Member States to "authorize air carriers licensed in another

---

[6] Case 352/88R, *Re Scheduled Air Services: Commission* v *Italy* [1989] ECR 267.
[7] Art. 4.

Member State, which have been authorized by their State of registration, to exercise third- and fourth-freedom traffic rights".[8]

Although the Regulation retained the condition that the exercise of fifth freedom rights was still dependent on the services constituting an extension of a service from, or being preliminary to a service to, the State of registration, it relaxed the capacity threshold of the traffic that can be carried as fifth freedom traffic to 50 per cent of the annual traffic which would have been carried under third and fourth freedom rights. The previous threshold was 30 per cent.

Overriding exemptions

7.10   Under Decision 87/602, Member States may claim a derogation from the obligations in the Decision either on the ground that the airport in question "has insufficient facilities to accommodate the service" or that the "navigational aids are insufficient to accommodate the service".[9]

Regulation 2343/90, however, introduced a more structured regime of exemptions which Member States were permitted to invoke, including discretion to derogate from the general principle of the Regulation in circumstances where a *public service obligation* had been imposed. A public service obligation was defined by the Regulation as "an obligation imposed upon an air carrier to take, in respect of any route which it is licensed to operate by a Member State, all necessary measures to ensure the provision of a service satisfying fixed standards of continuity, regularity and capacity which standards the carrier would not assume if it were solely considering its commercial interest". Likewise, the exercise of the traffic rights conferred by virtue of this Regulation was also subject to the right of Member States to regulate the distribution of air traffic between airports within an airport system, for which an airport system was defined by the Regulation as "two or more airports grouped together as serving the same city" including for example London (Heathrow, Gatwick and Stanstead), provided the system of distribution was not discriminatory on the basis of nationality.[10] In this latter case, Member States had the power either to impose conditions on, or to refuse, the exercise of the traffic rights.

3. The law on market access

7.11   Both Council Decision 87/602, as amended, and Council Regulation 2343/90 were measures designed to introduce greater freedom of access to air transport markets to bring about a single market for air transport, albeit gradually. The adoption of the final market access measure, in the form of Council Regulation 2408/92, was consequently far-reaching in that it aimed to remove the restrictions

---

[8] Art. 5(1).
[9] Art. 9.
[10] Arts. 9 and 10 respectively.

which had been established by previous legislation, subject as always to a limited number of exemptions.[11] It is also significant to the extent that the conferment of a general freedom of access has removed a substantial margin of discretion from the national authorities of Member States in the licensing of Community carriers and routes.

Scope

Regulation 2408/92 applies to routes within the Community and to scheduled   7.12
and non-scheduled services. It makes provision for the exclusion of the Gibraltar airport and airports in the Greek and Atlantic islands to take account of the sovereignty dispute between the United Kingdom and Spain, and the inadequacy of the air traffic system in the Greek islands and the Azores region respectively.

Access rights

Article 3(1) of the Regulation states explicitly that "Community air carriers shall   7.13
be permitted by the Member State(s) concerned to exercise traffic rights on routes within the Community".

A Community air carrier is defined by the Regulation as "an air carrier with a valid operating licence granted by a Member State in accordance with Council Regulation 2407/92" which thus requires Member States to respect the principle of reciprocity in recognising the validity or non-validity of operating licences issued by another Member State.[12] In this respect then, it is possible for a Community air carrier to operate and provide services which hitherto have been classified as domestic or cabotage given that the general right applies to "routes within the Community". This would include, for example, the right of a carrier registered in and licensed by Germany such as Lufthansa to operate between London and Glasgow, or between Milan and Rome. A cabotage right is known under the Chicago Convention as the eighth freedom. This national cabotage right, however, is subject to the derogation provided by the Regulation for Member States to refuse the authorisation of such services, but which must expire by 1 April 1997. Likewise, it is also possible for a Community carrier to operate Community cabotage services such as the "free-standing" services provided by the Spanish-registered Viva Air between Paris and Lisbon which does not involve a stop in the State of registration. Since this is not a domestic service in the sense in which it has traditionally been understood, any derogation from this right will have to be justified by reference to other provisions in the Regulation. The notion of a Community cabotage right is, however, fraught with numerous difficulties.[13]

Although Regulation 2408/92 applies only to routes within the Community, the   7.14
collective effect of this Regulation, of Council Regulation 2407/92 and of the right of establishment and movement recognised by the Treaty enables a

---

[11] [1992] OJ L240/8.
[12] See Ch. 6 *supra*.
[13] See Ch. 15 *infra*.

Community carrier to operate free-standing services between an airport in the territory of another Member State destined for a third country outside the Community: for example, a BA service between Dublin and the USA which has been incorporated into the draft air services agreement between the United Kingdom and the USA for a revised Bermuda Agreement. This is also known as the seventh freedom.

This general right of access, however, is subject to a number of exemptions which may be invoked by Member States in deciding whether to authorise the operation of the services in question by conferring the traffic rights. However, both the decisions of the Commission and the jurisprudence of the European Court of Justice point to a strict interpretation of these exemptions.

Viva Air

7.15   In the first case under the Regulation, Viva Air complained to the Commission concerning the refusal of the French authorities to authorise its proposed services between Paris (Charles de Gaulle) and Madrid despite it having been granted the necessary slots to operate twice daily return flights.[14] The refusal was justified on the grounds that Member States had the right to regulate traffic distribution within an airport system according to Article 8, and that the Decree adopted for the Paris airport system "does not allow an airline to operate services on the same medium-haul international route into both Paris (Orly) and Paris (CDG)". Although Viva Air was not operating into Paris (Orly), this rule was seen as relevant by the French authorities since they considered Viva Air a subsidiary of the Iberia Group and that Iberia was already operating on the Orly–Madrid sector. According to the French authorities, if Viva Air was to be authorised on the Charles de Gaulle–Madrid sector, then it "would create a precedent which would undermine the present system of allocating airport facilities". Consequently, for Viva Air to operate on that route, it had to have been granted traffic rights explicitly in accordance with Article 3 of the Regulation.

7.16   The questions for the Commission were two-fold. The first was whether the effect of Article 3 enabling Community carriers to exercise traffic rights was such that it left no discretion in Member States to regulate traffic rights except under terms of the Regulation. That is to say, whether an express authorisation is required from Member States on the basis of Article 3. In relation to Viva Air's case specifically, this included the question of whether the granting of slots amounted to an authorisation. Depending on the extent of the discretion that Member States continued to enjoy, the second question was whether the refusal by the French authorities represented a proper implementation of Article 8, that is without discrimination and according to published criteria.[15]

7.17   On the first question, the Commission began its analysis on the basis that Article 3(1) was a general provision conferring freedom of access to Community carriers on Community routes including domestic routes. However, it decided that "these provisions do not in themselves authorize Community air carriers to

---

[14] Commission Decision 93/347, [1993] OJ L140/51.
[15] See *infra* on Art. 8.

exercise traffic rights". There is a residual discretion, on the part of the Member States, to impose, for example a formal authorisation procedure, as the French authorities had in that case, without prejudice to the instances when exemptions under the Regulation can be invoked by Member States. Crucially however, it held that "authorisation is automatic and Member States no longer have any discretion in the matter" if none of the exemptions can be invoked. In any event, the Commission submitted that the use of exemptions which, in essence, would restrict the freedom of access "must be kept to the minimum necessary". In the case of a formal authorisation procedure, for example, the period for replying to applications from airlines must be kept short. The Commission thought this was crucial because first, the principle of freedom of access implies that carriers will be informed of decisions promptly so they can implement their proposals, or not implement them as the case may be. This was particularly true in respect of new services where substantial investment may have been committed. Secondly, the Commission felt that the time needed to consider applications and determine whether the exemptions provided in the Regulation applied, did not have to be inordinately long. Freedom of access was the rule; refusal was the exception. This approach was capable of giving rise to the implication that "where no reply is received by the stated deadline, authorisation to operate is implicit". Since it took the French authorities two months to come to a final decision refusing authorisation, the Commission concluded that there had been undue delay. Consequently, the Decree of 12 September 1980 which laid down the authorisation procedures was contrary to a fundamental principle of the Community.

This reasoning is consistent with the jurisprudence of the European Court of   7.18
Justice. In *Stichting* for example, which concerned the imposition of fines on 10 operators of cable networks in the The Netherlands, the Court said that Article 59 of the EC Treaty stipulated a general rule which abolishes discrimination on the basis of nationality for the provision of services in a Member State other than the Member State in which the service provider is established. An exception to this general rule was only possible in two circumstances. First, where there is a derogation provided by the Treaty, or secondly, where the applicable national law mirrors the law in the Member State in which the provider is established so that requirements established by that Member State would have to be satisfied in any event.[16]

Cabotage

Member States are not required to authorise the exercise of traffic rights within   7.19
their territory by Community carriers licensed by another Member State. This discretion is transitional and must expire by 1 April 1997. Under Article 3(2), a Member State is nevertheless under an obligation to authorise such traffic rights if they are exercised for the purposes of a scheduled service which is constituted "as an extension of a service from, or as a preliminary of a service to, the State

---

[16] Case C-288/89, *Stichting Collective Antennevoorziening Gouda* v *Commissariaat voor de Media* [1991] ECR I-4007.

of registration of the carrier" and the carrier in question does not use more than 50 per cent of its annual capacity on that route for the cabotage service.

7.20   During that transitional period also, a Member State is empowered to regulate "access to routes within its territory for air carriers licensed by it" under Council Regulation 2407/92 without prejudice to established Community law and principles. However, this discretion is subject to the requirement that there is no discrimination on the basis of "nationality of ownership and air carrier identity". This is a significant provision given the increasing complexity of ownership structure which includes cross-border equity, subsidiaries, and belatedly, franchising. TAT–European Airlines, for example, is part owned by BA (49.9 per cent); likewise Deutsche BA (49 per cent). KLM has a 45 per cent stake in Air UK, and SAS has a 40 per cent shareholding in Airlines of Britain which is represented by BMA.[17]

7.21   In a land-mark case which went to the core of Regulation 2408/92, and which is also considered in detail below, the Commission reasoned that the principle of non-discrimination had to be assessed according to both the nationality of the carrier and its identity. Although it is clear from the EC Treaty, the Regulation and the jurisprudence of the European Court of Justice that discrimination is prohibited on the ground of nationality, its mere absence cannot suffice in certain cases. In respect of these cases, the complicated structure of ownership in Community air transport demands that allegations of discrimination are also assessed on the basis of carrier identity. According to the Commission, the aim of prohibiting discrimination on this basis was to prevent Member States withholding from one or more carrier "the traffic rights granted to a limited number of *other* carriers who are or can be precisely identified to operate the same service on comparable terms" unless objective grounds could be established. Likewise, it would prevent Member States from granting traffic rights to one or more carriers which they do not propose to confer on *other* carriers who are or can be precisely identified as able to operate the same service on comparable terms.[18] This can be ascertained either on the basis of the effect arising directly from the measure taken or indirectly from the *de facto* circumstances by reference to the limited number and identity of Community carriers who benefit from, or are penalized by, the action or actions. This case arose from the decision of the French authorities to refuse permission to TAT to operate the Paris (Orly)–Marseille and Paris (Orly)–Toulouse routes despite the permission being granted to Air Inter, a subsidiary of Air France group.

Exclusive concession

7.22   Article 5 of Regulation 2408/92 provides a further derogation from the general right of access on domestic routes if Member States can demonstrate that "an exclusive concession has been granted by law or contract, and where other forms of transport cannot ensure an adequate and uninterrupted service". This is subject to two conditions so that, first, the exclusive concession would only apply if it was

---

[17] As at September 1995. Source: Civil Aviation Authority, *The Single European Aviation Market: Progress So Far* CAP 654 (1995). BA's share in TAT has since been increased to 100 per cent: [1996] OJ C316/11.
[18] Commission Decision 94/291, [1993] OJ L127/32.

operative at the time the Regulation came into effect, that is 1 January 1993. Secondly, the derogation is transitional in that the concession must expire at the end of its period of validity, or after a maximum period of three years, whichever was earlier. In practice, therefore, no exclusive concession can be granted today since the period for which such concessions can continue to be operative expired on 31 December 1995.

TAT: Paris–Marseille–Toulouse

The questions of whether an exclusive concession was in force at the time of the   7.23
Regulation coming into effect, and whether there was also an adequate and uninterrupted service provided by other transport forms, and if so what form of
transport was envisaged by the Regulation, were the subject of a lengthy analysis
by the Commission in its investigation of the TAT complaints against the refusal
by the French authorities to authorise its proposed services between Paris
(Orly)–Marseille and Paris (Orly)–Toulouse.[19] The application to serve on that
route was rejected by the French Director-General of Civil Aviation on the basis
that an exclusive concession had been agreed between France and Air Inter and
protected by Article 5 of the Regulation. The key submissions of TAT were that
the French authorities had acted contrary to its own published policy of encouraging domestic services to both Charles de Gaulle and Orly. In addition, TAT
argued that the Contrat de Plan struck between the Commission, France and the
Air France Group on 30 October 1990 following the takeover of Union des
Transports Aériens (UTA) by the latter had required the French authorities to
adopt multiple designation by 1 March 1992 for the Paris–Marseille and Paris–
Toulouse routes inter alia,[20] and in that respect, they had failed to comply with the
Contrat. TAT also submitted that the Paris–Marseille and Paris–Toulouse
reference in the Contrat applied to the Paris airport system and accordingly the
argument of exclusive concession could not stand since TAT was already operating from Charles de Gaulle to both destinations. Therefore, there was an
adequate means of alternative transport between Paris and Marseille and
Toulouse. A further issue relating to Article 8 of the Regulation on traffic distribution arose in the course of the proceedings.

In response to the allegations, the French authorities argued that the multiple   7.24
designation referred to in the Contrat was limited to services from and to Charles
de Gaulle within the Paris airport system because Article 5 applied only in
the context of services on an airport–airport basis rather a city–city basis.
Furthermore, they counter-claimed that "other forms of transport" in Article 5
referred to transport modes other than by air. In setting out its opinion, the
Commission referred to the general principle of interpretation in respect of the
Regulation which it first formulated in the Viva Air case.[21] According to the
Commission, the aim of the Regulation was to confer a general right of access to
Community carriers, subject to the exemptions which Member States may invoke.

---

[19] Ibid.
[20] See Ch. 5 supra.
[21] Commission Decision 93/347, [1993] OJ L140/51.

However, the "right to exercise the freedom is now the rule and refusal the exception". Hence, where an exemption has been invoked, it will be construed strictly and must be subject to transparent, objective and consistent criteria which do not discriminate on the basis of nationality.

7.25   The question of whether there was a valid or operative exclusive concession at the time the Regulation came into effect invited the Commission to consider two issues. First, the simple question of fact of whether, at 1 January 1993, there was a valid exclusive concession, and second the question of law of whether the Contrat of 1990 amounted to an exclusive concession. To deal with the first issue, a determination had to be made of the second. In the Commission's opinion, the application of Article 5 was not restricted to airport–airport services but had a wider application to city–city services so that in authorising TAT and indeed Air Inter to operate from and to Charles de Gaulle, but limiting access to Orly only to Air Inter, the French authorities were discriminating to the advantage of Air Inter in the allocation of traffic within the Paris airport system. In any event, the Commission referred to the Contrat of 1985 between itself, France and the Air France Group which defined the routes granted to Air Inter on an exclusive basis as "point-to-point rather than airport-to-airport routes and include no reference to the different airports of the Paris airport system". Furthermore, according to the Contrat of 1985, express permission was given to Air France and Air Afrique to operate on the Paris–Marseille route at the same time as Air Inter "thereby eliminating the exclusive nature of the concession held by that airline." According to the Commission, the exclusive concession derived from the Contrat of 1990 was of no consequence since it expired on 1 March 1992. The Commission thus concluded that this, together with the TAT authorisation and that of others to operate to Marseille and Toulouse from Charles de Gaulle, meant that "the French authorities have put an end to the exclusive rights that Air Inter might otherwise have enjoyed".

7.26   Although these considerations would have been sufficient for the Commission to rule that the derogation under Article 5 could not be invoked to refuse TAT permission to operate to Marseille and Toulouse from Orly, it ventured neverthe-less to consider the other limbs of the complaint. First, the issue of whether there were "other forms of transport" serving the Paris–Marseille and Paris–Toulouse sectors. The Commission reasoned that since Article 5 was designed to ensure the survival of adequate transport services between two points in the transitional period of adjustment, it therefore meant that Article 5 included "all other facilities for transport between two cities, including intermodal means – that is, mainly transport by train and by bus". However, the Article also includes "transport by plane in the case of indirect flights or where an alternative airport is available".

7.27   If the Paris–Marseille and Paris–Toulouse sectors were vulnerable to disruption or curtailment of services, then the Commission suggested that Article 4 on the imposition of public service obligations should have been invoked to ensure Air Inter's services were not subject to competition which could undermine an objec-tive of public policy. On the contrary, the Paris–Marseille and Paris–Toulouse routes were among the busiest in the Community with an annual traffic of approximately two million passengers. Protection of this route from competition would therefore be difficult to justify.

Having therefore resolved the question of whether air transport was a form of alternative transport envisaged by Article 5, the Commission then had to consider whether the alternative transport services between Paris and Marseille and Toulouse constituted "an adequate and uninterrupted service". First, the Commission cited the five daily return services provided by TAT from Charles de Gaulle which it considered as adequate and uninterrupted. Secondly, it thought that there were other forms of transport besides air transport which would ensure that the criteria of adequacy and interruption were fulfilled.

The consequential effect of these findings was that exclusive rights could only   7.28
arise if there was no other way of travelling from one *city* to another by an adequate and uninterrupted means. For airport systems in particular, if exclusive rights were to be maintained, they must apply to all the airports in the system and they must "expressly refer to an entire airport system and not just to a single airport". This decision is now the subject of a judicial review application by France and Air Inter who are alleging that the Commission had left Air Inter and its interests "in total ignorance". In particular also, it argues that the Commission had been wrong to adopt a wide interpretation of the rules on freedom, while construing the restrictions on that freedom only narrowly.[22]

Public service obligation

Article 4 of the Regulation sets out the concept of a "public service obligation"   7.29
(PSO) in Community air transport. A PSO is defined in Article 2(o) as an:

> "obligation imposed upon an air carrier to take, in respect of any route which it is licensed to operate by a Member State, all necessary measures to ensure the provision of a service satisfying fixed standards of continuity, regularity, capacity and pricing, which standards the air carrier would not assume if it were solely considering its commercial interest."

The scope of PSOs, however, is limited to two sets of circumstances. PSOs can   7.30
only be imposed on a route served by scheduled services "to an airport serving a peripheral or development region" or to a regional airport on a "thin route" but which is considered "vital for the economic development of the region in which the airport is located". According to Article 4(1)(a), PSOs can only be imposed "to the extent necessary to ensure on that route the adequate provision of scheduled air services" which meet the criteria of continuity, capacity and pricing which otherwise would not be met on a commercial basis[22a].

In practice, PSOs have two possible effects. The first is that they provide a measure of protection for the carrier or carriers on that route from competition coming from other carriers. In that respect, there is likely to be stability in income so that the development of services on that route will not be neglected or prejudiced. Secondly, however, where the income is insufficient to meet the operating costs,

[22] Case C-174/94, *France v Commission*, [1994] OJ C227/31 and Case C-301/94 *Air Inter v Commission*, [1994] OJ C275/28.
[22a] See [1996] OJ C387/6 and [1996] OJ C387/7.

PSOs can entail the provision of subsidies to the carrier since a public policy would have been declared that continuity of services on that route was vital.

Conditions

7.31 Whether the services on that route are adequate or otherwise will need to be determined in accordance with the principal considerations laid down in the Regulation:

- the public interest;
- the availability of other forms of transport, their access and their ability to meet the transport needs in question;
- the air fares and conditions of sale which can be quoted to users;
- the combined effect of all carriers operating or planning to operate on the route in question.

Where the alternative forms of transport cannot ensure an adequate and uninterrupted service, Member States have the discretion to include in the PSO a guarantee from the carrier that it will operate on that route for a certain specified period.

Tendering process and exclusivity

7.32 In general, a route which has been designated for a PSO may be served by more than one carrier. Where such a route has been so designated but no carrier is operating or likely to operate the services, access to that route may be limited to one carrier for a maximum period of three years. The carrier may also be entitled to reimbursement or subsidy from the Member State. This exclusive right will only apply following an open tendering process.

7.33 The tender must be advertised in the *Official Journal* and it must include the following as a minimum:

- standards required by the PSO;
- provisions for variation and termination of the contract particularly given unforeseen circumstances;
- length of contract;
- penalties for contractual failure.

Member States are prohibited by Article 4(1)(g) of the Regulation from making a decision on the tenders until after two months has elapsed following the closing date of the tender. The aim of this provision is to allow other Member States "to submit comments" given that a PSO designation can affect competition in Community air transport and ought therefore to have the benefit of wider consultation.

7.34 Two conditions apply before a Member State can designate a PSO to be performed by one carrier under the terms of the exclusivity paragraph. First of all, where "another Member State concerned proposes a satisfactory alternative means of fulfilling the same public service obligation" that route in question cannot be exclusively served by one carrier. "Another" Member State would seem to suggest that this condition is limited to services between two Member States, unless "another" Member State concerned is given a broad interpretation to mean a third party having the right of intervention to propose alternative means of performing a PSO. There is also the further difficulty of ascertaining whether the alternative proposed is "satisfactory". What constitutes "alternative means" in this context would arguably include alternative methodology although in all probability it refers to alternative forms of transport, including air transport as determined in the complaint of TAT against the French authorities relating to the Paris–Marseille and Paris–Toulouse routes.

However, the issue of alternative transport means is dealt with in Article 4(2)   **7.35** which will not allow the services on a route to be designated as a PSO for one carrier "where other forms of transport can ensure an adequate and uninterrupted service" and when the capacity offered on the route in question exceeds 30,000 per year. This means a route designated for PSO does not have to be open to multiple-carrier services if the capacity remains below the 30,000 threshold even if adequate and uninterrupted services were available from other forms of transport. According to the Commission in the TAT (Marseille–Toulouse) case, other forms of transport included air transport if the services in question were provided from a different airport within an airport system. This means air transport is included on a city-to-city route. If this construction of "other forms of transport" was adopted in respect of PSOs, then it would mean that where services were being provided by another carrier from an alternative airport within an airport system, it could be deemed as providing adequate and uninterrupted services so that the effect would be to put an end to the exclusive PSO. This would seem to be consistent with the jurisprudence of the European Court of Justice and the Commission in that derogations to a general right should be given as narrow an interpretation as possible.

Regional services

A further derogation is provided in Article 6 which empowers a Member State to   **7.36** exempt certain regional services from the general right of access under Article 3. The scope of the derogation, however, is limited to scheduled services on a new route between two regional airports.

The nature of the derogation takes the form of a refusal by a Member State to license a scheduled service by another carrier for a maximum period of two years if a carrier has already been licensed by that Member State to commence services on a new regional route. For this derogation to be invoked, two conditions need to exist. First, the licensed carrier must be using an aircraft which has no more than 80 seats, and secondly, the capacity does not exceed 30,000 seats per year. There is, however, a margin of discretion for Member States to license another carrier. The applicant carrier must be proposing to operate with an aircraft having no more than 80 seats or if a larger aircraft is to be used, no more than 80 seats are available for sale for travel on that route.

Traffic distribution

7.37   Although a policy on traffic distribution between airports is seemingly innocuous in that it usually seeks to achieve certain public policy objectives relating to the environment and the relief of congestion, such a policy can be a hornet's nest. Article 8 of the Regulation enables Member States to regulate the distribution of traffic between airports in an airport system. Hence, the scope of this Article is necessarily confined to cases involving an airport system.

The right to regulate traffic distribution, however, is subject to the requirement of non-discrimination either on the basis of nationality or identity of the carrier concerned. The justification for maintaining a distinction between nationality and identity has already been raised and discussed in relation to the TAT (Marseille–Toulouse) case. This is simply that discrimination on the basis of carrier's identity by virtue of its ownership structure may still possible even if no apparent discrimination is detectable in respect of nationality.

Viva Air: Paris–Madrid

7.38   Article 8(2) envisages that, in the context of traffic distribution, the exercise of such traffic rights are to be subject to Community or national law on air transport safety, the environment and slot allocation. The Commission has already made it clear in its decision in the Viva Air case that while traffic distribution and the allocation of slots may be inextricably linked, they were distinct from the authorisation of traffic rights.[23] This seems logical since Article 8(2) appears to be referring to the "exercise of traffic rights" which makes a certain presumption that the rights have been duly granted. The authorisation of traffic rights does not therefore give rise to the presumption that slots would automatically follow nor *vice versa*.

7.39   Since a derogation must be construed narrowly, the Commission had to consider in that case whether the implementation of Article 8 was improper. In addition to the necessarily narrow construction that should be given to a derogation, the interpretation of any derogation "must be based on transparent and objective criteria which remain constant over a given period and are non-discriminatory". To secure transparency, the rules implementing that derogation must be published and made known in advance so that any uncertainty will be confined to the minimum. Since they were not so published, the Commission concluded that the rules could not be applied to Viva Air. This was a relatively simple question of fact.

7.40   The more difficult issue of discrimination required the Commission to enter into an in-depth analysis of traffic density and the substantive effect of the rules distributing traffic between airports. The case submitted by the French authorities in explaining its policy of prohibiting the same airline to serve both Orly and Charles de Gaulle simply referred to the "type of market involved". First, they eliminated the case of long-haul services into both airports, since the length of the

---

[23] Commission Decision 93/347, [1993] OJ L140/51.

journey does not usually warrant the duplication of services. For domestic services, however, they argued that services into both airports were encouraged "in order to allow airlines wishing to do so to improve their services to Paris" and by the same token promote the expansion of Charles de Gaulle. The submission in respect of medium-haul services, which included Paris-Madrid, was different. They argued that "concentrating the flights of one airline at one airport will ensure the best possible service for users and the optimization of airport capacity use". To further ensure that there was no discrimination, all such services were directed to Charles de Gaulle. Given the limited capacity at Charles de Gaulle, certain services to the Iberian peninsula would continue, albeit temporarily, to be operated out of Orly.

The Commission was less than convinced. On long-haul services, it noted the **7.41** services which were being provided by Air France from both Orly and Charles de Gaulle such as those to New York. On domestic and medium-haul (intra-Community) services, the Commission saw little to distinguish between them. Indeed, the separation of domestic and medium-haul services was contrary to the principle of a single market. Furthermore, this was evident from the distances involving certain domestic routes which could be more aptly classified as medium-haul, *a fortiori* if the difference in traffic level on these comparable routes was not significant. If that was so, such domestic services should be subject to the same policy of diverting them to Charles de Gaulle, or alternatively medium-haul intra-Community services should be subject to the same policy for domestic services which would allow flights to both Orly and Charles de Gaulle "to improve services to Paris and expand CDG". Any distinction between domestic and intra-Community services was therefore prohibited, and was permitted only to the extent provided by Article 3(2) on cabotage services.

The Commission also concluded that Viva Air should not have been refused **7.42** permission on the basis that Iberia, which owns Viva Air, was already operating on the Orly–Madrid route. The rule which the French authorities had cited was therefore inapplicable. The Commission considered Viva Air as a separate entity from the Iberia Group for the purposes of the Regulation by reason of the fact that Viva Air was a carrier holding a valid operating licence under the terms of Regulation 2407/92 which was not dependent on the issue of control, and also for the reason that it had been founded for a long time with an established staff and fleet, and its own brand of service and policy.

TAT: Paris–London

The case of Viva Air was in many respects an important precedent under Article 8 **7.43** of the Regulation. If nothing else, it laid down the general principles for the interpretation of that Article and its objective application. Even so, the Commission was presented with another case alleging infringement of Article 8, again by the French authorities.[24] TAT had applied to operate four daily return services on the London (Gatwick)–Paris (Orly) route which the French authorities had refused to authorise. The decision to refuse was made on the ground that, "as part of the airport allocation policy for the Paris region, scheduled international services to

---

[24] Commission Decision 94/290, [1993] OJ L127/22.

most European countries, and the United Kingdom in particular, had been authorized only from Charles-de-Gaulle airport". TAT duly made a complaint to the Commission claiming that:

- the rules providing for the different treatment of Paris–London and French domestic services was discriminatory and lacked an objective basis since in particular, Pakistan International Airways (PIA) was permitted to exercise fifth-freedom rights between London–Paris–Karachi;
- the rules governing traffic distribution had not been published, and cannot therefore be applied even assuming they existed;
- there were no substantive reasons for the refusal except a reference to the right to regulate in Article 8;
- other exemptions could not be applied including congestion since it was already in possession of the slots necessary for the services.

7.44   As part of its investigation, but also to establish their existence, the Commission requested a copy of the rules on which the French authorities had based their decisions. The reply claimed that the French Minister of Transport had decided to clarify the policy, and would therefore adopt a decree in due course. This was adopted three months following the complaint by TAT. Nevertheless, it provided, *inter alia*, that French domestic services may be operated to and from Orly and Charles de Gaulle. In addition, Orly may be used for scheduled services to and from Spain, Greece and Portugal provided they exceeded three-weekly return frequencies, for non-scheduled international services whose principal place of business was at Orly, and for scheduled international services between Community airports operated by non-Community carriers in accordance with an air service agreement, provided that trade between Member States was not affected. This last provision was essentially to cover services such as those provided by PIA. All other services of an intra-Community character were to be operated at Charles de Gaulle.

7.45   The aim of this policy, according to the French authorities, was three-fold. First, it aimed to allow the introduction of competition on a gradual basis. They stated:

"The abrupt application of a new airport policy cannot be countenanced in view of previous investment, both in commercial and in physical terms, by the airlines concerned. Initially, therefore, a new policy approach can only be implemented with regard to new services, and to measures of an incentive and progressive nature."

7.46   The second aim of the policy was to relieve congestion at both Orly and Charles de Gaulle. The third was to "make CDG 'the gateway to Europe'" thereby promoting flight transfers, and "to confirm Orly as 'the gateway to Paris'". Even with this new policy, TAT made the observation that London–Orly services would still be prohibited, and if French domestic services as well as services to Spain, Greece and Portugal could be operated at Orly, then that was a discriminatory policy which contravened the fundamental freedoms established by the Community.

7.47   This case raised a number of questions. First, whether the effect of the distribution policy was discriminatory. The Commission's assessment began by looking at the distinction between domestic and intra-Community services. Although it was clear that the policy excluded intra-Community services at Orly, it was also capable of excluding domestic services which are permitted at Orly even by a French-registered carrier such as TAT if these depended on an intra-Community connection flight. For example, London–Paris–Lyon. Thus, consecutive-cabotage, that is cabotage services either as an extension of or preliminary to a service in the State of registration, would effectively have been abandoned. The only exception was in relation to intra-Community services to and from Spain, Greece and Portugal which have access to Orly under the terms of the policy. This would result in a disproportionate number of carriers being excluded from competing on a dense route. The reasonable conclusion must be that such a policy operated towards the partitioning of dense routes to the benefit of certain carriers.

"In these circumstances, the Decree in question must be regarded as introducing, in practice, discrimination against Community carriers other than those established in France, and to a lesser extent, other than Greek, Portuguese and Spanish carriers as regards the operation of French domestic routes terminating at Paris."

The essential consideration to the issue of discrimination was whether the   7.48
discrimination had been based on objective and transparent criteria given that its essence was a restriction on a general freedom of access. The Commission found that it was hard-pressed to identify any objectivity in that policy, nor was it justified on available data. It was driven to conclude in the way it had concluded in previous cases, particularly in the Viva Air case, that Regulation 2408/92 was an integral measure of a programme designed to create a single European aviation market by abolishing barriers to access. That means that the invocation of any restrictions permitted by the Regulation can only be warranted if reference to "objective and overriding grounds in the common interest" can be made or if the same result cannot be secured by less burdensome means – that is, proportionality. For instance, in certain circumstances such as the saturation of facilities or congestion, requiring a traffic allocation policy may be justified as an overriding consideration. In this case, the limitation of intra-Community services to Charles de Gaulle was not substantiated by any evidence that Charles de Gaulle was less congested than Orly.

In the same breath, the Commission admitted that Orly was a popular airport   7.49
for users, thus making it one of the leading airports in the world. Orly airport serves about 85 per cent of French domestic traffic, with the remaining 15 per cent served by Charles de Gaulle. Hence, by prohibiting virtually all intra-Community flights into or out of Orly, that would have the consequence of depriving a significant number of users of the benefit which the Regulation sought to confer. This was not consistent with France's own Decree of promoting Orly as a "hub of the domestic network" and the "gateway to Paris". Nor was it consistent with the aim of the EC Treaty since trade between Paris–France and most other Member States would be affected. On the contrary, it would nullify the practical effect of cabotage rights under Article 3(2) of the Regulation, notwithstanding the rights granted for services to and from Spain, Greece and Portugal.

Indeed, the authorisation of these latter services should, *a fortiori*, augment the authorisation of other carriers.

Review of traffic distribution rules: Paris

7.50   Article 8(3) of the Regulation empowers a Member State to request the Commission to examine whether the provisions in Article 8(1) and (2) have been properly implemented by another Member State, and on such a request, the Commission is obliged to decide if the latter Member State may continue to apply its traffic distribution rules. Subsequent to the decisions of the Commission regarding the complaints of TAT, and in accordance with Article 8(3), the United Kingdom submitted a request to the Commission to examine the traffic distribution rules governing the Paris airport system.[25]

7.51   In particular, the United Kingdom submitted that Articles 4, 5 and 7 of the French decree of 15 November 1994 were incompatible with Community law and the Commission's decision in *TAT: Paris–London*. The relevant provisions were:

- *Article 3*: Provided that the exercise of the relevant traffic rights has been authorised in accordance with Regulation 2408/92, intra-Community air services shall be operated from the airports of Charles de Gaulle and Orly under the conditions provided for in Articles 4 and 5 of the decree.

- *Article 4*: No carrier may operate more than four outward flights and four return flights per day between the airport of Orly and any other Community airport or airport system.

7.52   - *Article 5*: The limits in Article 4 shall not apply where the carrier uses on the Orly pad for the operation of the services mentioned in the said Article between 0700 and 0930 local time and between 1800 and 2030 local time, only aircraft whose minimum size is fixed as follows on the basis of the annual traffic of such services:

Minimum aircraft size	Total annual passengers
40	less than 100,001
70	100,001–250,00
100	250,001–1,000,000
140	1,000,001–3,000,000
200	more than 3,000,000

  The total annual traffic as fixed above is defined as the aggregate traffic from 1 January to 31 December for all air services between a given Community airport or, where appropriate, the airport system to which it belongs and the Paris airport system.

- *Article 7*: Any air carrier wishing to operate an air service from one of the airports belonging to the Paris airport system shall, when submitting its operating schedule, provide the information required by the competent authority to ensure compliance with the provisions of the decree and to verify, in particular, that the marketing conditions of the air services submitted to them affect neither directly or indirectly the application of Articles 4, 5 and 6.

---

[25] Commission Decision 95/259, [1995] OJ L162/25.

The contention of the United Kingdom revolved around the discriminatory   7.53
effect of the rules and the lack of objective justifications for them, especially
because they required the use of larger aircraft even when traffic between two
airports did not justify it. Accordingly, the rules did not provide for "a genuine
distribution of traffic". The French authorities submitted that the rules were
intended to encourage the development of Charles de Gaulle which had the
potential for a sizeable expansion while controlling the development of traffic
at Orly.

(a) *Scope of Article 8(1)*. In assessing the scope of Article 8(1), the Commission stated   7.54
that in the first instance, that Article had to be construed as recognising "in principle the legitimacy of an active airport planning policy which complies with the
general principles of Community law and, in particular, the third aviation package". In executing that policy, a large range of matters would have to be considered, which in some cases would restrict to some extent access to individual airports
within an airport system if the policy was to be effective. Member States must be
recognised as having the right to develop systematically an airport system. On this
basis, Article 8(1) could not exclude "*a priori* the possibility of pursuing a specific
airport policy for a given airport system". Indeed, according to the Commission:

> "a Member State may legitimately wish to promote the development of one airport of
> an airport system at the expense of the other airports located therein. In such a case,
> the imposition of restrictions on access to those other airports alone may constitute a
> reasonable means of pursuing that objective."

Hence, the French decree of 15 November 1995 must be considered as measures for the distribution of traffic within an airport system under the terms
of Article 8(1).

(b) *Discrimination*. An important characteristic of Article 8(1) is that discrim-   7.55
ination on the basis of the nationality or identity of air carriers is prohibited in
the implementation of traffic distribution rules. In this regard, the Commission
concluded that Article 4 of the decree was not discriminatory because it applied
in the same way to all airlines. Likewise, it concluded that Article 5 of the decree
did not constitute "an overt discrimination on the grounds of the nationality or
identity of the air carrier". This was because the restriction on the size of aircraft
was related to the annual traffic volume.

Referring to its earlier decision in *TAT: Paris–London*, the Commission stressed   7.56
that discrimination could not be determined conclusively by having regard merely
to the measures *per se*. More importantly, the principle of non-discrimination
extended to the "discriminatory effects" of the measures in practice even if only
indirectly. Therefore, Article 5 of the decree had to be assessed in that light. On
the basis of the evidence available, the Commission was not satisfied that the
restrictions in Article 5 resulted in any form of discrimination in favour of French
carriers. Although the United Kingdom had referred to the plight of Air UK and
Manx Airlines in its submission, the Commission said that there were other UK
airlines such as Virgin Atlantic, Monarch Airlines and Britannia Airways which
possess aircraft capable of meeting the restrictions. In addition, it said that the

United Kingdom submission referred only to the fleet of French and UK carriers affected by Article 5 of the decree without explaining how carriers of other Member States might be affected. In the absence of more specific evidence pointing to the discriminatory nature or effect of that Article, the Commission concluded that it was not in violation of the non-discrimination principle.

7.57   (c) *Proportionality*. The Commission began this part of its analysis by stating that the general right to provide services under the EC Treaty meant that the "any restriction of the freedom to provide services must be justified on grounds of overriding considerations of public interest".[26] By implication, this required the restrictions to be proportionate to the objectives sought. In applying this principle to the case, the Commission remarked that while the nature of Articles 4 and 5 of the decree did not impose an absolute restriction on frequencies and size of aircraft, they were "capable of affecting the ability of air carriers to operate an unlimited number of services to and from Orly in accordance with their own commercial preferences". Consequently, this amounted to an obstruction of the freedom envisaged by Regulation 2408/92. However, the Commission reiterated that the right of a Member State to pursue actively an airport planning policy could not be denied. Moreover, the restrictions stipulated in Articles 4 and 5, which discouraged certain operations from Orly, were based on objective criteria and were capable of contributing to the objectives of the policy.

7.58   Nevertheless, the Commission pointed out that the annual traffic volume used by the French authorities were not specifically related to Orly airport to which the restrictions applied. It rejected the submission of the French authorities that the calculation of the annual traffic volume must be taken in the context of the airport system. Instead:

> "the annual traffic volume on any given route may only validly be used for determining the minimum aircraft size pursuant to Article 5 if such volume is defined as the total number of passengers travelling between that airport [Orly] and any other airport located within the EEA. In particular, traffic volume cannot be defined in these circumstances by reference to the airport system of Paris, nor by reference to the airport system of which the other airport may be a part."

7.59   Such a method of calculation would run the risk of enacting barriers to entry which would be disproportionate to the aims, in this case the control of traffic development at Orly airport. The need to make such a distinction was essential in the view of the Commission because the nature and relative importance of traffic into one airport of the system could vary significantly from another airport belonging to the same system. In the context of this complaint, traffic between London and Paris was served by a permutation of routes between Heathrow, Gatwick and Stansted on the one hand and, Orly and Charles de Gaulle on the other. Thus, for example, the traffic between Gatwick or Stansted and Orly may only represent a fraction of the total volume between Heathrow and Orly, but all

---

[26] See Commission interpretative communication concerning the free movement of services across frontiers, [1993] OJ C334/3.

three routes would fall within the stipulations of Article 5 on minimum aircraft size. The implementation of this policy would mean that an airline wishing to operate services, say, between Stansted and Orly would risk being required to use a larger aircraft that was inappropriate to the traffic level simply because of the volume of traffic between Heathrow and Orly. Likewise, this analysis would apply to the comparison between Heathrow–Charles de Gaulle and Stansted–Charles de Gaulle. An airline operating on the latter route could be required to use a larger aircraft on the unrelated ground that the traffic volume between Heathrow–Charles de Gaulle was high. On the basis of these considerations, the Commission decided that the method of calculating the traffic volume was not proportionate to the objectives sought, and required the French authorities to make the amendments accordingly.

On the whole, however, the Commission did not regard the restrictions of **7.60** Articles 4 and 5 of the decree to be disproportionate to the objectives pursued by the French authorities within the traffic distribution policy for the Paris airport system. On the contrary, it was possible for any airline to develop a commercially viable operation at Orly airport within the latitude permitted by that policy. In particular, the Commission noted that the permission for an airline to operate up to four frequencies per route from Orly, without restrictions, was generally suffic- ient even for a new airline to commence competing services against the incum- bents. At any rate, the majority of the routes to and from Orly were being operated with four or more daily frequencies, and traffic volumes were generally in excess of 500,000.

Airport systems

Article 8(5) places an obligation on Member States to inform the Commission if **7.61** a new airport system is to be constituted or an existing airport system is to be modified. At present, airport systems for the purposes of the Regulation are listed in Annex II.

(a)	Denmark:	Copenhagen (Kastrup–Roskilde)
(b)	Germany:	Berlin (Tegel–Schönefeld–Tempelhof)
(c)	France:	Paris (CDG–Orly–Le Bourget)
		Lyon–Bron–Satolas
(d)	Italy:	Rome (Fiumicino–Ciampino)
		Milan (Linate–Malpensa–Bergamo)
		Venice (Tessera–Treviso)
(e)	United Kingdom:	London (Heathrow–Gatwick–Stansted)

Infrastructural limitations

The Regulation provides in Article 9(1) a substantive derogation from the general **7.62** right of access if Member States deem that there is "serious congestion and/or environmental problems". This derogation will be particularly relevant in cases where "other modes of transport can provide satisfactory levels of service".

Nevertheless, the Regulation stipulates that the implementation of this derogation has to be in accordance with the following principles:

- be non-discriminatory on the grounds of nationality or identity of carriers;
- be valid for a limited period, not exceeding three years;
- not unduly affect the objectives of the Regulation or distort competition
  between carriers;
- not be more restrictive than is necessary to relieve the congestion or environmental problems.

7.63 Although all the relevant derogations in the Regulation refer to the requirement
of non-discrimination either of carrier nationality or identity, Article 9 explicitly
requires Member States to adhere to the principle of proportionality when implementing the derogation. In most cases, proportionality would be read into the
provisions of the Regulation so that the exceptions were not unduly applied to
frustrate the objectives of the Regulation. The case law of the Commission bears
testimony to this.

In addition to these principles, Article 9(7) lays down explicitly that any decision
to limit the exercise of traffic rights by a Community carrier on an intra-
Community route must be applied uniformly to all Community carriers in the
same route. Likewise, if the decision entails the refusal to authorise new or additional services, this decision should be applied to all Community carriers seeking
to operate new or additional services on that same route. In the light of the
decisions handed down by the Commission in the application of this Regulation,
it would seem unavoidable to include in the notion of an "intra-Community
route" all domestic routes unless the derogation under Article 3(2) on cabotage
has been claimed.

7.64 Member States are also required to respect the principle of reciprocity. If a
Member State has refused to authorise a new or additional service proposed by
a Community carrier licensed by another Member State, then it is not permitted
to authorise "an air carrier" to operate services between the airports in question
for such period as that other carrier is not permitted to operate. This reciprocity,
however, is subject to the right of Member States to regulate the distribution of
traffic in accordance with Article 8(1), or it may be waived if the opposite Member
State agrees to the authorisation of such new or additional services.

Procedure

7.65 The procedural requirements applicable to this derogation are extensive. Member
States seeking to declare the application of Article 9(1) must first notify all other
Member States and the Commission of the proposal and provide "adequate justification for the action" three months in advance as required by Article 9(3). Unless
"a Member State concerned" or the Commission objects to the proposal within
one month of the notice, the proposal may be implemented. Clearly the requirement of *locus standi* is aimed at restricting the right to object to those Member
States with a clear interest in the matter. The approach of the European Court
of Justice in interpreting similar provisions has been strict. In respect of Article

173 of the EC Treaty for example, which provides for persons who have a "direct and individual concern" in relation to a Community action or measure to seek judicial review, the Court has taken a narrow scope of application.[27]

On a complaint, or on its own initiative, the Commission is required to   7.66 investigate the action and decide within one month of having received all necessary information. This decision is subject to an appellate procedure in accordance with Article 9(6) which empowers the Council to take a different decision "in exceptional circumstances" by a qualified majority vote. Pending a final decision, the Commission is also empowered by Article 9(4) to impose interim measures "taking into account in particular the possibility of irreversible effects".

4. Conclusion

It is without doubt that the measure providing for a general right of access to market is one of the most important legislation with far-reaching consequences. Since its introduction, the Commission has reported that the number of intra-Community routes has increased although ironically, "there has been a marked drop in the number of routes with two carriers".[28] However, the Commission accepted that the majority of these monopoly or duopoly routes were either low-traffic density sectors or were subject to indirect competition from neighbouring routes or charter services. In addition, the number of routes where more than two carriers operated also remained small, accounting for only about 6 per cent of all intra-Community routes. Nevertheless, the operating frequencies on these latter routes have increased sharply.

On specific market sectors, the Commission noted that competition was most notable on domestic routes particularly in France and Spain. Furthermore, the general freedoms provided by the market access measure have yet to be fully exploited by the carriers. The Commission observed that the use of the fifth freedom right was typically restricted to national carriers because these services tend to be expensive and which are therefore unsuitable to many of the new low-cost carriers. Likewise, the use of the cabotage right has been limited chiefly because of the various restrictions still being applied while the seventh freedom right has largely been used only by subsidiaries of national carriers such as TAT.

Although the results achieved so far have been fairly modest, there is little doubt that the general right of market access has much in store for Community air transport. Over 80 new airlines were established since the third package in 1993. National carriers have also suffered a reduction in their market shares as a consequence of the direct competition from some of these new carriers. But the Commission concedes that there remains an urgent programme of action to overcome the obstacles to effective competition. These include the infrastructural limitations of air space and airport capacity, and the high costs of ground-handling services.

---

[27] Case 25/62, *Plaumann v Commission* [1963] ECR 95.
[28] *Impact of the Third Package of Air Transport Liberalization Measures*, COM(96) 514.

Chapter 8

DEREGULATION OF FARES

As with access to routes, the liberalisation of air fares for scheduled services was initiated in 1987 with the adoption of the first package of liberalisation measures. The two subsequent sets of measures brought greater competitiveness in air fares by vesting in air carriers greater freedom to set fares according to their commercial judgement.

Competition in air fares is arguably the most effective form of air transport competition designed to benefit users and to increase levels of airline efficiency. Competition in fares, however, is not simply an end in itself. Often it is a catalyst to competition in the quality of service and the range of products offered to users. Quality of service is important where demand is usually inelastic, and this is particularly evident in the case of premium air fares such as first or business class fares. This inelasticity provides little incentive to compete on fares; competition for a larger market share must therefore depend on the quality of service.

Airlines which compete in air fares frequently find the need to introduce a variety of fare products either to attract additional custom or to sustain the loyalty of existing customers, for example, "Advance Purchase Excursion Fares" (APEX), "3-Day Executive Fares" and so on. Some may involve inflexible conditions relating to the dates of travel and overnight stays. Others may be less restrictive. Experience in fares deregulation elsewhere is instructive of the need for greater commercial freedom for airlines to set fares, within the rules of fair play, which meet to the maximum extent possible the demand for air travel. While some passengers are prepared to adhere to the conditions of a cheaper fare, others such as business travellers are less amenable to restrictive conditions for time is often the vital factor for such passengers and thus maximum flexibility in the conditions of travel becomes essential. In other cases, fares were reduced significantly on what are known as "no-frill" services where food and drink can be purchased on board the flight, rather than being served as a matter of course. EasyJet which operates out of Luton airport is a prominent example. EasyJet is a new entrant in the post-liberalised period, whose fares are offered at substantially reduced levels to tempt travellers who otherwise would not have chosen to fly. Another new entrant to have emerged to compete with the incumbents is Debonair.

In addition, some air carriers have departed from the traditional three-class cabin configuration to include a fourth, for instance, "Economy Deluxe" or "Economy SuperDeluxe" class offering more leg-room or higher pitch of seat reclination. Without such freedom to set air fares and improve on service quality, competition in fares will not exist because there will be little incentive in doing so, whether to increase market share or lower the unit cost of production.

1. Background to fares liberalisation

8.4 The first phase of fares liberalisation was introduced with the passage of Council Directive 87/601 which aimed to provide for greater flexibility in the setting of fares by air carriers so as to enable them "to develop markets and better meet consumer needs".[1] The second stage was initiated in 1990 when the Council adopted Regulation 2342/90.[2] The greater part of this Regulation repeated much of what was contained in Council Directive 87/601, which it also repealed.

At the time Directive 87/601 was adopted it applied only to scheduled air fares and in respect of those routes which involved travel between an airport in one Member State and an airport in another Member State. By implication then, scheduled domestic services and scheduled services which involved a third country airport were excluded. This scope was retained in Regulation 2342/90.

Criteria

8.5 Subject to the approval system, both Directive 87/601 and Regulation 2342/90 required Member States to approve all air fares which were "reasonably related to the long-term fully allocated costs of the applicant air carrier". Member States were also required to take into account other relevant factors. These included:

- the needs of the consumer;
- the need for a satisfactory return on capital;
- the market situation such as air fares charged by other carriers on the same route;
- the need to prevent dumping particularly through the use of excessively low fares.

8.6 Member States were, however, expressly prohibited from withholding approval simply on the ground that the proposed air fare was lower than that offered by another carrier on the same route. The simple logic of this prohibition was to prevent Member States from protecting any particular air carrier from price competition. Thus, a Member State was under an obligation to permit an air carrier of another Member State to match an air fare already approved for a route between two points in the Community. While the air carrier must be operating a scheduled service, it could, however, be a direct or indirect service. If the services concerned were indirect, the Member State concerned would then be exempted from the obligation if the services exceeded the length of the shortest direct service by more than 20 per cent.

8.7 In 1991, the United Kingdom invoked on two occasions the complaint procedure pursuant to Article 5(1) of Regulation 2342/90 which enabled a Member State claiming to have "a legitimate interest in the route concerned" to request the Commission to examine an air fare which that Member State believed was

---

[1] [1987] OJ L374/12.
[2] [1990] OJ L217/1.

not in compliance with the criteria for approval or the conditions of the fare zones. The complaint by the UK Government alleged that a number of fare increases for certain routes to and from the United Kingdom were not in conformity with Article 3 of the Regulation which required Member States to have regard to long-term fully-allocated costs, satisfactory return on capital and adequate cost margin for maintaining safety standards. The complaint in respect of some fare increases was subsequently withdrawn. Thus, of the 59 routes which the Commission investigated in accordance with the complaint, it found the fares on 32 of the routes to be in compliance with Article 3 while the remaining 27 were not. The majority of the fare increases investigated by the Commission related to British Airways services. The five airlines whose fare increases were approved by the relevant aviation authorities and were found to have infringed the Regulation were BA, Alitalia, Scandinavian Airline System, Air France and Olympic Airways. In addition, the Commission investigated the fare increases on those routes as to which the United Kingdom had withdrawn the complaint. The fares of two airlines, BA and Lufthansa, were found to have failed to comply with the Regulation. Culpability for these infringements, however, rested with the Member States or their aviation authorities rather than the airlines.[3] In the second complaint, the Commission found a number of fares offered by BA, Alitalia, Luxair and Iberia were in contravention of Article 3(1).[4]

Approval of fares

Under Directive 87/601, air fares were subject to the express approval of the relevant aviation authority of the two Member States concerned. Hence, fares were subject to a system of double approval which entailed an express or implied approval of the two Member States concerned. They were required to approve fares which fell within the "zones of flexibility". However, approval would be implied if neither of the relevant aviation authorities had disapproved the proposed air fare within 30 days of submission.   8.8

Fares could be submitted individually by an air carrier, or following consultations with other carriers provided of course the consultations comply with the requirements laid down in Council Regulation 3976/87.[5]

With the advent of Regulation 2342/90, the discretion exercised by Member States in approving air fares was further reduced. In particular, any rejection of "a fully flexible fare above 105% of the reference fare" must be disapproved by *both* Member States failing which the fare was deemed approved – "double disapproval" system. This was in addition to the obligation of Member States to approve fares which fell within the expanded zones of flexibility. By implication also, Member States retained the right to disapprove fares which failed to meet the terms applicable to the zones in force, and also fares which were "excessively high to the disadvantage of users or unjustifiably low in view of the competitive market situation".   8.9

[3] Commission Decision 92/8, [1992] OJ L5/26.
[4] Commission Decision 92/398, [1992] OJ L220/35.
[5] See Ch. 4 *supra*.

Zonal concept

8.10   The most significant feature of the fares liberalisation programme was the introduction of the zonal concept in Directive 87/601. In a number ways, the concept
of fare zones was an interesting and innovative means of liberalising air transport
competition in the Community. In particular, while it was important that competition be introduced gradually, the zonal concept enabled a limited degree of
competition in air fares to be achieved. Air fares which fell within a particular zone
would no longer require the approval of Member States, thus conferring on air
carriers a much wider discretion to set fares in accordance with the law of demand
and supply. Article 2(b) of the Directive defined the zonal concept as a zone of
flexibility within which "air fares meeting the conditions in Annex II qualify for
automatic approval by the aeronautical authorities of the Member States".

8.11   Two zones of flexibility were provided for in Article 2(c) of the Directive: a discount zone and a deep-discount zone. The limits of a zone were expressed as a
percentage of the reference fare which was defined as "the normal economy air
fare charged by a third- or fourth-freedom air carrier on the route in question".[6]
Accordingly, the Directive set the limits of the discount zone as between 65 per
cent (floor) and 90 per cent (ceiling) of the reference fare, while the limits of the
deep-discount zone were set at between 45 per cent and 65 per cent. Hence,
within these zones, third- and fourth-freedom air carriers were free to set whatever air fare they deemed appropriate subject to the condition that the fares met
the Annex II conditions and were filed 21 days prior to them taking effect.

8.12   The Directive also provided that the obligations of Member States under it
would not prejudice the right of Member States "from concluding arrangements
which are more flexible". In a case where a bilaterally agreed fare between the
Member States qualified for automatic approval in the deep-discount zone and
where the fare was below the floor of that zone, "there shall be additional flexibility as to the level of that fare". It was provided that the floor of the zone would
be 10 per cent below the bilaterally agreed fare, extending to the ceiling of the
deep-discount zone. Clearly though, the conditions of Annex II must be met.

8.13   Under Regulation 2342/90 the zones of flexibility for fares were extended.
Three zones were established:

- *normal economy zone*: limits between 95 per cent and 105 per cent of the
reference fare;

- *discount zone*: limits between 80 per cent and 94 per cent of the reference fare;

- *deep-discount zone*: limits between 30 per cent and 79 per cent of the reference
fare.

The application of these zones depended on the fares meeting the conditions
set out in Annex II of the Regulation. All fares which fell outside these zones of
flexibility continued to be subject to the jurisdiction of Member States.

---

[6] In this sense, only third- and fourth-freedom air carriers were permitted to act as price leaders.

Annex II conditions

An air fare that could be the subject of the discount or deep-discount zone was 8.14
required to satisfy the conditions laid down in Annex II of either the Directive or
Regulation. *Inter alia*, this required that the air fare was in respect of a round or
return trip, provided for a maximum and minimum period of stay, and set out
the conditions for off-peak travel.

2. Deregulation of fares

By far, the most important piece of legislation governing air fares is Council 8.15
Regulation 2409/92 adopted as part of the final package of liberalisation measures for Community air transport.[7] A principal aim of the Regulation is to enable
air fares to be "determined freely by market forces" while at the same time ensuring that price freedom is accompanied by "adequate safeguards for the interests
of consumers and industry". Subject to these safeguards, the intention of the
Regulation is to deregulate air fares for Community air transport.

Scope

While hitherto Council Directive 87/601 and Council Regulation 2342/90 were 8.16
applicable only to air fares for scheduled services between Member States,
Council Regulation 2409/92 establishes criteria and procedures for "fares and
rates on air services for carriage wholly within the Community". The effect of the
Regulation is not only to expand the regulatory scope to include domestic services
within a particular Member State, but also to expand the types of air services
subject to the Regulation including charter and cargo services. Accordingly, charter fares, seat rates paid by charterers to air carriers, and cargo rates would be
set by free agreement between the parties.

Two exceptions, however, apply. First, the Regulation does not apply to fares 8.17
charged by carriers which are not Community carriers. A Community carrier is
defined in the Regulation as a carrier with a valid operating licence issued in
accordance with Council Regulation 2407/92. The clear intention of this exception is to continue to subject air fares for services operated by non-Community
carriers to bilateral agreements between Member States and the third country
concerned. The Regulation also continues to restrict "price leadership" to
Community carriers, thus limiting the commercial freedom it has established for
the setting of fares and introduction of new products only to Community carriers.

The second exception applies to fares for services operated as a matter of public
service obligation. A public service obligation is defined as an obligation imposed
on an air carrier to operate a particular service in accordance with fixed standards
of continuity, regularity, capacity and pricing, which the air carrier would not
otherwise assume if it was based solely on a commercial basis.[8]

---

[7] [1992] OJ L240/15.
[8] See Ch. 7 *supra* and Council Regulation 2408/92, [1992] OJ L240/8.

Regulatory framework

Filing of fares

8.18   The ability to set air fares freely must logically mean that the zones of flexibility established by previous legislation would no longer be needed. Article 5(2), however, empowers Member States to require air fares to be filed with the relevant national authorities provided that the system of filing does not discriminate between air carriers on grounds of nationality or identity, nor require fares to be filed more than 24 hours before they take effect. In a case where a new fare is being introduced to match an existing fare, the Regulation requires no more than prior notification. The requirement of filing charter fares, charter rates or cargo rates does not, however, apply to such services since Article 5(2) expressly refers to "air fares to be filed", although Article 4 requires air carriers operating within the Community to inform the general public, on request, of all air fares including cargo rates.

   The importance of filing fares lies in the ability of the relevant national authority to conduct proper supervision of fares that they have not been set either excessively high by abusing a market position, or excessively low with a predatory intent. This is critical if the safeguards in the Regulation are to be enforced effectively. The two complaints lodged by the United Kingdom are illustrative of this.

Safeguards

8.19   Of specific relevance to the Regulation, the requirement of filing enables Member States to regulate any "upward" or "downward" spiral of fares as conceived under Article 6 of the Regulation. Article 6 empowers Member States to do two things. First, it enables a Member State at any time to "withdraw a basic fare which . . . is excessively high to the disadvantage of users". A basic fare would be considered as excessively high if it is not related to the long-term fully-allocated costs of the carrier and a satisfactory return on capital. Whether or not fares have spiralled upwards without being reasonably related to costs would depend on a number of factors including the entire fare structure on the route in question and the competitive market situation as well as the overall profitability in the relevant market.

8.20   Secondly, a Member State is empowered to act by terminating any downward spiral of fares to prevent further fare decreases in a market. It is a condition precedent to the exercise of this power that the Member State needs to be satisfied that market forces have led to the sustained downward development "deviating from ordinary seasonal pricing movements and resulting in widespread losses among all air carriers concerned for the air services concerned". Such losses will need to be assessed in accordance with the long-term fully-allocated costs of the carriers. It is significant that the provision requires losses among "all carriers" so that one or two carriers making losses while others are not, will not be entitled to claim protection under Article 6, but may instead need to improve on efficiency. Fourteen days must elapse before any decision of the Member State either to withdraw the basic fare or terminate the fare decrease is to take effect. This is to provide Member States "concerned" with the opportunity to notify their disagreement with the proposed action in which case "consultations to review the situation" may be requested.

According to the Commission, the concept of "long-term" meant that "short-term fluctuations in costs cannot be taken into account" on the one hand, while "fully-allocated costs" meant that "all costs which relate to an air fare must be allocated fully and not only to the route in question" on the other hand. In this latter respect, any marginal approach in cost allocation would not be acceptable, notwithstanding that it might be commercially sustainable.[9] As far as route-related costs are concerned, the Commission will require that all directly attributable costs to the routes in question, such as fuel, airport and crew expenses, must be taken into account. However, the more complex issue of indirect costs would need to be determined on the basis of a number of assumptions. The Commission accepts that a variety of accounting methods may be used to calculate the indirect costs, and while it does not intend to specify a preferred method, an airline must use the method chosen "in a consistent and controllable way".   **8.21**

Equally, as regards specific fare-related costs, a number of assumptions will have to be made so that, for example, the different costs of producing a seat in first class may be differentiated from those of producing a seat in the economy cabin. In the Commission's view, the real difference as to the cost of different fare-types flows from "the conditions attached to the air fare or lack of the same" because these conditions can have a significant bearing on the load factor of a particular service. For instance, in the case of a business fare where no restrictions are usually attached, passengers have the flexibility of cancelling their reservation on the flight in question without incurring a penalty. By contrast, a promotional fare which is usually accompanied by restrictions will not usually result in cancellations because of the penalties. Consequently, the load factor on business fares may be lower than if it was on promotional fares. A reasonable load factor, typically at 55 per cent, must therefore be assumed. This load factor will then be applied as a function of the fares charged by the airlines to determine profitability.   **8.22**

In terms of the relationship between fares and costs, the Commission generally regards a profit margin of 10 per cent–15 per cent as reasonable. This would produce an Operating Ratio (OR) of between 110 and 115. However, this ratio cannot be applied directly on a route-to-route basis since an average air carrier may be assumed to have some profitable routes and some un-profitable routes. This means "a certain degree of cross-subsidization between routes is justifiable". If a calculation on a route-to-route basis has to be made, the Commission will assume a further margin of 10 per cent, thus raising the OR to 125. A further 10 per cent margin will need to be added to take into account errors in allocating costs. It is therefore reasonable to apply an OR of between 135 and 140. Fares with an OR above 140 will only be approved if "the route showed overall negative results for at least two seasons".   **8.23**

Where, for example, a high OR is applied to business fares, but the route nevertheless produces negative results, it may be reasonable for the Commission to imply that "these airlines attempt to have very low fares for the leisure traffic   **8.24**

---

[9] Commission Decision 92/398, [1992] OJ L220/39.

with cross-subsidization from the business traffic". Accordingly, these fares would not be acceptable, particularly where there is little or no competition on business fares and where competition in the promotional fare sector is important. By the same token, a high OR cannot be acceptable if the airline concerned was simply raising its fares to match those of its competitors precisely because they will not be cost-related.

8.25   During the gestation period of the Regulation, these safeguards were reportedly seen as essential to ensure that the full competitive effect of deregulating fares was brought in gradually and to assuage the "fear of inducing the kind of airline bankruptcies that have swept the United States since it deregulated its air travel market".[10] It is not clear from the terms of the Regulation whether the safeguards against upward and downward spirals apply to cargo rates and charter fares. A strict interpretation would seem to suggest that at least in the case of cargo services, these safeguards do not apply since the charge for cargo services is usually denoted as "rates" rather than fares. In addition, this would seem consistent with the history of cargo rates regulation where previous legislation has afforded a large measure of freedom for setting the rates. Indeed, this was evident in Council Regulation 294/91 adopted in 1991 designed to liberalise cargo services.[11] The Regulation stated in recital 13 that "to be better able to compete, air cargo carriers need flexibility in setting cargo rates". In as much as Article 9 provided that rates charged by Community cargo carriers could be set freely by agreement between the parties to the contract of carriage, there were no safeguard provisions in that legislation. Nor should they be implied.

Basic fare

8.26   A basic fare, for the purposes of the Regulation, means "the lowest fully flexible fare, available on a one way and return basis, which is offered for sale at least to the same extent as that of any other fully flexible fare offered on the same air service".

Review procedure

8.27   The decision of a Member State whether or not to act under Article 6 is subject to review by the Commission at the request of another Member State. During the period of investigation, the Commission has, at its disposal, the power to impose an interim measure to require that the air fare in question be withdrawn during the investigation. It may do so either because in the six months prior to the investigation it had decided that "a similar or lower level of the basic fare on the city-pair concerned" did not comply with the criteria of Article 6(1)(a) or the carrier from which information was requested had supplied incorrect or incomplete information. In addition, the Commission has independent powers to investigate a complaint relating to compliance with Article 6 by "a party with a legitimate interest".

---

[10] *The Independent*, 27 March 1992.
[11] [1991] OJ L36/1.

3. Relationship with Articles 85 and 86

Any regulatory action by Member States under the Regulation is principally   8.28
aimed at correcting certain market failures which have led to significant and sustained changes in air fares. This must therefore seem distinct from, and independent of, any action that may be taken under Articles 85 and 86 for the breach of
Community competition law, since in particular the Regulation expressly requires
Member States to have regard to the market conditions and structure of competition on the route in question if they were proposing to withdraw or terminate
the upward or downward spiral of fares.

If, consequently, the upward spiral of fares was the product of an agreement   8.29
between several airlines or reflected an abuse of a dominant market position, then
an action under Article 85 or 86 pursuant to Council Regulation 3975/87 can be
taken. The Commission has already warned that abuses of a dominant position
to charge high fares will be dealt with severely, especially with respect to fares on
duopoly routes.[12] Likewise, if the spiral of fares, particularly a downward spiral,
has been the consequence of a concerted practice or an agreement between a
number of carriers with predatory intent, or a deliberate exercise of market power
to suppress fares, an action can be taken pursuant to those measures. In fact, the
Court of Justice has already sanctioned the use of Article 86 to deal with unfair
trading conditions resulting from excessively high or low fares, and in particular,
where the exclusive application of only one tariff on a given route arises because
of "the conduct of an undertaking in a dominant position, and not because of the
policy of the aeronautical authorities".[13] However, the difficulties that may be
associated with an enforcement action under Articles 85 and 86, particularly in
determining the relevant market, whether market dominance exists as much as
whether there has been an abuse of that dominance, cannot be ignored.

4. Conclusion

In October 1996, the Commission published its evaluation of the liberalisation   8.28
programme.[14] Its findings on the issue of fares competition were mixed. While the
deregulation of fares have led to a reduction in fares, these were limited to those
routes operated by more than two carriers. Indeed, as the Commission found,
flexible fares on a large number of monopoly and duopoly routes have continued
to rise. More specifically, it concluded that "fares competition has been
characterized, by and large, by the launching of new promotional and special fares
rather than reductions in existing fares." It is clear from the report that fares
deregulation has yet to produce significant changes to fare structures and levels.
Much of this is the consequence of the continuing tradition of monopoly and
duopoly routes in a substantial part of the intra-Community air transport market.

---

[12] *The Times*, 30 May 1996.
[13] Case 66/86, *Ahmed Saeed Flugreisen & Silver Line Reisebüro* v *Zentrale Zur Bekämpfung Unlauteren Wettbewerbs* [1989] ECR 803, at 850.
[14] *Impact of the Third Package of Air Transport Liberalization Measures*, COM(96) 514.

Chapter 9

DEREGULATION OF CAPACITY

Apart from the possible enforcement of Articles 85 and 86 of the EC Treaty 9.1
against agreements to limit or restrict passenger capacity between air carriers, the
regulation of passenger capacity in European air transport was first introduced in
1987 when the Council adopted the first tranche of liberalisation measures.

In international air transport, capacity has been and continues to be a highly
regulated area. This is sometimes referred to as frequency since the frequency of
services will have a direct bearing on the overall capacity for any given period.
With the exception of "open-skies" bilateral agreements and those agreements
which purport to provide a measure of flexibility within specified zones, passenger
capacity is often shared by the participating countries on a 50 per cent basis.
Increasingly, however, flexibility has been introduced into the sharing of capacity
where the carrier(s) of each country has a 5 per cent margin of flexibility so that
it is able to carry a minimum of 45 per cent and a maximum 55 per cent of the
capacity agreed for the season or year. Total capacity is seasonally adjusted, and
often in accordance with the density of traffic in the previous corresponding season or seasons. Capacity controls in Community air transport were abolished in
1992 when the final package of liberalisation measures was adopted.

1. Background to capacity liberalisation

Council Decision 87/602[1] was adopted against the background of the objective 9.2
that flexibility and competition in Community air transport ought to be increased,
and in respect of capacity, air carriers ought to have the freedom to decide the
level of capacity that is commercially rational by relaxing the artificial constraints
which were imposed by bilateral agreements between Member States prior to the
advent of the Decision.

The scope of the Decision, however, was limited to the sharing of passenger
capacity between carriers of two Member States on scheduled air services between
the two States. Air services which were the subject of Council Directive 83/416
on inter-regional services were not affected by the Decision.[2] This was followed

---

[1] [1987] OJ L374/19.
[2] [1983] OJ L237/19.

by Regulation 2343/90 as the Community moved into the second phase of the liberalisation programme.[3]

Zones of flexibility

9.3   The significance of the Decision was to move away from the rigidities of the bilateral system in determining capacity and the traditional division of 50 per cent–50 per cent between the carriers of the respective Member States. It did so by authorising the flexibility for carriers which operated air services between the territories of the two Member States concerned to adjust capacity on the routes operated, provided that the adjustment did not result in capacity shares exceeding the upper limit of 55 per cent or the lower limit of 45 per cent. More significantly, the Decision provided a default clause that unless a decision to the contrary was taken by the Commission following a review, the zone of flexibility was to be extended to capacity shares of 60 per cent–40 per cent on 1 October 1989. The power of the Commission in this respect was, however, conditional upon a Member State requesting such a review under Article 4(1) on the ground that the application of the initial zone of flexibility "has led to serious financial damage for its air carrier(s)".

9.4   The freedom to make capacity adjustments was subject to a number of important conditions. Assume airline A and airline B of two different Member States, and airline B under the first automatic approval had chosen to offer a lower capacity. Its freedom to adjust the level of capacity upwards subsequently was restricted by the limit of the capacity offered by airline A. Airline A would be permitted to respond to the decision of airline B by having one further automatic increase up to the limit of its capacity file at the beginning of the season. In return, airline B would be permitted a further automatic approval of another increase but only to match the new level of capacity offered by airline A. Any further proposal to increase capacity during the season would need the bilateral approval of the Member States concerned; decreases in capacity were, however, excluded.

9.5   The complications of these restrictions were removed when Regulation 2343/90 was adopted. The Regulation introduced an incremental concept in that the air carrier of one Member State will be permitted by the other Member State to increase its capacity share for any season by 7.5 per cent of the capacity in the previous corresponding season. It further provided that in any event, Member States could claim a 60 per cent share of the capacity recorded in the previous corresponding season. By introducing the 7.5 per cent flexibility, the Council raised the stakes in competition by granting a greater degree of freedom to carriers to decide and to increase the level of capacity. Although the Regulation provided the default claim of 60 per cent share, this would benefit only a carrier which carried less than 60 per cent of the traffic in the previous season. A carrier which transported more than 60 per cent of the total capacity would lay claim to the 7.5 per cent flexibility to achieve a higher upper limit. Indeed, Member States were not prevented from concluding more flexible arrangements, although Article

---

[3] [1990] OJ L217/8.

13 of the Regulation expressly prohibited the conclusion of more restrictive capacity arrangements.

The removal of some of the conditions governing adjustments to increase   9.6
capacity shares provided an important foundation for the complete deregulation of capacity by 1993. At the insistence of the Mediterranean States during the gestation period of the legislation, however, the Regulation complemented the greater degree of capacity freedom with two safeguards. First, it enabled a Member State whose air carrier had suffered serious financial damage as a result of any capacity increase under the Regulation to request the Commission to initiate a review. This would include the assessment of the market situation, the financial position of the carrier in question and the extent of its capacity utilization in order to ascertain whether the sharing of capacity on the routes between the Member States concerned should be "stabilized for a limited period".[4]

Secondly, it enabled a Member State to request the Commission to initiate a   9.7
review of the capacity sharing arrangements and to decide whether the application of the 7.5 per cent increment should be reduced for the routes between the two Member States concerned. Such a request could only be made where the scheduled air services of the complainant Member State had been "exposed to substantial competition from non-scheduled services and where a situation exists whereby the opportunities of carriers of that Member State to effectively compete in the market are unduly affected".[5]

Regional services

While those inter-regional services which fell to be covered under Council   9.8
Directive 83/416 were excluded from the scope of Council Decision 87/602, Regulation 2343/90 went a step further by revoking the Directive, and instead prohibited any limitations on capacity sharing for services between regional airports regardless of the size of the aircraft.

2. Deregulation of capacity

Council Regulation 2408/92[6] marks the culmination of the process of gradual   9.9
liberalisation with respect to capacity controls in Community air transport. The effect of the provision is simple. All forms of capacity limitations in respect of air services covered by the Regulation are prohibited, unless the services in question are the subject of a condition imposed by virtue of Article 8, Article 9 or Article 10(2) of the Regulation.

---

[4] Council Regulation 2343/90, Art. 12(1).
[5] Council Regulation 2343/90, Art. 12(2).
[6] [1992] OJ L240/8.

3. Safeguards

Air traffic distribution

9.10 Article 8 of Regulation 2408/92 makes provision for Member States to regulate the distribution of traffic within an airport system provided that this is done in accordance with the principle of non-discrimination in respect of nationality and identity. The application of Article 8 has already been discussed in Chapter 7.

Congestion and environmental restrictions

9.11 The issue of congestion and the power of Member States to impose restrictions on capacity or frequency was examined by the Commission in 1992 pursuant to a complaint made under Regulation 2343/90.[7] The applicable provisions in that case, however, have not changed under Regulation 2408/92 in that the latter continues to impose infrastructural conditions for the exercise of traffic rights on Community routes. In particular, the exercise of the freedom relating to capacity is subject to the condition that "a Member State shall not authorize an air carrier (a) to establish a new service; or (b) to increase the frequency of an existing service between a specific airport in its territory and another Member State for such time as an air carrier licensed by that other Member State is not permitted" on the basis of published Community, national, regional or local rules relating to safety, the protection of the environment and the allocation of slots.[8] This was repeated in Article 9(8) of Regulation 2408/92.

9.12 In that case, the Belgian Government lodged a complaint with the Commission alleging that the United Kingdom had acted contrary to the Regulation in that it had failed to give effect to the principle of reciprocity. It argued that if Sabena was not authorised to increase its frequency on the London (Heathrow)–Brussels route, then British Midland (BMA) should not be authorised to increase its six daily services to eight. In any event, the Belgian Government resorted to the argument that Article 10(3) embodied the "teleological" principle which envisaged the possibility of a Member State (*i.e.* Belgium) taking counter-measures against the carrier concerned by refusing to authorise its proposed increase in services.

9.13 The response from the United Kingdom was simply that Article 10(3) did not provide for reciprocal action, and was in fact contrary to Article 4 of the Regulation which authorised Community carriers to operate third- and fourth-freedom services between Member States. Furthermore, it argued that Sabena did not seem to have been refused permission to increase its frequencies. In any event, the United Kingdom took the view that the services in question were authorised under the bilateral agreement between the two Member States rather than the Regulation, and if that was accepted then Member States were prohibited by

---

[7] Commission Decision 92/552, [1992] OJ L353/32.
[8] Council Regulation 2343/90, Art. 10(3). Art. 10(1) provided further conditions which have not been incorporated into Council Regulation 2408/92: the airport or airport system concerned must have sufficient facilities to accommodate the service and the navigational aids must be equally sufficient.

Article 13(2) from using the provisions of the Regulation "to make existing capacity arrangements more restrictive".

The case therefore revolved around two key questions. The first was the meaning of authorisation, and in the light of that definition, whether Sabena had been authorised to increase frequencies on the route in question. It was agreed, however, that Sabena had been authorised by the Belgian authorities. The second focused on the issue of reciprocity and the right of a Member State to take counter-measures against the carrier of that other Member State.

Authorisation

It is axiomatic that London (Heathrow) airport suffers from chronic congestion.   9.14
Securing slots to implement the additional frequencies was always going to be a difficult issue. For BMA, however, additional frequencies on that route would be met by re-assigning the slots which it had been allocated. It was a question of opportunity cost. Sabena, on the other hand, had to request additional slots from the Heathrow airport co-ordinator: four were requested, two in the morning and two in the afternoon. A further issue arose during the consideration of the case that Sabena's requests for these additional slots were not in compliance with the published rules on slot allocation at Heathrow airport which required all requests to be submitted by 1 November 1991 for the season in question.

Although Sabena failed in its requests initially, the co-ordinator managed to   9.15
secure a combination of slots for Sabena. These were, however, outside the times which Sabena had requested although it was given a choice of slot-pairs (arrival and departure). According to the co-ordinator, these were nonetheless the best available slots which could be found given the circumstances.

In its assessment, the Commission stated that the aim of Article 10(3) was to strike a balance in the traffic rights between the carriers licensed to operate on a particular route. However, "this balance in traffic rights must be numerical" so that Article 10(3) had to be read as implying a certain obligation in a Member State "to withdraw the traffic rights already granted to an air carrier licensed by this State" to achieve that balance. Accordingly, a carrier had the right to expect a Member State to refuse to authorise its competitor for, *inter alia*, an increase in frequency. It did not, however, provide for a "matching right" such that every slot given to one carrier must be matched by a corresponding slot to the carrier in competition. This would defeat the object of the derogations provided in the Regulation.

The criteria for determining whether there was a numerical balance of the   9.16
traffic rights in this case were, first of all, whether sufficient slots had been allocated by the co-ordinator to enable Sabena to increase its frequencies. In that case, additional slots albeit at different times were found by the co-ordinator for Sabena some of which did not permit a fast turn around of aircraft because an aircraft would have to wait for a considerable period on the ground. The question then was whether "best available" slots would suffice for the purposes of the Regulation. On the basis of the slots offered, the Commission concluded that Sabena would still suffer from a more unfavourable position than BMA in using the allocated slots profitably. Aircraft utility would be low and consequently deny Sabena a commercially efficient operation. Nevertheless, it was important to

recognise that allocating slots in precise accordance with the times requested could not always be possible in practice. Hence, the best available slots offered to Sabena should be considered "as a starting point for further improvements" as if in a slot allocation conference. This would require the slot co-ordinator to put the carrier (Sabena) at the front of the waiting list so as "to provide Sabena eventually with slots which permit a commercial operation of the frequency increase".

9.17   This was a necessary compromise since the Regulation did not explicitly require that "the slots offered at the time of the requests be exactly the ones requested". Indeed, the Commission reasoned that the Regulation did not provide that "the slots offered must *immediately* be economically viable" (emphasis added). By implication, therefore, it would be sufficient that a Member State "offers the best slots which are available at the time of the request". It is noteworthy also that the Commission emphasised the importance of the "best available slots" being offered if discrimination is to be avoided.

The fact that Sabena had not requested the slots prior to the published closing date of 1 November 1991 was immaterial since "the interest of Sabena to increase its flights on the abovementioned route arose when it became acquainted with the authorisation of British Midland to increase its flights". It was acceptable that the request was made in time and before the proposed starting date of the services.

Counter-measures

9.18   A refusal to authorise new services or additional services on the basis that the conditions under Article 10(1) have not been met has to be seen as an exception to the general freedom conferred on carriers to decide on the appropriate levels of capacity or frequency. Accordingly, the discretion of Member States in refusing such authorisation must be interpreted narrowly. The Commission had no hesitation in concluding that:

> "Article 10(3) on the contrary does not provide for a Member State to take counter-measures against an air carrier licensed in another Member State (A), which has been authorized by the latter . . . to operate additional flights to the first Member State (B)."

9.19   Indeed, the Commission rejected the right to take counter-measures as "a retortion measure against a decision taken by another Member State". Such a step was prohibited by Community law. Any grievance relating to the implementation of Article 10 was provided with the specific redress procedure under Article 10(4) in the form of a request to the Commission to investigate. Hence, the decision of the Belgian authorities to refuse BMA authorisation was contrary to the Regulation.

Bilateral agreement

9.20   In respect of the claim by the United Kingdom that traffic on the route was governed by the existing bilateral agreement and that the provisions of the Regulation could not be used to restrict the bilateral arrangements pursuant to Article 13(2), the Commission took into account the procedure provided in the agreement for adjustments to capacity arrangements. In particular, it provided that:

"Each aeronautical authority will allow an airline designated by the other to mount such capacity as the airline considers appropriate . . . so long as the principal objective of the service is to provide adequate capacity at a reasonable load factor for third/fourth freedom traffic between its own country and the other."

The crucial criterion of limiting increase in frequency to "adequate capacity at a reasonable load factor", argued the Commission, was indicative of the requirement that "any increase in capacity must be based on a corresponding increase in traffic". This provision appeared to be more restrictive than the provisions of the Regulation.   **9.21**

Furthermore, the bilateral agreement provided that "each authority will retain the right to require consultations with the other in the event that it considers that the interests of any of its own airlines on a particular route or routes are being seriously damaged as a result of the capacity being mounted by the airline or airlines of the other country". The Commission felt that this amounted to a reciprocity clause which was more restrictive and in any event not provided for by the Regulation. Accordingly, since the bilateral agreement was already more restrictive than the provisions of the Regulation, Article 13(2) did not apply in that case.

Serious financial damage

This safeguard was retained from the previous legislation which had been inserted at the insistence of the southern Member States (Greece, Italy, Portugal, Spain) on the ground that their national carriers would require protection from non-scheduled carriers operating to their country.[9] It enables a Member State to request the Commission to investigate a claim that the freedom conferred by Article 10 has led to serious financial damage for the scheduled carrier licensed by that Member State. In assessing whether there is such damage, the Commission is obliged to have regard to the market situation, the opportunities for the carriers of that Member State to compete effectively, the financial position of the carriers concerned and the capacity utilization achieved. If such damage exists, the Commission is empowered to take measures to ensure that "scheduled air services to and from that State should be stabilized for a limited period".   **9.22**

This is an important balance which seeks to distinguish between efficiency and genuine constraints on competition opportunities. Where, for example, a carrier has not availed itself of the opportunities to compete, and consequently suffers from low capacity, it is unlikely that this safeguard will be invoked to rally to its rescue. Likewise, if a carrier misallocates its assets by using an inappropriate aircraft for the level of market demand, any consequential damage is unlikely to be seen as a result of market constraints. The damage must, of course, be *serious*, though this is a pre-condition which frequently defies precise definition, and must accordingly be determined from case to case. Likewise, the meaning of "limited period", which under the terms of Article 10(3) necessarily involves an artificial regulatory judgement. No doubt, the limited period within which services should   **9.23**

---

[9] F.De Coninck, *European Air Law: New Skies for Europe* (1992), p.70.

be stabilised must be subject to periodic review to restrict the application of the safeguard to the minimum.

4. Control of capacity under Articles 85 and 86

9.24   The nature of the safeguards in the Regulation are in essence regulatory, concerned primarily with the proper allocation of traffic between airports in the light of infrastructural constraints and ensuring equitable access to markets and capacity optimalization. They do not, however, apply to anti-competitive practices in capacity except to a very limited extent. Such practices or agreements come within the scope of Articles 85 and 86 as implemented by Regulation 3975/87.[10]

The most obvious form of anti-competitive practice relating to capacity is "dumping" or excess capacity with a predatory intent. Of course, the ability to dump capacity by increasing frequency is conditional upon the ability to secure or to have access to additional slots, unless existing slots are reorganised for the purposes of the services in question. Alternatively, dumping may also be achieved by using a larger aircraft than usual so that more seats are offered for the route in question. This is an extremely difficult issue since the use of a larger aircraft to offer more seats *per se* cannot be classified as anti-competitive or an abuse of dominant position.

9.25   A predatory intent, or abuse, has to be established. Mounting additional capacity is a competitive response in accordance with the terms of Community policy on air transport competition if the object is to meet additional demand. This is therefore not incompatible with Community law. If this was otherwise, then much of the freedom conferred on carriers could be readily frustrated and possibly in an arbitrary way. The experience of the UK Civil Aviation Authority provides a very clear testimony to the difficulty of dealing with the fine line of whether a significant increase in capacity by a carrier is anti-competitive or merely a legitimate response to fair competition. In the majority of cases, the difference will only be a matter of degree. In dealing with such cases, the CAA asks three key questions: do the actions complained of have a serious effect on the complaining carrier; if so, is there an offsetting benefit to the users; and, is the remedy requested proportional to the perceived ill?[11]

9.26   Agreements relating to capacity which have the effect of restricting competition as prohibited by Article 85 may, however, be the subject of a block or individual exemption under Article 85(3) as implemented by Regulation 3976/87. It is therefore possible that capacity pooling as result of an agreement relating to joint planning and co-ordination of schedules or joint operations may be exempted provided of course the conditions set out in the applicable legislation have been met: in this case, Council Regulation 1617/93.[12]

---

[10] [1987] OJ L374/1.
[11] CAA Decision 7/90 (8 November 1990).
[12] [1993] OJ L155/18. See Ch. 4 *supra*.

Chapter 10

SLOT ALLOCATION

1. Introduction

There is little doubt that the most significant barrier to effective air transport competition today is the lack of runway capacity measured against the overall demand at congested airports. By implication, these are the more popular airports among air transport users, whether because of their convenience or superior inter-line connections. Therefore, the more popular an airport, the more limited will be the number of available slots to be allocated. This problem is not unique to the Community, but is indeed an international concern as more airports face the growing lack of capacity as well as environmental limitations on capacity expansion.

Significance of slots to competition

Airport slots are required for the take-off and landing of aircraft without which no service is possible. An authorisation to provide services is very much a licence without substance if no slots to facilitate the services are available in reality. Thus, the promise of the market access measure under the third phase of liberalisation would run the danger of not being realised if airport capacity cannot meet the demand stemming from the industry's growth. The obvious effect of the lack of such slots is to deny new airlines the opportunity to enter the market to stimulate competition against the incumbents. The barrier for entry into the airport or for increasing frequency to satisfy demand becomes inevitably high.

The further effect of this infrastructural constraint on competition is to reinforce the dominance of an incumbent, creating a vicious circle into which new entrants will find it difficult to break. For a dominant carrier which possesses a substantial number of slots at a congested airport, its response to competitive changes is seldom restricted by the lack of slots. Ultimately, it will only be a matter of opportunity cost in switching the use of one slot for a particular service or destination at a given time, to another. The problem for the new entrant in gaining slots is compounded by the economic fact that a minimum number of slots is usually required to operate viable services. For short-haul services, there will need to be a minimum threshold of frequency to compete effectively against the incumbents by maximising aircraft utilization. For longer flights, the typical size of the aircraft and journey time do not usually demand more than two daily services. Accordingly, the demand for slots will be proportionally lower. Equally, the slot

10.1

10.2

10.3

time for such longer flights is less crucial and will consequently have a lower demand for peak time slots. On the other hand, synergy and maximum aircraft utilisation are important considerations in the co-ordination of short-haul flights. Dependence on peak time slots will be naturally higher.

10.4   The most significant cause underlying this problem is the use of "grandfather rights" where the allocation of slots is conducted by reference to historical precedence. This long-standing practice means an airline holding and using a slot in one scheduling season has a first claim on that slot in the next equivalent season. A scheduling season is either the summer or winter season. An airline which dominates a particular busy airport, whether by reason of historical privilege or endowment or a monopoly position, will usually enjoy a strong presence as a result of its claim to the slots under the historical precedence rule. Alternative methods of allocation include slots trading and peak pricing of slots. A system of slot trading involves the buying and selling of slots between airlines, although a likely consequence of this system may be higher fares and the strengthening of the position of dominant airlines which are more able to outbid smaller airlines. Slots trading is widely practised in the USA and to a lesser extent at those airports where a slot-control regime operates. Slot trading also exists within the Community to a limited extent although the transparency of these transactions is still wanting.

10.5   The peak pricing of slots calls for a premium to be attached to peak period slots so that airlines will be required to weigh the higher cost of operation against a service which lacks demand so that it might consider switching the service to an off-peak slot. In practice, however, the general inelasticity of demand for peak time slots means that the transfer from a peak to an off-peak slot will only take place if there has been an excessive change in the demand for that service or in circumstances when the likely loss cannot be rationally subsidised by gains from operations elsewhere. In spite of the anti-competitive overtones of the way in which slots are allocated under the historical precedence approach, it is generally accepted as the best available method for distributing airport slots. Coupled with the inevitable, but limited, trading of slots between airlines, the rule of historical precedence has not only worked but has no better alternative to it at the present time. To that end, power was given to the Commission under the first package of liberalisation measures to adopt further measures to exempt slot allocation procedures.[1]

Slot allocation procedures under IATA

10.6   The current practice of slot allocation owes much of its existence to the procedures developed by IATA. These procedures are set out in its *Scheduling Procedures Guide* which incorporates a number of principles such as the rule on historical precedence, new entrants and emergencies. Slots are typically allocated by a scheduling committee of an airport consisting of representatives from the airlines, the airport and the regulatory authority. Allocated slots, however, need not be used. This may be attributed to the lack of demand for services at that particular

---

[1] Council Regulation 3976/87, [1987] OJ L374/9.

time, or to extraneous circumstances such as international embargoes, hostilities or industrial action. This scheduling practice under IATA is charged with anti-competitive concerns. However, much of the work carried out by IATA, which goes beyond scheduling, is of vital importance to the structure of international air transport today. Several of the benefits are patently obvious, such as single ticketing and single currency transaction for multiple journeys. Its contributions are recognised by the Community in the form of exemptions granted to certain practices which have evolved.[2]

Community response to slot allocation problems

The first measure adopted by the Community on the issue of slot allocation was to   10.7
exempt the long-standing practice of scheduling between the airlines concerned, and typically presided over by the dominant airline at the airport in question. Although the practice falls within the scope of Article 85(1) as an agreement between undertakings or a decision by associations of undertakings which prevents, restricts or distorts competition, there were sufficient recognised benefits derived from it to justify an exemption under Article 85(3). In the preamble of Council Regulation 3976/87, it was accepted as "desirable" that exemption be given to certain agreements and practices which otherwise would constitute an infraction of Article 85(1). The task of adopting specific legislation for exemption was entrusted to the Commission. Accordingly, Commission Regulation 2671/88 was adopted which *inter alia* exempted agreements on slot allocation and airport scheduling subject to certain *a priori* conditions.[3] This was replaced by Commission Regulation 84/91[4] and more recently by Commission Regulation 1617/93.[5] The latter states in recital 6:

> "Arrangements on slot allocation at airports and airport scheduling can improve the utilization of airport capacity and airspace, facilitate air traffic control and help to spread the supply of air transport service from the airport. However, if competition is [not][6] to be eliminated, entry to congested airports must remain possible."

To reconcile these demands, the block exemption which expires on 30 June   10.8
1998, is subject to several conditions:

- Consultations on allocation and scheduling must be open to all interested carriers.
- Non-discriminatory rules on priority of allocation are established. These rules must take into account any air traffic distribution rules laid down by national or international authorities and the needs of users and the airport

---

[2] See Ch. 4 *supra* and Commission Regulation 1617/93, [1993] OJ L155/18.
[3] [1988] OJ L239/9.
[4] [1991] OJ L10/14.
[5] [1993] OJ L155/18.
[6] Corrigendum: [1994] OJ L15/20.

concerned. Where account is taken of any historical rights on slots, it must be subject to the rules on new entrants below. Once established, these rules must be available to any interested party.

- New entrants are allocated 50 per cent of either newly created or unused slots or slots returned by an incumbent or otherwise becoming available.

- Participating carriers in the consultations are to have access to information on historical slots, requested slots, allocated slots, outstanding requests, remaining slots and criteria for allocation. Rejected requests must be supplied with reasons.

10.9   In 1990, the Commission instigated a consultation exercise to formulate a set of common rules on slot allocation in anticipation of the growing problem of infra-structural limitations and its effect on the liberalisation programme to achieve greater competition. Although there were some objections against the proposed intervention, including amongst others the Economic and Social Committee, on the basis that the present system was working satisfactorily, the Commission saw the need to reinforce the system to ensure that the procedures were always applied and the principles of neutrality and transparency were adopted beyond doubt. More importantly, the Commission pointed to the need for abandoning the rule of his-torical precedence in certain circumstances to safeguard the objectives and to har-ness the opportunities envisaged in the Community's air transport policy. It stated:

> "in certain cases the priority of grandfather rights should be superseded by the interest to promote competition on routes where there is presently a monopoly or duopoly. Subject to certain conditions this can mean that carriers holding grandfather rights will be required to give up these slots for reallocation to a new entrant."[7]

10.10   Accordingly, on the basis of the conclusions which emerged from the consul-tation, Council Regulation 95/93 on common rules for the allocation of slots at Community airports was adopted.[7a] These rules, however, are without prejudice to the application of Articles 85 and 86.

2. Scope of the rules

10.11   The common rules apply only at Community airports. They make provision for two classes of airports, namely "co-ordinated airports" and "fully co-ordinated airports". A co-ordinated airport is defined in the Regulation as "an airport where a co-ordinator has been appointed to facilitate the operations of air carriers oper-ating or intending to operate at that airport". On the other hand, a fully co-ordinated airport is "a co-ordinated airport where, in order to land or take off, during the periods for which it is fully co-ordinated, it is necessary for an air carrier to have a slot allocated". By implication, therefore, an un-coordinated airport is one which does not meet these conditions.

---

[7] Explanatory Memorandum (COM(90) 576), para. 15.
[7a] [1993] OJ L14/1.

The responsibility for classifying an airport as un-coordinated, co-ordinated or   10.12
fully co-ordinated rests with the Member States subject to a number of conditions
specified in Article 3 of the Regulation. In particular, a Member State is obliged
to ensure that a thorough analysis is carried out as soon as possible in circumstances where:

- air carriers representing more than half of the operations at the airport consider that capacity is insufficient to meet actual or planned operations;
- new entrants encounter serious problems in securing slots;
- the Member State itself considers it necessary.

The analysis should have regard to the possibilities of increasing the capacity in   10.13
the short-term either through infrastructural or operational changes. It should
also determine the anticipated time frame within which the problems are to be
resolved. In the event that the analysis cannot suggest a short-term solution to the
problems, following consultations with the airlines using the airport, airport
authorities, air traffic control authorities and representative bodies, the Member
State is required to designate the airport in question as fully co-ordinated for the
periods during which capacity problems occur. This designation may be lifted but
only when the capacity is sufficient to meet actual and planned operations.

These rules, however, do not apply in the case of Gibraltar airport until such   10.14
time as the joint declarations made by Spain and the United Kingdom have come
into effect. Nevertheless, in 1993, the Government of Gibraltar and the Gibraltar
Development Corporation applied for judicial review to challenge the provision
on a number of substantive grounds. They submitted in the first place that the
provision contravened Community law by allowing bilateral agreements to have
superior effect over Community law and violated the principle of legitimate expectations since other Community measures on slot allocation applied to Gibraltar
airport. Furthermore, they argued that the suspension was discriminatory because
it selected Gibraltar for inferior treatment and denied it the benefits of economic
development envisaged by the Regulation. In the event, the European Court of
Justice dismissed the application as inadmissible.[8]

3. Co-ordinated and fully co-ordinated airports

Airport co-ordinator

An airport which has been designated either as co-ordinated or fully co-ordinated   10.15
by a Member State must have an airport co-ordinator whose appointment is the
responsibility of that Member State. Prior to appointment, the Member State is
required to consult with airlines using the airport regularly, airport authorities and

---

[8] Case C-168/93, *Government of Gibraltar & Gibraltar Development Council* v *Council* [1993] OJ C269/12.

representative bodies. The co-ordinator needs to be a natural or legal person with detailed knowledge of scheduling co-ordination for airlines and may be appointed for more than one airport.

The co-ordinator, who is responsible for allocating and monitoring the use of slots, is required to perform his duties in an independent manner and in accordance with the principles of neutrality, non-discrimination and transparency. He is also required to supply, upon request and within a reasonable time, information on slots allocated on the basis of historical rights, slots requested and allocated, outstanding requests, remaining available slots and the criteria used for allocation.

Co-ordination committee

10.16   In the case of a fully co-ordinated airport only, the Member State is required to establish a co-ordination committee to assist in a consultative capacity the airport co-ordinator. Member States are given the discretion to decide on the setting up of a committee in the case of co-ordinated airports.

The committee is to be made up of at least the airlines using the airport regularly, relevant airport authorities and air traffic control representatives. The remit of the committee is to advise on the possibilities of capacity expansion, improvement of traffic conditions, complaints on allocation, methods of monitoring the use of slots, guidelines for allocation and serious problems encountered by new entrants.

Airport capacity

10.17   At fully co-ordinated airports, competent authorities of Member States are required to determine, on an objective basis and having regard to the types of traffic at that airport, the capacity available for slot allocation twice annually. This requirement becomes discretionary in the case of co-ordinated airports. This is to be done in co-operation with airlines regularly using the airport, the airport co-ordinator, representatives of air traffic control and customs and immigration authorities. The results are to be submitted to the airport co-ordinator prior to the slot allocation conferences.

4. Rules of slot allocation

Priority rules

10.18   The fundamental rule of allocation is based on the concept of grandfather rights. Article 8(1) stipulates that:

> "a slot that has been operated by an air carrier as cleared by the co-ordinator shall entitle that air carrier to claim the same slot in the next equivalent scheduling period."

Nevertheless, slots may be exchanged freely between carriers or switched by a carrier from one route or service to another. Any change must be transparent and subject to confirmation by the co-ordinator to ensure that airport operations would not be prejudiced or otherwise affect the application of the Regulation. This freedom, however, is not available to new entrants operating a service between two Community airports for a period of two seasons.

Where all slot requests cannot be met, the co-ordinator is required to give **10.19** priority to "commercial air services and in particular to scheduled services and programmed non-scheduled services". In addition, the co-ordinator is required to take into account additional priority rules established by the industry and any additional guidelines recommended by the co-ordination committee provided they do not contravene Community law. In the Commission's explanatory memorandum proposing the common rules, for example, it stated that priority should be given to an airline with a longer period of operation in the same season in circumstances where two or more airlines compete for the same slot.[9] Reasons must always be given by the co-ordinator for any refusal and the nearest alternative slot indicated.

The co-ordinator is required by Article 8(3) to endeavour to accommodate *ad hoc* slot requests for all types of aviation at an airport. The slots may be available from the slot pool established in accordance with the Regulation, or as a result of a surrender at short notice.

Slot pool

Article 10 of the Regulation requires the setting up of a "slot pool" for each co- **10.20** ordinated period at an airport where slot allocation takes place. The slot pool is a repository for newly created slots, unused slots, surrendered slots, or slots which otherwise became available.

Newly created slots may be available for allocation as a result of operational changes or improvement, or infrastructural expansion. Unused slots are the product of mandatory confiscation due to non-utilisation. However, non-utilisation may be justified by reason of the grounding of an aircraft, closure of an airport or airspace, or other similarly exceptional situations. Slots which are allocated but which vary substantially from the time requested are often surrendered, and are then placed in the slot pool for redistribution.

Minimum usage of allocated slots

In addition, Article 10 requires an airline to demonstrate that at least 80 per cent **10.21** of the slots allocated to it over a recognisable period up to one scheduling period for scheduled or programmed non-scheduled services have been used. Failure to do so will disentitle the airline to the same series of slots in the next equivalent period. Consequently, these slots will be placed in the slot pool.

---

[9] COM(90) 576, Annex.

10.22   In calculating the minimum usage, account need not be taken of those slots which have been allocated and returned to the co-ordinator for reallocation before 31 January for the following summer season or 31 August for the following winter season. Non-utilisation can also be justified on the basis of:

- unforeseeable circumstances beyond the control of the airline resulting for example in the grounding of an aircraft or closure of an airport or airspace, or hostilities such as the Gulf War;[10]
- problems concerning the commencement of a new scheduled passenger service with an aircraft of no more than 80 seats on a route between a regional airport and the co-ordinated airport, and where the capacity does not exceed 30,000 seats per annum;
- serious financial damage of the airline, the consequence of which is a temporary operating licence pending financial reorganisation;
- an interruption to a series of non-scheduled services due to cancellations by tour operators, particularly during the off-peak seasons, provided that overall usage does not fall below 70 per cent;
- an interruption to a series of services due to action intended to affect such services so that it becomes impossible for the airline to operate the services, such as industrial actions.

New entrants

10.23   A new entrant is defined at length as either:

- an air carrier requesting slots at an airport on any day and holding or having been allocated fewer than four slots at that airport on that day or,
- an air carrier requesting slots for a non-stop service between two Community airports where at most two other air carriers operate a direct service between these airports or airport systems on that day, and holding or having been allocated fewer than four slots at that airport on that day for that non-stop service.

10.24   In addition, an air carrier which holds more than 3 per cent of the total slots available on the day and at the airport in question, or more than 2 per cent of the total slots in respect of an airport system of which the airport concerned is part, shall not be considered as a new entrant at that airport. An air carrier will lose the status of a new entrant if slots offered to it within two hours before or after the time requested are not accepted.

The fundamental right of new entrants, without prejudice to Article 8 of Council Regulation 2408/92 on the distribution of traffic within an airport system,[11] is the entitlement to 50 per cent of the slots available for distribution from the slot pool. Where serious problems are experienced by new entrants in securing slots, the Member State responsible is obliged to convene the airport co-ordination committee to examine the possibilities of remedying the problems.

---

[10] COM (91) 422.
[11] [1992] OJ L240/8.

5. Derogations from the rules

In several circumstances, the common rules on slot allocation may be disapplied   10.25
subject always to a number of conditions. These relate to regional services, constraints at airports and third country reciprocity.

Regional services

Article 9 of the Regulation enables a Member State to reserve certain slots at fully   10.26
co-ordinated airports for two classes of domestic scheduled services. First, this
derogation may be claimed in respect of services on a route between the fully co-
ordinated airport and an airport located in a peripheral or development region
where such a route is considered vital for the economic development of that
region. This is, however, conditional upon:

- the slots being used on that route at the time the Regulation came into force;
- the route being served by only one air carrier;
- the absence of an adequate service provided by other modes of transport;
- the termination of the reservation when a second air carrier has established
  a domestic scheduled service on that route with the same number of frequencies as the incumbent and operated it for at least one season.

Secondly, the derogation may be claimed in respect of routes which have been   10.27
designated as public service obligations under Community legislation, particularly
under Council Regulation 2408/92. The procedures in Article 4(1)(d)–(i) of that
Regulation on the invitation to tender to provide services must be invoked if a
second air carrier demonstrates an interest in operating on the routes in question
but has failed to obtain the necessary slots within one hour before or after the
requested times.[12]

Reciprocal access to intra-Community slots

Although Article 8(4) allows an air carrier the flexibility to freely exchange with   10.28
another carrier its slots or to switch the use of its slots between different routes, a
restriction applies in respect of certain routes between a fully co-ordinated airport
and an airport in another Member State. This "safeguard mechanism" prevents
a carrier from using that flexibility to introduce additional frequencies on such
routes if another Community carrier licensed by another Member State has not
been able to secure the necessary slots within two hours before or after the times
requested which can be reasonably used to match the additional frequencies.
Naturally, this mechanism will not apply if the air carrier using the flexibility does
not exceed the frequencies of the other carrier in question.

A pre-requisite to this claim is that "serious and consistent efforts" must have
been made to secure the slots, in addition to which the carriers concerned must

---

[12] *Ibid.* See Ch. 7 *supra*.

have failed to reach a mutual agreement to the problem. Member States responsible for the fully co-ordinated airports are obliged to facilitate a solution such as endeavouring to ensure that the slot requests of the carrier licensed by another Member State are accommodated, or to ensure the reasonable use of the flexibility provided for in Article 8(4).

10.29   This derogation has its genesis in the second package of liberalisation measures. Article 10(3) of Council Regulation 2343/90 required a Member State to refuse a carrier the authorisation to establish a new service or increase its frequency between two airports in the Community if a carrier from that other Member State was unable to do so on an existing service to the airport in question.[13] This was a transitional provision pending the adoption of a set of common rules on slot allocation. When British Midland (BMA) sought to increase its frequency on the London (Heathrow)–Brussels service by switching its slots at Heathrow Airport, the Belgian Government requested the Commission to examine the application of Article 10(3) in the light of Sabena's failure to secure the slots it desired in order to increase its frequency on the same service.[14] Although the Commission recognised that the advantages derived from such flexibility for carriers in the position of BMA "may lead to a *de facto* discrimination", ultimately it had to accept that the slots offered by the co-ordinator of a busy airport need only be the best available.

Third countries

10.30   Article 12 of the Regulation enables a Member State, *inter alia*, to suspend wholly or partially the obligations arising from the common rules on slot allocation in respect of an air carrier of a third country if the mutual treatment of Community carriers was lacking. In particular, a Member State may take appropriate remedial actions if a third country:

- does not grant Community carriers treatment comparable to that afforded by the Member State to the carriers of the third country; or
- does not grant Community carriers *de facto* national treatment; or
- grants carriers from other third countries more favourable treatment than Community carriers.

6. Relationship between slots and traffic rights

10.31   The authorisation of traffic rights is governed by the provisions of Council Regulation 2408/92.[15] The possession of an authorisation to exercise traffic rights does not ensure the opportunity to provide the services if the necessary slots are

---

[13] [1990] OJ L217/8.
[14] Commission Decision 92/552, [1992] OJ L353/32.
[15] [1992] OJ L240/8.

unavailable. By the same token, the possession of slots does not give rise to the presumption of a right to exercise traffic rights. The Commission explained in *Viva Air* that the issues of slots and traffic rights are legally distinct. Accordingly, traffic rights cannot be refused on the ground of an air carrier not having the necessary airport slots. A carrier can therefore decline to provide to the authorities information on slots when seeking authorisation to exercise traffic rights. In that case, Viva Air's argument that the slots it possessed was equivalent to an authorisation was rejected by the Commission. According to the Commission, the possession of slots may only be equivalent to an authorisation if the Member State does not impose any special formalities for obtaining such authorisation.[16]

7. Experience in the USA

In 1968, as a result of growth in the air transport sector, several airports in the USA began to show signs of capacity limitations. Delays were common and particularly acute at major airports. Some flights never made it, and for some of those which made it, flight times were substantially longer because of the delay. This led to the introduction of the "High Density Rule" (HDR) to limit the hourly and daily operations at five of the most congested airports, namely, Washington (National), New York (Kennedy, La Guardia and Newark) and Chicago (O'Hare). At the multi-runway O'Hare, for example, there are currently an average of 155 slot operations per hour. The HDR was originally intended as a temporary measure to counter the congestion problems and would be lifted unless it resolved significantly those problems.

    10.32

The first significant change to the HDR took place in 1970 which lifted its application at Newark after experience had shown that the nature of congestion there was gate accessibility rather than slots capacity. A period of lull ensued until the advent of airline deregulation in 1978. Although the history of slot allocation at the HDR airports was characterised by scheduling committees responsible for slot co-ordination, the Federal Aviation Administration opted to experiment with the system of slot trading to cope with the demands arising from the aftermath of deregulation, and more particularly in the light of the failure of the voluntary scheduling system to resolve the deadlock at the four HDR airports in 1984 and 1985.

    10.33

To reflect the uniqueness of local characteristics, each slot-controlled period at the HDR airports is divided into three classes of slots: air carrier slots, commuter slots, and others (which include general aviation). Slots at HDR airports are also given withdrawal priority tags which may have to be surrendered under the "Essential Air Service" rule to ensure the regularity of services to small communities,[17] or in accordance with the obligations of an international air service agreement. Furthermore, new entrants have a guaranteed claim to 25 per cent of new,

    10.34

---

[16] Commission Decision 93/347, [1993] OJ L140/51.
[17] The Essential Air Service programme was sanctioned by Congress at the time of the deregulation: Federal Aviation Act 1958, s. 419.

unused or returned slots at HDR airports which are allocated on the basis of a lottery system.

10.35   In response to a wider review of competitiveness of the air transport industry, in 1994 the Department of Transportation carried out the most comprehensive review of the HDR in 25 years. A key question of the review was whether the HDR should be lifted, and if so, whether immediately or phased. In the final analysis, it concluded that the evidence from its review demonstrated that the costs to consumers and airlines of lifting or modifying the HDR would outweigh the benefits that may be derived. In particular, it noted that only at O'Hare would there be a net-dollar benefit of US$205m while there would be significant losses measured in terms of revenue and delay costs to consumers, airlines and airports at the other three airports.[18]

8. Conclusions

10.36   The lack of airport slots to facilitate the demands arising from growth in the sector is only one, but a more obvious, constraint on competition. Less obvious infrastructural constraints exist in the form of airspace congestion and capacity limitations at airport terminals. Both have a critical effect on competition if they limit the number of permitted movements, particularly in and around congested airports. Yet the simple answer to these problems of expanding airspace or terminal capacity or constructing additional runways, is more complex than it first seems. Foremost of all, expansion of this nature and scale is both a politically and environmentally contentious issue. So often, the difficulty has been to make a stark choice between development and preserving the status quo.

In the context of airport slots, the concept of grandfather rights has proved to be one of the most formidable barriers to air transport competition. While the radical solution of abolishing this practice would open up substantially the opportunities of competition, the proposal to do so would indubitably encounter political opposition of monumental proportions, and destroy the legitimate expectations of incumbents who have invested heavily and committed themselves to the development of services which depend on the slots. Hence, the fundamental aim of the common rules has been to strike an acceptable balance between these claims. Still, there is much to be done.[18a]

10.37   One of the major shortcomings of the Regulation, as research by the UK Civil Aviation Authority reveals, has been the implementation of the "new entrant" concept.[19] Under the Regulation, a new entrant is defined principally on a quantitative basis which does not therefore distinguish between passenger and cargo services. Nor does it distinguish the routes on which a new entrant wishes to serve. Thus, for example, it does not differentiate between short- and long-haul services since as journey length increases, the desired number of slots for rotations

---

[18] Department of Transportation, *Report to the Congress: A Study of the High Density Rule* (1995).
[18a] The Commission has already indicated that it is prepared to sanction slot trading at airports so as to regularise existing practice: *Financial Times*, 4 October 1996.
[19] Civil Aviation Authority, *Slot Allocation: A Proposal for Europe's Airports* CAP 644 (1994).

decreases. The effect of this lack of guiding details is to encourage spreading the slots from the pool thinly among as many applicants as possible. Consequently, the number of slots allocated to a carrier is likely to be small and are often slots which vary significantly from the times requested.

Likewise, the Regulation does not allow for the number of slots held by an   10.38
incumbent at a particular airport to be taken into account in distributing slots to new entrants. The present framework makes it possible for an incumbent to enjoy the status of a new entrant in respect of those intra-Community routes from the same airport on which it does not have more than a double daily service (*i.e.* four slots) and on which no more than two carriers operate a direct service. Since the problems of slot allocation are most acute at congested airports, which by defin-ition suffer from scarcity of slots, the number of slots available from the pool for distribution to new entrants at 50 per cent is arguably insufficient to secure an environment in which new entrants can seriously compete with the incumbents. The "S-curve" theory, a general measure to analyse demand and growth in the frequency of services, suggests that new entrants need to operate at a frequency close to the incumbent to sustain commercially viable and competitive services. If, therefore, all slots from the pool were earmarked for new entrants, the cumulative effect of this approach over successive scheduling seasons may be to provide a series of slots which will enable a new entrant to compete seriously with an incum-bent. A further shortcoming identified in the study of the CAA is the exclusion of competitive carriers such as BMA at Heathrow and Air UK at Gatwick from the definition of new entrant because they possess more than 3 per cent of the slots at the airport concerned or 2 per cent of the slots at the airport system.

In the long-term, the equitable balance which the Regulation intends to strike   10.39
will be difficult to achieve without substantial modifications to the provisions. If competition means providing genuine alternatives to the incumbents, particularly on monopoly and duopoly routes, rather than indiscriminately allocating as many slots to new entrants as possible for any service, then the concept of a new entrant will need to be redefined to create more effective competition.

Chapter 11

COMPUTER RESERVATION SYSTEMS

1. Introduction

The use of computer reservation systems (CRSs) assumed popularity in mid-1970s in the USA. They began as off-shoots of internal computerisation programmes introduced by the major airlines. Hence, it is of no real coincidence that most CRSs today are owned by airlines. CRSs were first leased to travel agents as a reservation tool before being commercially vended to other airlines and information providers. Since their introduction, CRSs have come to represent one of the most important tools for airline marketing and distribution of products. Indeed, their use has extended into other sectors including car rental.   11.1

The likes of BA, Virgin Atlantic, Air France, Lufthansa, United Airlines, American Airlines, amongst others, recognise the importance of CRS either as owners, developers or participants. "Apollo", for example, is owned by United, "Sabre" by American, "WorldSpan" by Trans-World Airlines, "Saphir" by Sabena, "Amadeus" by a combination of Air France, Iberia, Lufthansa, SAS and others, and "Galileo International" is co-owned by United (through "Cavio"), BA, KLM, Swissair, Alitalia, Austrian Airlines, Olympic Airways and TAP. It is not surprising therefore that today the bulk of airline sales and reservations are conducted through CRSs. It provides a ready and easy access to information relating to flight schedules, fares, seat availability as well as instantaneous reservation and issuing of tickets. The more sophisticated systems also provide for car rental and hotel reservation.   11.2

A travel agent or other subscriber of the CRS will retrieve information from a central database to display on a monitor flight schedules, fares, availability and other related information. This information will have been supplied by the participating airline or information providers, such as the Official Airline Guide and ABC International, and downloaded by the CRS vendor or operator. Instantaneous reservations can then be made and transmitted by the subscriber to the central database. This process removes the traditional method of having to conduct the transaction over the telephone between the travel agent and the respective airlines. The scope for savings is consequently considerable. One study in the USA shows that reservations were made typically in one-third of the time it would have taken previously.[1] In addition, a CRS can generate sophisticated and   11.3

---

[1] M.Levine, "Airline Competition in Deregulated Markets: Theory, Firm Strategy and Public Policy" (1987) 4 *Yale Journal on Regulation* 393.

detailed statistical information for use by the airlines and travel agents, enables them to monitor market trends and customer preferences, and produces accurate, computer-processed accounts thus removing the mountain of paperwork consequent on the growth of air travel; *a fortiori*, as products become more complex and varied as a result of deregulation and liberalisation. In return for these, participating airlines and subscribers of the systems pay a certain fee.

Implications of CRS for competition

11.4   Given the way in which the CRS industry has developed, that most of the CRSs have been developed and owned by either one or a combination of major airlines, and the way in which a CRS operates, the potential for abuse is considerable – not least in respect of smaller and new entrants who will need access to such systems if effective competition is to be secured.[2] The dominance of such major CRS-owning carriers has led Alfred Kahn, the architect of American air transport deregulation, to reflect that:

> "No one counted on the muscle of the big carriers, which protected their own markets and devoured most smaller entrants. Their biggest weapons were the computerised reservation systems, lifeline of travel agents . . ."[3]

11.5   Equally, there is scope for abuse by a CRS owner against another CRS-owning airline, by refusing the latter airline access to the former's CRS. Thus, there is a two-fold problem between CRS owners on the one hand, and between CRS owners and participating carriers on the other. This is by no means to understate the competition issues stemming from restrictive contracts between CRS owners and subscribers of the systems, namely travel agents.

The main difficulty between CRS owners is the use of "lock-in" clauses in contracts with subscribers. Typically, a subscriber will not be permitted to switch to a different CRS for a period of five years. This is justified by the CRS owner on the need to recoup the substantial investment made by it in developing the system. Dependence on that system to secure sales is therefore necessary to both the subscriber and participating airlines, whether or not these airlines are also owners of other CRSs. Indeed, the high capital cost of developing a CRS constitutes a significant barrier to entry, and consequently few can devote the resources to do so. Hence, the structure of the CRS market is readily characterised by dominance.

11.6   The limited number of CRS operators inevitably affects the market structure and competition between participating airlines who have to gain access to the CRS, and invariably the CRS-owning airline. Access to the CRS has been a troubling issue, as has the neutrality of information displayed. In an un-regulated world, there is every incentive for the CRS-owning airline to either refuse access

---

[2] See Transport Committee, *Airline Competition: Computer Reservation Systems* (3rd Report), HC 461 (1987–88) and US Department of Transportation, *Study of airline computer reservation system* (1988), Report DOT-P-37-88-2.

[3] *Independent on Sunday*, Business Supplement, 13 January 1991.

to the system of convenience by a competitor, or to charge prohibitive fees for access. Either way, this is potentially an abuse of a dominant position. Yet, most airlines accept the inevitable fact of having access to a CRS and accepting reservations from a travel agent as sales are increasingly made through a CRS. In other words, the revenue losses from refusing to pay the access and booking fees, and thus be denied reservations made through that system, would frequently outweigh the costs of access. In fact, the thorny issue of access has been the subject of litigation on both sides of the Atlantic.[4] Smaller low-cost airlines, however, may be less dependent on CRSs, particularly if their route structures are less sophisticated or extensive. Airlines such as EasyJet and SouthWest Airlines in the USA who operate a non-ticketing system are able to enjoy a much simplified system of reservation and ticketing.

Having gained access, accuracy, timeliness and neutrality of the information   **11.7**
displayed on the screen become important. In the competitive world of air transport, the temptation remains for a CRS-owning airline to discriminate in the information displayed on the first screen so that its own products are given the first option of refusal by the customer. Research has shown that busy travel agents were more likely to be influenced by what appeared on the first screen. Indeed, there is a tendency for travel agents to book passengers on flights operated by the CRS-owning airline, for a variety of reasons including reliability and accuracy of information. This is known as the "halo effect" which consists of:

> "subtle forms of bias in favour of the CRS-owning or 'host' airline that continue to characterize the structure and operation of each system. In addition, each CRS appears to provide more convenient access to – and more accurate – information on fares and seat availability on flights operated by its airline owner, as well as superior reliability in recording reservations for travel on its own flights."[5]

Such approaches may, in addition, be reinforced by higher commissions paid to   **11.8**
travel agents for making reservations with the host airline.

A further point of concern relates to the extent to which the data of products loaded into the CRS by a participating airline can be used to the advantage of the airline owning that CRS. The possibility of a CRS-owning airline monitoring its competitors' products and pricing policy will give the former a competitive edge by pre-empting new services or fares proposed by a competitor who participates in the system.

The marginal profit from the diversion of passenger from a competitor to the   **11.9**
CRS-owning airline either as a result of screen display bias, the halo effect or a more attractive and immediate product is an important resource for cross-subsidising other related activities of the CRS owner. The effects of such practices on the structure of competition are serious. The high entry barriers into the CRS

[4] Commission Decision 88/589, *London European Airways* v *Sabena* [1988] OJ L317/47; *Alaska Airlines* v *United Airlines* [1992] ECLR R-28 and *United Airlines* v *CAB* 766 F 2d 1107 (1985).
[5] D.Pickrell, "The Regulation and Deregulation of US airlines" in K.Button (ed.), *Airline Deregulation: International Experiences* (1991) at p.39. See also US Department of Transportation, *Study of airline computer reservation system* (1988), Report DOT-P-37-88-2.

market, and consequently the need to gain access to an established system invariably owned by a dominant airline, have an overall effect on the ability of competing airlines, particularly smaller airlines and new entrants, to compete successfully and to establish a market share viable for operation. To that end, regulatory intervention has become necessary. At the international level, for example, the ICAO has recently adopted a revised Code of Conduct to regulate cross-border CRS operations. In particular, it aims to expand the applicability of the Code to non-scheduled services, to require that passengers be informed of code-shared flights, to establish additional criteria for CRSs fees and to develop more specific criteria for the order of flight displays.[6]

11.10   In the USA, measures to counter the potential for anti-competitive practices were adopted in 1984 by the Civil Aeronautics Board.[7] The regulations require, *inter alia*, that screen displays must be comprehensive and free from bias, that fees must be non-discriminatory although there may be price differentials to reflect cost differentials, that system enhancements must be offered to all participating carriers equally, that the terms of access must be directly related to the CRS participation, that subscribers of CRSs are permitted to use multiple systems and contracts must be limited to five years in any event.

11.11   The response of the Community to the competition concerns of CRSs in the air transport sector has been two-fold. Like the CAB, the measures adopted in the Community seek to strike a balance between the need to prevent the exploitation of market power on the one hand, and the need to maintain a reasonable scope for scientific and technical progress on the other. Accordingly, a Code of Conduct has been adopted which in essence incorporates the principles of the Code of Conduct issued by the ECAC. In this respect, the Code of Conduct which has been enacted as a Council Regulation is binding in its entirety in the Member States, although at the time of the Code coming into effect, no CRSs operating in the Community were immediately able to fulfil the requirements which led to a variety of waivers granted under Article 21(2) of the Code so as to allow them to adapt. In addition, the Commission has also adopted a Regulation pre-dating the Code of Conduct to grant a block exemption to certain agreements relating to CRSs, as subsequently amended.

2. Code of Conduct on CRS

11.12   The Code of Conduct was first adopted in 1989,[8] and subsequently amended in 1993 to take account of needed changes in the light of experience.[9] In particular, an evaluation report was published in 1992, which among other things revealed the need to clarify certain provisions of the earlier Code.[10] The Code will now expire on 31 December 1997.

---

[6] Press Release PIO 7/96.
[7] *Carrier-Owned Computer Reservations Systems* 14 CFR § 255 (1984), as amended in 1988.
[8] Council Regulation 2299/89, [1989] OJ L220/1.
[9] Council Regulation 3089/93, [1993] OJ L278/1.
[10] *Report on the Application of Council Regulation 2299/89 on a Code of Conduct for Computerized Reservation Systems* (COM(92) 404).

The purpose of the Code is primarily to regulate the behaviour of CRS owners and operators by imposing upon them certain obligations. It is intended to harmonise the diversity of approaches adopted in Member States towards CRSs. The Commission has stated that "since the code of conduct is a Regulation and directly legally binding in the Community, all relevant contracts will have to be brought in line with the provisions of the code". However, it does not expect the need for existing contracts to be re-negotiated, but simply to be brought into line by an amendment that would refer to the "direct applicability of the code of conduct and indicating the way in which certain clauses of the contracts would consequently have to be understood".[11] In its first year of operation, approximately 30 complaints were made under the Code, the bulk of which related to the manner in which information on schedules and fares was displayed.

Scope of the Code

The scope of the Code is set out in Article 1 of the Regulation. It applies to computer reservation systems which are used to provide information on air transport products within the Community. The Code will apply regardless of: 11.13

- the status or nationality of the system vendor, which is defined as an entity responsible for the operation or marketing of a CRS;

- the source of information or location of the relevant central data processing unit. Increasingly, data processing centres are located outside the country in which the CRS-owners are registered to exploit more economic opportunities such as lower labour cost;

- the geographical location of the airports between which the product is intended for use, for example the purchase of a ticket through a CRS in the United Kingdom for travel between Miami and Los Angeles. Air transport products are defined in the Code as comprising of "un-bundled" and "bundled" products. The former means a product which is used for the carriage of a passenger by air between two airports including other ancillary services and additional benefits offered for sale as an integral part of the product. A bundled product, on the other hand, consists of a pre-arranged combination of an un-bundled product with "other services not ancillary to air transport, offered for sale and/or sold at an inclusive price". This distinction was included in the later Code as a result of the Commission's evaluation report of 1992. Since the third package of liberalisation measures has effectively abolished the distinction between scheduled and non-scheduled services, and since the majority of air transport users in the Community travelled on non-scheduled services, there was an undisputed need for equal treatment so that non-scheduled carriers were also given the possibility of offering their products through the same medium.[12]   11.14

---

[11] *Explanatory Note on the EEC Code of Conduct for Computer Reservation Systems* [1990] OJ C184/2.

[12] *Report on the Application of Council Regulation 2299/89 on a Code of Conduct for Computerized Reservation Systems* (COM(92) 404), pp.15–16.

11.15   The Code anticipates that Community airlines will be given equal treatment by a system vendor or CRS operators outside the Community in respect of the obligations imposed on Community CRS operators. To that end, Article 7(1) exempts a system vendor from the obligations laid down in the Code if reciprocity of treatment is lacking. Specifically, it provides that the obligations of a system vendor under the Code will not apply in respect of a CRS-owning carrier of a third country to the extent that its CRS outside the territory of the Community does not offer Community air carriers equivalent treatment to that provided under the Community regime. This derogation also extends to the obligations of participating airlines in respect of a CRS controlled by an airline of a third country.

3. CRS owners and participating airlines

11.16   A participating airline is also known in the Code as a "participating carrier" and defined to mean an air carrier which has an agreement with a system vendor for the distribution of air transport products through the CRS, including the CRS-owning carrier itself. Under the Code, the relationship between a CRS owner and participating carriers is characterised by the obligations of access, information display and reciprocity.

Access

11.17   Access to a CRS is undoubtedly a vital lifeline for an airline. Yet, as has been made evident, this issue itself raises a host of others such as loading of data, misuse of data, fees for access, reciprocity, all of which are addressed in the Code and which need further examination.

The basic governing provision on access is laid down in Article 3(2). It states that a system vendor must enable any air carrier to participate, on an equal and non-discriminatory basis, in its distribution facilities designed to produce information on air transport products. This obligation is subject to the available capacity of the system concerned and may be limited by technical constraints outside the control of the vendor. Where system enhancements have been introduced, they are expected to be offered to all participating carriers on similar terms and in a way which does not result in a time lapse for their implementation between the parent carrier and participating carriers.

11.18   More specifically, a system vendor is prohibited from:

- attaching unreasonable conditions to any contract with a participating carrier. What amounts to unreasonableness must of course be assessed in the given context;

- requiring the participating carrier to accept supplementary conditions "which, by their nature or according to commercial usage, have no connection with the participation in its CRS";

- imposing an exclusive clause such that participation in that CRS is conditional upon the carrier not participating in another CRS.

In addition, a participating carrier is entitled to withdraw from the participation by giving a notice of not more than six months although the contract of participation cannot be terminated before the expiry of the first year. Recoverable costs by the system vendor are restricted to costs directly related to the termination of the contract, and not punitive damages.

Fees[13]

The Code recognises that a certain fee must be payable for participation in the system to enable the system vendor to recoup the costs of development. However, the fee charged by the vendor cannot be discriminatory and must be reasonably structured and related to the cost of service. Price differentials are permitted to the extent that they reflect cost differentials.   **11.19**

To enable the effective monitoring of the relationship between fees and cost of service, the Code further requires that the billing for CRS services must contain the following minimum: type of CRS booking, booking date, flight date and number, passenger name, country, IATA identification code, city-code, city-pair, status of booking code, class of service, passenger-name-record locator, and booking/cancellation indicator.

Loading[14]

System vendors are also required to offer all loading and processing facilities of the system to all participating carriers without discrimination. This includes distribution facilities, which a system vendor must ensure are separated in a clear and verifiable manner from the marketing inventory of a participating carrier, including the CRS-owning carrier. The importance of this "de-hosting", where the CRS functions are separated from the internal reservation and inventory functions of the carrier owning the CRS, is illustrated in cases where the CRS-owning carrier can exercise a competitive advantage over participating carriers in its CRS precisely because it is able to submit real time information such as last seat availability and latest fares into the system as well as having access to the marketing information of participating carriers. The idea of wholesale de-hosting or divestment was, however, rejected as an option earlier. This was because of the doubt over whether the bias would be eliminated completely and also the difficulty stemming from relations with third countries whose carriers owned CRSs. Consequently, Article 4(4) and Article 6 seek to establish "Chinese Walls" by technical means and appropriate software safeguards between the internal reservation of a parent carrier and the CRS, and prohibiting the parent carrier reserving for itself specific loading and up-dating methods.[15]   **11.20**

---

[13] Art. 10.
[14] Arts. 4 and 4a.
[15] See *Report on the Application of Council Regulation 2299/89 on a Code of Conduct for Computerized Reservation Systems* (COM(92) 404).

11.21   In addition, the information which has been submitted to the CRS must be loaded and processed with care and timeliness and must not be manipulated by the system vendor so as to lead to inaccurate, misleading and discriminatory information. In return, participating carriers and other information providers are obliged to ensure that the information which they submit to the CRS is "accurate, non-misleading, transparent and no less comprehensive than for any other CRS". These participants must ensure that the information which they submit will enable the vendor to discharge its obligations under the Code, for example, in distinguishing between a change of aircraft and a transit stop *en route*.[16] This obligation extends to intermediaries who are employed to submit the information.

Use of information

11.22   The Code restricts the use of statistical and other information concerning individual bookings to the air carriers participating in the service covered by the booking and to the subscriber involved. In any event, the provision of such information by the system vendor is subject to the principle of equality.

However, marketing, booking and sales data which are made available must be offered without delay and discrimination to all participating carriers, but such data is not to include any identification or personal information on a passenger or a corporate user. Personal information of a passenger can only be divulged with the consent of the passenger.

Compliance with technical requirements

11.23   A system vendor is required under the Code to appoint an independent auditor to monitor the technical compliance of its CRS in respect of information loading and availability, in particular the software used to implement those obligations. To expedite the monitoring, the auditor will have access to any programmes, procedures, operations and safeguards used by the system vendor. The auditor's report is then to be submitted to the Commission.

Display

11.24   The provisions governing the display of information on the CRS are set out in Article 5 of the Code. The basic obligation of a system vendor is to display information in a clear, accurate and non-discriminatory manner. The system vendor is required to provide a principal display for each transaction which is defined in the Code as "a comprehensive neutral display of data concerning air services between city-pairs, within a specified time period". It should therefore provide information relating to flight schedules, fare types and seat availability on the city-pair in question as submitted by participating carriers or information providers.

In this respect, the ranking of information and flight options becomes crucial. In addition to the prohibition that ranking is not to be related to carrier identity, the Code provides in the Annex the ranking criteria for un-bundled air transport

---

[16] *Explanatory Note on the EEC Code of Conduct for Computer Reservation Systems* [1990] OJ C184/2, para. 3.

products.[17] The order in which the flight options between the city-pairs concerned should appear, unless otherwise requested by the customer, is:

- all non-stop direct flights;
- other direct flights which may include an intermediate stop, but not involving a change of aircraft;
- connecting flights where an intermediate stop is made. In constructing the principal display, the system vendor is required to use a minimum number of nine connecting points.

For non-stop flights, they should be ranked according to departure time, while   11.25
for other direct and connecting flights, ranking should be in accordance with the elapsed journey time, that is the time difference between departure and arrival time. A system vendor must include in the principal display all indirect flights requested by participating carriers which fall within the limits of the elapsed journey time unless the routing is in excess of 130 per cent of the great circle distance between the two points. Inclusion of the latter is at the discretion of the system vendor.

In addition, the Annex sets out the information which a principal display is to contain:

- that the information on the number of direct flights and identity of carriers is not comprehensive, if the system vendor believes this to be the case;
- that the flight is a non-scheduled service or involves stops *en route*;
- that the actual operator is not the carrier identified by the carrier designator code, particularly in cases involving code-sharing services.

On fares, a system vendor must ensure that the principal display is complete   11.26
and shows all publicly available fares without discrimination. This means all fares provided by the airline in question must be shown by the CRS and the display is not to be limited only to fares approved or co-ordinated under IATA. However, fares which have not been approved by the authorities can only be included if accompanied by the appropriate annotation.

A system vendor is also obliged to ensure that the principal display does not   11.27
give excessive exposure to a particular product, or display a particular travel option including unrealistic options. An unrealistic travel option may include a connecting flight with a considerably longer journey time but which offers little specific advantages. Likewise, no flight for direct services nor combination of flights for multi-sector services must be displayed more than once in a principal display, lest a competing flight is relegated to the next page of display. Where a change of aircraft is involved, it shall be displayed as connecting flights, with one line per aircraft segment on the display. A limited exception is, however, provided to allow for separate displays according to individual carrier designator codes in cases where certain participating carriers have a joint venture arrangement requiring each of them to assume separate responsibility for the sale of air transport products on a flight or combination of flights.

---

[17] An un-bundled product is defined by Article 2(a) of the Code as "the carriage by air of a passenger between two airports, including any related ancillary services and additional benefits offered for sale and/or sold as an integral part of that product". Details on bundled products need not feature in the principal display.

Derogation

11.28   The obligations of display, however, do not apply to a CRS used by a carrier in its own office and at sales counters where the non-application is clearly identified. Equally, the obligations respecting principal displays may be disregarded at the request of a customer, where for example a specific airline has been requested. Such displays are known as secondary displays. Details of bundled products may also be relegated to the secondary display because full inclusion in the principal display of such information would severely limit the transparency of displays.[18]

Non-participating carriers

11.29   Where a CRS vendor agrees to display information supplied by non-participating carriers, it must do so on an accurate, non-misleading and non-discriminatory basis. However, in respect of the ranking of information according to different flight categories, participating carriers may be given priority or more favourable treatment.[19]

Reciprocity

11.30   Article 3a of the Code lays down the obligation of a CRS-owning airline in relation to the supply of information to a competing CRS. It requires the former to provide to a competing CRS, on request, information on schedules, fares and availability on its own services which it submits to its own CRS, or to distribute or confirm the reservation of such air transport products through that competing CRS. This obligation will not apply if the competing system vendor is in breach of the loading and processing obligations under Article 4a or it cannot give sufficient guarantees on unauthorised access by its parent carrier as stipulated in Article 6. The basis for this mandatory participation is simply to avoid the non-participation of a carrier in a competing CRS, particularly in the case of a dominant carrier which also owns a CRS, because this would seriously disadvantage the competing CRS and thereby distort CRS competition. Nevertheless, the Commission recognises that mandatory participation *in extremis* would also affect the ability of carriers to compete, weaken their ability to negotiate with system vendors and result in a higher cost element which would ultimately penalise smaller carriers. In addition, it was crucial to avoid imposing an undue economic burden, no less so on smaller carriers, through mandatory participation in other CRSs. To that end, any fees payable for participation would be limited to the costs of reproducing information generated by the CRS and booking fees. Article 3a therefore seeks to strike that balance, albeit limited to parent carriers and their affiliates.[20] This amendment was the consequence of an experience stemming from a complaint by "Sabre" against the subsidiaries of Air France and Sabena for refusing to participate in "Sabre"'s distribution facilities. "Sabre" claimed that the

[18] *Report on the Application of Council Regulation 2299/89 on a Code of Conduct for Computerized Reservation Systems* (COM(92) 404), p.16.
[19] *Explanatory Note on the EEC Code of Conduct for Computer Reservation Systems* [1990] OJ C184/2, para. 11.
[20] See *Report on the Application of Council Regulation 2299/89 on a Code of Conduct for Computerized Reservation Systems* (COM(92) 404).

refusal of the subsidiaries had the effect of preventing effective competition in national markets because the sale of domestic services could not be distributed through that system. Moreover, Air France and Sabena were shareholders of a rival CRS. Both carriers had maintained that their CRS was providing adequate distribution facilities by virtue of the 80 per cent market share which they held. They argued further that the "Sabre" system gave rise to potential discrimination against participating carriers because American Airlines' ownership of it meant that it was a "hosted" rather than a "de-hosted" system. In the end, however, a settlement was made between the parties.[21]

4. CRS owners and subscribers

A CRS cannot function without the intervention of intermediaries who represent the interface between customers and their requests and the sale of air transport products. These are usually the travel agents who subscribe to the CRS. To ensure that the relationship between the CRS owners and subscribers does not lead to anti-competitive effects, the Code regulates that relationship by reference to three areas: access, fees and termination of contract.   **11.31**

Access[22]

Foremost of all, a system vendor is required to provide, without discrimination, to a subscriber all the relevant distribution facilities of a CRS for access to information on air transport products and the making of reservations to a subscriber. This obligation of equality in treatment extends to the offer of any service enhancement which if offered to one subscriber must also be offered to all subscribers.   **11.32**

Article 9(2) of the Code requires that the contract for access cannot be exclusive so that it prevents the subscriber from subscribing to another competing CRS. By the same token, a CRS-owning airline cannot directly or indirectly require a subscriber to use a specific CRS for the sale of any of its products. In addition, Article 9(4) prohibits a system vendor from attaching unreasonable conditions in the contract, including the requirement that the subscriber accepts an offer of technical equipment or software from the vendor, although the contract may specify that the equipment and software used must be compatible with the vendor's own system. The contract for access must incorporate at the minimum the right to access the principal display and the obligation of the subscriber not to manipulate material supplied by the CRS in such a way as to produce misleading and inaccurate information.

Premium and commission
Travel agents who make a sale are usually paid a certain commission. The higher the commission, the greater will be the incentive for the travel agent to offer for   **11.33**

---

[21] *Twenty-Third Report on Competition Policy* (1993), p.156.
[22] Art. 9.

sale the products of the airline in question in favour of other competing products. Smaller airlines who are less able to absorb the cost of a high commission will inevitably be disadvantaged competitively. The use of such market power by a dominant airline may well constitute an infraction of the provisions of Article 86, and be prohibited accordingly.

11.34   In the context of CRSs, it is equally possible for a CRS-owning airline to pay a travel agent or subscriber a higher commission for using its CRS or alternatively for selling its products through a particular CRS. Such practices are expressly prohibited under Article 8 of the Code which provides that a CRS-owning airline shall not directly nor indirectly link the use of any specific CRS by a subscriber with the receipt of any commission or other incentive or disincentive for the sale of its air transport products. The purpose of this prohibition reflects the nature of a CRS which is basically to provide information relating to the air transport products of the participating carriers. The sale of such products and the authorisation for ticketing are a matter between the travel agent and the airline concerned, unless the system vendor has been given ticketing authorisation by that airline.[23]

Fees

11.35   The access to and use of a CRS by a subscriber is characteristically subject to a certain fee. To ensure that such fees do not distort competition in the CRS market, Article 10 of the Code requires that the fees be reasonably structured and related to the cost of service, allowing at the same time for different fees to reflect cost differentials in the service provided, which must be adequately demonstrated. The Commission has, however, explained in its 1990 statement that this provision can be interpreted as permitting the linking of fees by a CRS-owning airline with the *number of bookings* made by the subscriber through its CRS where such fees are cost-related. It does not, on the other hand, permit the linking of fees with the *percentage of bookings* because "the difference in fee level could not be justified by differences in costs".[24]

Termination of contract

11.36   In addition to the requirement that a contract for access must not be exclusive nor subject to unreasonable conditions, Article 9(4) of the Code further states that the termination of the contract by a subscriber may be effected without penalty by a notice which need not exceed three months although any termination cannot be effective within the first year of the agreement. Where the contract is terminated within the first year, damages may accrue to the system vendor. In other cases, compensation is limited to the costs directly related to the termination. The difficulty, of course, will arise in circumstances where the system vendor has a long-term contract with a third party, for example to supply hardware. In such

---

[23] *Explanatory Note on the EEC Code of Conduct for Computer Reservation Systems* [1990] OJ C184/2, para. 7.
[24] *Explanatory Note on the EEC Code of Conduct for Computer Reservation Systems* [1990] OJ C184/2, para. 8.

cases, the Commission believes that the use of separate contracts, one for the CRS and the other for hardware supply, would be more appropriate.[25]

5. Complaints procedure

A complaint against an infringement of the Code may be initiated by Member States or any natural or legal person having a legitimate interest in the matter. The Commission may also act on its own initiative to terminate such infringements. To facilitate its duties under the Code, the Commission has been given extensive powers of investigation. It has the authority to obtain all the necessary information to expedite its investigation as well as to undertake investigations into undertakings by examining their books and business accounts and to enter premises. To ensure the effectiveness of these investigative powers, Article 16 empowers the Commission to impose fines of between ECU 1,000 and 50,000 for the incorrect supply of information or the failure to produce the relevant business records, whether intentionally or negligently. Furthermore, a fine to the maximum of 10 per cent of the annual turnover may be imposed on system vendors, CRS-owning and participating airlines, and subscribers for infringements of the Code. The decisions of the Commission, however, are ultimately subject to the review jurisdiction of the European Court of Justice.

11.37

6. Exemption from the competition rules

Agreements, decisions or concerted practices relating to CRSs may be granted an exemption from the competition rules in two ways. First, when the initial package of liberalisation measures was adopted in 1987, a provision was made in the implementing of Council Regulation 3976/87 to exempt certain categories of CRSs agreements from Article 85(1) of the EC Treaty.[26] This was a block exemption which benefited only agreements which satisfied the conditions stipulated in the Regulation and subsequent measures adopted by the Commission.

11.38

Secondly, a notification for individual exemption must still be submitted to the Commission under the provisions of Council Regulation 17/62.[27] An example of such a notification, which did not enjoy the block exemption under Regulation 3976/87, was given in 1993 under Article 19(3) of Regulation 17/62 on the merger between "Galileo" and "Covia" to form "Galileo International".[28] This agreement was authorised by the Commission on the strength of the benefits cited

11.39

---

[25] *Report on the Application of Council Regulation 2299/89 on a Code of Conduct for Computerized Reservation Systems* (COM(92) 404), p.13.
[26] [1987] OJ L374/9.
[27] [1959–1962] OJ (Sp. edn.), p.204.
[28] Case IV/34.632, [1993] OJ C107/4.

in accordance with the conditions of Article 85(3). Likewise, the Commission took a favourable view of the agreement to develop the "Acriss" system on car rental reservation in the Community.[29] This dual system is attributed to the way in which CRSs have been treated as an "ancillary service" in air transport. This was confirmed by the Commission in the case of *London European Airways* v *Sabena*.[30] Accordingly, CRSs fall outside the scope of Council Regulation 3975/87 for the purposes of individual exemptions.

11.40   In accordance with the enabling powers of Regulation 3976/87, Commission Regulation 2672/88 was adopted to exempt certain CRS agreements.[31] This expired on 31 January 1991. A further Regulation 83/91 was consequently adopted to extend the application of the exemption, which itself expired on 31 December 1992.[32] This expiry date was amended by Regulation 3618/92 to 30 June 1993,[33] and subsequently by Regulation 1618/93 to 31 December 1993.[34] Although recital 7 of Regulation 3976/87 explains that "exemptions should be granted for a limited period during which air carriers can adapt to a more competitive environment", the thinking seems to have changed at least in respect of CRSs. This is evident in the decision of the Commission to extend the expiry date of the block exemption for CRS agreements by adopting Regulation 3652/93 which will now expire on 30 June 1998.[35] In part, this revised Regulation was made in the light of its experience and in particular the issues which arose when it examined the co-operation agreement between "Amadeus" and "Sabre". The proposal was to produce a joint product to which subscribers would have access. Although the Commission considered that the agreement would lead to a reduction in price competition, it was prepared to accept the improvement that the agreement would make to the distribution of air transport products within and outside of the Community, provided that undertakings were given to ensure that competition in the CRS market and in air transport would not be affected, for example by requiring the flights of "Amadeus" and "Sabre" owners to be displayed by other CRSs. Subsequently, however, the negotiations failed and the agreement was abandoned.[36]

Scope of exemption

11.41   The block exemption under Regulation 3652/93 extends to agreements between undertakings the purpose of which is either:

- to purchase or develop a CRS in common;
- to create a system vendor to market and operate the CRS; or
- to regulate the provision of distribution facilities by the system vendor or by distributors.

---

[29] Case IV/34.342, [1993] OJ C149/9.
[30] Commission Decision 88/589, [1988] OJ L317/47.
[31] [1988] OJ L239/13.
[32] [1991] OJ L10/9.
[33] [1992] OJ L367/16.
[34] [1993] OJ L155/23.
[35] [1993] OJ L333/37.
[36] *Twenty-First Report on Competition Policy* (1991), p.73.

This exemption, however, applies only to a limited number of obligations. It **11.42** exempts from Article 85(1):

- the obligation not to engage directly or indirectly in the development, marketing or operation of another CRS;
- the obligation of a system vendor to appoint a parent or participating carrier as providers of distribution facilities to all or certain subscribers in a defined area of the common market;
- the obligation of the system vendor to grant a distributor of facilities exclusive rights to solicit all or certain subscribers;
- the obligation of the system vendor not to allow the distributors to sell distribution facilities provided by other system vendors.

Conditions

To attract an automatic exemption, the Regulation requires an agreement on **11.43** CRS to observe a number of conditions. Most of these reflect the obligations set out in the Code of Conduct. The interesting effect of this overlap, therefore, is that a CRS owner who demonstrates an intention to adopt the Code as part of its agreement with participating carriers and subscribers will almost certainly benefit from an exemption either for the purchase or development of a CRS, the creation of a system vendor or the regulation of provision of distribution facilities.

On the relationship between a system vendor and a participating airline, the Regulation requires, first, that the system vendor allow any air carrier the opportunity to participate in an equal and non-discriminatory manner in the CRS. Other obligations of the system vendors relate to the processing and loading of information as well as the use of statistical and personal information derived from the use of the CRS and the display of information. A similar derogation as that provided in the Code in respect of equal treatment by CRS-owning airlines of a third country applies to Community system vendors.

On the other hand, the obligations of the system vendor with regard to sub- **11.44** scribers relate principally to equal access and reasonableness of its conditions, and the linking of commission with the use of certain CRS. In addition, the fees for access by subscribers, and for access by participating carriers, must be reasonably structured and cost-related.

Revocation

The benefit of the automatic exemption is of course conditional upon compliance **11.45** with the obligations stipulated in the Regulation. Where an agreement produces effects incompatible with the conditions of Article 85(3) or the provisions of Article 86, the benefit may be withdrawn. In particular, this may include an agreement which hinders the maintenance of effective competition in the CRS market, or restricts air transport competition. In addition, the benefit may be withdrawn where the system vendor imposes unfair fees or charges on subscribers or participating carriers, or refuses to enter into an access contract or refuses access to other CRS-related facilities without objective and non-discriminatory reasons of a technical and commercial nature. Article 13 of the Regulation also provides expressly that a system vendor is not to enter into any agreement or engage in a concerted practice with other system vendors with the object or effect of partitioning the market.

Abuse of a dominant position

11.46   An automatic exemption from Article 85(1) of the EC Treaty by virtue of Commission Regulation 3652/93 does not, however, prejudice the application of Article 86 of the Treaty on abuse of a dominant position which affects trade between Member States, as the Court of First Instance has said in *Tetra Pak Rausing SA* v *Commission*.[37] The abuse of a dominant position in the CRS market has already been examined earlier in the case of *London European Airways* v *Sabena* in which the alleged abuse by Sabena in refusing London European Airways access to its "Saphir" system was upheld by the Commission.[38] First, the dominant position of "Saphir" was derived from its 50 per cent share of the CRS market in Belgium and the large number of subscribers and participating airlines in the system. The Commission concluded that this position was abused by virtue of the conditions required of London European for access which were not related to the use of the CRS, in particular the requirement that London European concluded a ground-handling contract with Sabena. The condition that London European charged a higher fare on the Luton–Brussels route for access to "Saphir" was also judged by the Commission as unreasonable and incompatible with the common market.

7. Future of CRSs

11.47   Air transport is a complex operation and will become more so as greater liberalisation takes place. Advancement in technology to support air transport services is an important requisite for the overall growth of the industry. Without any shadow of doubt, CRSs have emerged to become one of the most important marketing tools in the air transport business. Indeed, the recognition of its role in the globalisation of air transport services is explicit in the Annex of the General Agreement on Trade in Services. Airlines today could not conceivably have achieved their success without the supreme convenience of CRSs, nor could travel agents have avoided the morass of paperwork and the large volume of telephone reservations without automated transactions, nor indeed could consumers have had the choice and range of information to make considered decisions. The move towards greater airline alliances of varying complexity and the introduction of

---

[37] Case T-51/89, [1990] ECR 309.
[38] Commission Decision 88/589, [1988] OJ L317/47.

ticketless air travel will have the ineluctable effect of demanding even more sophisticated systems of reservation. Consequently, regulatory surveillance against anti-competitive practices in the CRS industry becomes ever more important.

Part IV

COMPETITION AND STATE INTERVENTION

Chapter 12

STATE AIDS: THE PROHIBITION

1. Introduction

State intervention has been a characteristic of air transport for many years, and   12.1
in particular since the Second World War. This common practice is a manifestation of the political attributes of the sector which demand the involvement of the state. Whether this intervention takes the form of public ownership in airlines or state regulation of private airlines is immaterial. Both have the potential to distort competition and to create inequity between airlines by virtue of unequal access to finance, endowment of special rights or exclusive privileges and other conditions which cannot be described as normal commercial practice.

Given that a high number of airlines operating within the Community or the   12.2
European Economic Area (EEA) are either wholly or partially owned by the state, state aid is an issue of crucial importance; more so in the context of a liberalised market. Indeed, amongst the national flag carriers of the EEA countries, only two are entirely free of any public ownership.

Table 2: *Ownership of Flag Carriers as in 1996**

Flag Carrier	Country	State Ownership
Aer Lingus	Ireland	100%
Air France	France	94.2%
Alitalia	Italy	86.4%
Austrian Airlines	Austria	51.9%
British Airways	United Kingdom	0%
Finnair	Finland	60.7%
Iberia	Spain	99.8%
Icelandair	Iceland	0%
KLM	Netherlands	38.2%
Lufthansa	Germany	35.68%
Luxair	Luxembourg	23.11%
Olympic Airways	Greece	100%
Sabena	Belgium	33.8%
SAS	Sweden	50% of 42.85%
	Denmark	50% of 28.57%
	Norway	50% of 28.57%
TAP	Portugal	100%

*Source: *Association of European Airlines Yearbook 1996*. The ownership share does not take into account those which are held by public sector institutions or airlines of another State.

12.3   The disparity has provoked controversies of different kinds. In 1991, for example, the Commission authorised a restructuring programme for Sabena involving
the wiping out of losses to the value of Bfrs 22.6bn and Bfrs 7.6bn recapitalisation.[1]
This was followed more recently by the authorisation of another recapitalisation
programme for Air France worth FF 20bn, £Irl 175m to Aer Lingus, Esc 180bn
to TAP and in 1995 Pta 87bn to Iberia.[2] For those flag carriers which have limited
or no access to state finances and those which have been established privately, state
assistance of such magnitude is not likely to pass without their objections.

12.4   Since Article 222 of the EC Treaty provides for neutrality in the ownership of
undertakings, there cannot be any enforced privatisation of undertakings owned
by the state to achieve a level playing field in the competitive sector of air transport. There is thus a need for a system which controls the availability of aid ema-
nating from the state for the benefit of undertakings. In its broadest sense, of
course, undertakings must include private undertakings so that any assistance
received from the state outside normal market conditions can be seen as a state
aid within the terms of the Treaty.

The policy of the Commission on state aids in air transport was first consolidat-
ed in its Communication to the Council of 1984.[3] This was followed in 1992 by
a report setting out its evaluation of the state aid system[4] and a set of guidelines
in 1994 which replaces those contained in the 1984 memorandum to the
Council.[5] Prior to the publication of the 1994 guidelines, the Commission had
formed the Comité des Sages to look into the competitiveness of European air
transport, whose report also included an analysis of the state aids system.[6] These
are considered further below.

12.5   The timing of the 1994 guidelines has been important, in particular since the
adoption of the third liberalisation package which confers on Community carriers
a general right of access to the market. The aim of securing more air transport
competition within the EEA will be seriously prejudiced if state aids with distortive
effects are to be freely handed out. In the words of the Commission:

> "In the more competitive environment State aids might be of substantially increased
> strategic importance for governments looking for measures to protect the economic
> interest of their 'own' airlines. This could lead to a subsidy race which would jeopar-
> dise both the common interest and the basic objectives of the liberalisation process."[7]

12.6   The review of state aids must consequently be more stringent in the post-
liberalisation period. This review is comprised of three stages. The first stage is to

---

[1] Commission Decision 91/555, [1991] OJ L300/48.
[2] Commission Decision 94/653, [1994] OJ L254/73; Commission Decision 94/118, [1994] OJ
L54/30; Commission Decision 94/698, [1994] OJ L279/29; Commission Decision 96/278, [1996] OJ
L104/25 respectively.
[3] Memorandum 2, *Progress Towards The Development of A Community Air Transport Policy* (COM(84) 72),
Annex IV.
[4] *Report on the Evaluation of Aid Schemes Established in Favour of Community Air Carriers*, SEC(92) 431.
[5] *Application of Articles 92 and 93 to State Aids in the Aviation Sector*, [1994] OJ C350/5.
[6] *Expanding Horizons* (1994).
[7] [1994] OJ C350/5, para. 2.

determine whether an aid has been advanced, and if so whether it is incompatible with the Treaty. If the aid is prohibited as incompatible, it then needs to be determined whether the aid falls within the scope of the exemptions. These exemptions are either mandatory in that the Treaty provides for an automatic exemption, or discretionary so that the exemption is dependent on a decision of the Commission.

2. Scope of prohibition: Article 92(1)

Article 92(1) of the Treaty provides the following prohibition: 12.7

> "Save as otherwise provided in this Treaty, any aid granted by a Member State or through State resources in any form whatsoever which distorts or threatens to distort competition by favouring certain undertakings or the production of certain goods shall, insofar as it affects trade between Member States, be incompatible with the common market."

The saving provision in the Article allows for derogations from the prohibition   12.8
including the exemptions set out in Article 92(2) and (3) as well as Article 93(2) which empowers the Council to adopt specific measures which would exempt an aid from the prohibition. In addition, further derogations can be found in other parts of the Treaty including Articles 77 and 80 which accord special treatment to the transport sector, and Article 90(2) relating to certain public undertakings.

The "core" provisions of Article 92(1) will be discussed in four sections:

- aid granted by Member States or through state resources;
- aid of any form whatsoever;
- aid which distorts or threatens to distort competition by favouring certain undertakings;
- aid which affects trade between Member States.

Source of aid

The case law of the European Court of Justice on the term "Member States or   12.9
through State resources" suggests that a wide interpretation is necessary to ensure that Member States who employ methods which aim to circumvent the prohibition on state aids are prevented from doing so. In this respect, "State" will include central, regional and local authorities and such other undertakings which enjoy a certain nexus with the state. In 1991, the Court held that state funds channelled through a state holding company and its subsidiary amounted to resources flowing from the state. In that case, Alfa Romeo was the beneficiary of capital injection from Finmeccanica, a public holding company. Finmeccanica, however, is controlled by Instituto per la Ricostruzione Industriale (IRI) both in respect of capital and the appointment of members of the board. Since IRI derives its capital from the Italian state, the Court concluded that both IRI and Finmeccanica had

no full freedom of action regardless of the fact that they were to operate according to economic criteria.[8]

12.10   The Court's view on the issue of state influence was set out earlier in the case of *Steinike* concerning a levy imposed by the German authorities to fund other economic activities, specifically the agricultural, food and forestry industries. The responsibility for administering the collection was vested in a body established by law. The Court, in response to the question of whether the body in question could be classified as a recipient of aid under the terms of Article 92(1), reasoned that:

> "The prohibition contained in Article 92(1) covers aid granted by a Member State or through State resources without its being necessary to make a distinction whether the aid is granted directly or indirectly by the State or by public or private bodies established or appointed by it to administer the aid. In applying Article 92 regard must be had to the effects of the aid on the undertakings or producers favoured and not the status of the institutions entrusted with the distribution and administration of aid."[9]

12.11   Likewise, in the case of *Van der Kooy*, the fact that Gasunie, the gas supply undertaking in The Netherlands, was 50 per cent owned by the state and its decisions on tariffs including preferential tariffs were subject to ministerial approval, provided evidence for the conclusion that it did not enjoy full autonomy in its actions but was instead under the control and instructions of public authorities.[10]

12.12   In 1994, the Commission examined the subscription by CDC-Participations (CDC-P), a subsidiary of Caisse des Dépots et de Consignations, to two issues of bonds by Air France. Caisse is a state-owned company, and the question therefore arose as to whether the subscription was capable of amounting to aid incompatible with the EC Treaty. The view of the French authorities was simply that the Caisse and CDC-P were autonomous organisations subject to control by Parliament rather than the Government. In applying the principle laid down by the European Court of Justice in *Van der Kooy*, the Commission concluded that "CDC-P is not an autonomous entity from the Caisse, which is subject to the control of the French public authorities". Caisse was a public entity established by law and in addition to which its directors were appointed by the French Government. Since Caisse held 100 per cent of the CDC-P shares, appointed its directors and provided the funding for its operations, it was capable of directing the latter's investment decisions. Consequently, the subscription by CDC-P to the bonds issued by Air France was "imputable to the French State within the meaning of the Court's case law on Article 92(1)".[11]

12.13   A wide interpretation has also been given to the idea of "State resources" in that the Court has said in *Steinike* that the source of the aid can be private and procured by some state measure although the measure need not necessarily apply to the whole community or a wider class of persons or undertakings. In that case, it said:

---

[8] Case C-305/89, *Alfa Romeo: Italy v Commission* [1991] ECR I-1603.
[9] Case 78/76, *Firma Steinike und Weinlig v Germany* [1977] ECR 595, at 611.
[10] Cases 67, 68 and 70/85, *Kwekerij Gebroeders Van der Kooy v Commission* [1988] ECR 219.
[11] Commission Decision 94/662, [1994] OJ L258/26.

"A measure adopted by the public authority and favouring certain undertakings does not lose the character of a gratuitous advantage by the fact that it is wholly or partially financed by contributions imposed by the public authority and levied on the undertakings concerned."[12]

It re-stated this broad view in a later case that "aid need not necessarily be   12.14
financed from State resources to be classified as State aid". In that case, it had been accepted that the allowance paid by the Caisse nationale de crédit agricole (National Agriculture Credit Fund) to the poorest farmers was not state aid within the strict terms of Article 92(1) on the ground that the funds were generated from private sources, and not state resources. Nevertheless, on the evidence that the NACF was a public body whose decisions were subject to the approval of public authorities and was therefore subject to their influence, the European Court of Justice shared the Commission's view that the decision to allocate the allowance was attributable to the encouragement from the French Government.[13]

A major difficulty in the determination of whether aid had been granted by   12.15
Member States or through state resources to an undertaking is the lack of transparency in the relationship between them. This is particularly acute in the case of public undertakings. The Commission made the observation in its 1992 report that the implementation of the state aids rules was severely obstructed by the lack of both notification by Member States of aid schemes and the availability of information. This is in spite of a Commission Directive adopted in 1980 dealing with the transparency of financial relations between Member States and public undertakings[14] which was amended by Commission Directive 85/413 to include the transportation sector.[15] The Directive requires that public authorities demonstrated clearly the public funds which are made directly or indirectly available and the use to which the funds have been put. These transparency requirements apply in particular to the financial relations between public authorities and public undertakings on:

- the setting-off of operating losses;
- the provision of capital, or non-refundable grants or loans on privileged terms;
- forgoing of profits through financial advantages;
- forgoing a normal return on the public funds used;
- compensation for financial burdens imposed by public authorities.

---

[12] Case 78/76, *Firma Steinike und Weinlig v Germany* [1977] ECR 595, at 611.
[13] Case 290/83, *Commission v France* [1985] ECR 439, at 449.
[14] Commission Directive 80/723, [1980] OJ L195/35. The Directive was the subject of judicial review on an application by several Member States claiming that the Commission was acting *ultra vires* in adopting the measure since, *inter alia*, the requirements discriminated against public undertakings. This was rejected by the Court: Cases 188-190/80, *France, Italy and UK v Commission* [1982] ECR 2545.
[15] [1985] OJ L229/20.

Forms of aid

12.16   Article 92(1) does not define the form of aid which may be prohibited as incompatible with the EC Treaty. On the contrary, the expression "any form whatsoever" explicitly discourages the need for state aids to be of a specific or particular kind. Hence, the absence of an exhaustive list of aids. Aid in any form whatsoever can therefore include a positive payment by the state or a negative payment which results in a pecuniary advantage being conferred on the undertaking. In *Van der Kooy*, the European Court of Justice suggested that so long as there was a debit to state funds, it may be considered as an aid. In that case, which concerned preferential tariffs for the use of natural gas to farmers using glass houses, it remarked:

> "The State, or the entity on which it exerts influence, does not apply the tariff as an ordinary economic agent but uses it to confer a pecuniary advantage on energy consumers, in the same way as it grants aid to certain undertakings, forgoing the profit which it could normally realize."[16]

12.17   By way of contrast, the Court stated in *Norddeutsches* that an advantage derived from Community tariff quota was not an aid from the Member State in question since the resources which had been waived were Community resources rather than those of the Member State.[17]

Market economy investor principle

12.18   In the 1994 guidelines, the Commission outlined the three main categories of aid which are regarded as most common in the air transport sector: capital contributions, loan financing and guarantees. In considering these cases, the Commission adopts the "market economy investor principle" (MEIP). The MEIP is based on the concept of neutrality as regards ownership in undertakings. Article 90(1) of the EC Treaty provides that:

> "In the case of public undertakings and undertakings to which Member States grant special or exclusive rights, Member States shall neither enact nor maintain in force any measure contrary to the rules contained in the Treaty."

12.19   In essence then, the MEIP entails a comparison between "the terms on which the funds were made available by the State to the airline, and the terms which a private investor operating under normal market conditions would find acceptable in providing funds to a comparable private undertaking".[18] This principle has also been accepted by the European Court of Justice which stated comprehensively in *Belgium* v *Commission* that the test was "whether in similar circumstances a private shareholder, having regard to the foreseeability of obtaining a return and leaving

---

[16] Cases 67, 68 and 70/85, *Kwekerij Gebroeders Van der Kooy* v *Commission* [1988] ECR 219, at 270.
[17] Case 213-215/81, *Norddeutsches Vieh- Und Fleischkontor Herbert Will* v *Bundesanstalt Fuer Landwirtschaftliche Marktordnung* [1982] ECR 3583.
[18] [1994] OJ C350/5, para. 26.

aside all social, regional-policy and sectoral considerations, would have subscribed the capital in question".[19]

In applying the principle, the Commission expects that a market economy   12.20 investor will wish to see a restructuring programme which is capable of restoring the viability of the company. Hence, the quintessential need for any aid to be linked to a coherent restructuring programme. The Commission has already detailed in its decisions that unless it can be clearly established that any state assistance is linked to such a programme, it is likely to consider it as a prohibited aid within the terms of the EC Treaty: *Sabena, Aer Lingus, Air France, Olympic Airways, TAP* and *Iberia*.[20]

Capital contributions

Typically, this takes the form of a capital or equity injection by the state. Capital   12.21 contribution can also take the form of share acquisition as the European Court of Justice acknowledged in *Intermills*[21] or through convertible bonds as in the subscription by CDC-P to two bond issues by Air France.[22] Furthermore, a plan to write-off debts or losses accrued by an undertaking, particularly by way of the state assuming the responsibility for them, is tantamount to a capital injection. This was so, for example, in the case of *Sabena* and *Olympic Airways*.[23] In determining whether the capital contribution amounts to an aid, the Commission will consider a number of issues against the background of the market economy investor principle.

(a) *Return on investment.* The market economy investor principle states simply that   12.22 state provision of capital must be considered in the light of whether a private investor would have acted in the same way. To resolve this issue, the Commission must first consider the past, present and future financial performance of the undertaking in question to ascertain whether the structure and future prospects for the company are capable of providing a normal return within a reasonable period.

Short-term profitability will not be the sole determinant in its assessment of the   12.23 return on investment because the Commission believes that the correct analogy must consist of "a private company pursuing a structural policy and guided by profitability perspectives in the longer term".[24] This is consistent with the case law of the European Court of Justice.[25] In the case of a capital injection which does not suggest a normal return both in the short and long term, then it is likely that the Commission will conclude that the undertaking is in receipt of an aid by virtue of the state "forgoing the benefit which a market economy investor would expect".[26] In *ENI-Lanerossi*, where a capital injection was made into ENI, a state holding company, the Court pronounced that:

---

[19] Case 234/84, [1986] ECR 2263, at 2286.
[20] See *infra*.
[21] Case 323/82, *S.A. Intermills* v *Commission* [1984] ECR 3809.
[22] Commission Decision 94/662, [1994] OJ L258/26.
[23] Commission Decision 91/555, [1991] OJ L300/48 and Commission Decision 94/696, [1994] OJ L273/22.
[24] [1994] OJ C350/5, para. 28.
[25] See Case 323/82, *S.A. Intermills* v *Commission* [1984] ECR 3809; Case 234/84, *Belgium* v *Commission* [1991] ECR I-1433; Case C-305/89, *Alfa Romeo: Italy* v *Commission* [1991] ECR I-1603.
[26] [1994] OJ C350/5, para. 28.

"when injections of capital by a public investor disregard any prospects of profitability, even in the long term, such provision of capital must be regarded as aid."[27]

12.24   By contrast, the Commission authorised a capital injection of FF 300m into Air Outre-Mer (AOM) by Altus France, a subsidiary of Crédit Lyonnais. It raised no objections against the capital contribution because it considered that Crédit Lyonnais was acting in the capacity of a rational private investor since AOM was likely to return to profitability in the near future.[28]

Of course, in examining the rate of return, the Commission will have to adopt a realistic approach. The guidelines indicate that the undertaking's financial performance and commercial strategy will be examined against a variety of factors including:

- the gearing ratios and cashflow which will indicate the ability to finance investments and operating costs;
- projected operating and net results;
- future capital values and dividend payments;
- the markets in which the airline operates and intends to operate, the trends in those markets and its share in those markets.

12.25   The Commission will also have regard to changes in economic and technical efficiency by reference to:

- operating costs;
- labour productivity;
- average age of the fleet so that a higher than average age will mean the requirement of a substantial investment and is "usually associated with a lack of investment or with previous inopportune investment" towards which a market economy investor may be reluctant to contribute.[29] This was noted by the Commission in its examination of the FF 20bn capital injection into Air France although in that case it concluded, *inter alia*, that unless the investment was permitted, the average age of the fleet would deteriorate to the extent that it would prevent Air France from contributing to the competitiveness of the sector and thus the interest of the Community.[30]

12.26   One of the most controversial decisions delivered by the Commission on state aid relates to the recent proposal to capitalise Iberia with Pta 87bn. This followed a 1992 restructuring plan which involved a state contribution amounting to Pta 120bn. The case was cleared without the Commission having to examine the other elements of state aid such as for example whether the aid would distort competition, or whether the aid fell within one of the categories for exemption.[31]

---

[27] Case C-303/88, *ENI-Lanerossi: Italy v Commission* [1991] ECR I-1433.
[28] *Twenty-Fifth Report on Competition Policy* (1995), p.72.
[29] [1994] OJ C350/5, para. 29.
[30] Commission Decision 94/653, [1994] OJ L254/73.
[31] Commission Decision 96/278, [1996] OJ L104/25.

(b) *Economic environment.* In applying the MEIP, the Commission will need to refer   12.27
to the economic environment of the airline industry. This entails an assessment of
the market conditions and the way in which the airline in question is being
affected. For instance, during the short term crisis provoked by the Gulf War,
the Commission indicated its intention to look at state aids more favourably.[32]
Furthermore, in its decision to authorise a capital injection of £Irl 175m into Aer
Lingus, the Commission had to verify the conditions of the industry and in that
case observed that "most airlines are still experiencing a drastic downturn or
stagnation of revenues and profits which has lasted much longer than expected"
as a result the Gulf crisis of 1990 and the global economic recession.[33] In its later
decision of 1994 to authorise a capital injection of FF 20bn into Air France, the
Commission made a similar analysis of the market situation. It noted that:

> "One of the main causes of these losses resides in the world-wide economic recession,
> which has amplified the effects of the Gulf crisis and has had tremendous effects in
> the air transport sector, which is particularly sensitive to changes in the general level
> of economic activity . . . Another factor which has negatively affected the results of
> the companies is the fact that investments in aircraft made at the end of the 1980s
> were on the basis of optimistic commercial programmes. The delivery of these
> aeroplanes has caused over-capacity because the substantial increase in supply has not
> been off-set by a corresponding increase in demand."[34]

The Commission believes nevertheless that "a company whose structure is   12.28
basically sound may have good prospects for the future despite a general downturn in the performance of the industry".[35] This view is not shared by a
number of airlines who have commenced judicial review proceedings against the
Commission's decision. In one application, BA, SAS and Euralair, amongst
others, are claiming that the Commission had been mistaken to conclude that the
Air France's restructuring plan was adequate to restore long-term viability, that
the aid was proportionate to the plan, and that the aid did not affect trade to an
extent contrary to the common interest.[36] BMA is also seeking to annul the
decision in a separate application to the Court of First Instance.[37]

(c) *Proportional investment.* The Commission expects that any capital injection into   12.29
an airline will be made in accordance with the distribution of the shareholding in
the company. There is therefore unlikely to be any aid involved if the capital
injection was made simultaneously by the state and any private shareholders in
accordance with the proportion of shares they held in the company. In addition,
"the private investor's holding must have real economic significance".[38] This issue

---

[32] COM(91) 59.
[33] Commission Decision 94/118, [1994] OJ L54/30.
[34] Commission Decision 94/653, [1994] OJ L254/73.
[35] [1994] OJ C350/5, para. 30.
[36] Case T-371/94, *British Airways, Scandinavian Airlines System, Koninklijke Luchtvaart Maatschappij, Air UK, Euralair International, TAT* v *Commission* [1994] OJ C386/21.
[37] Case T-394/94, *British Midland Airways* v *Commission* [1994] OJ C392/14.
[38] [1994] OJ C350/5, para. 27.

was examined in 1994 by the Commission relating to the subscription by CDC-P to the two bond issues by Air France.

12.30   At the time of the investigation, Air France was owned by the state (99.3 per cent), by CDC-P (0.5 per cent) and private shareholders (0.1 per cent). The two bonds comprised 1.8m "obligations remboursables en actions" (ORA) worth over FF 749m and 0.4m progressive interest subordinated notes (TSIP-BSA) worth over FF 749m. The French Government had waived its intention, as a major shareholder, to subscribe to the bonds. In accordance with the remaining equity distribution in Air France, CDC-P's subscription to the ORA amounted to over FF 748m and almost all of the TSIP-BSA bonds. Of the total ORA bonds, 4516 were subscribed by the private shareholders and of the total TSIP-BSA bonds, only 14 were taken up by them. The Commission had to conclude that the subscription by the private shareholders was "negligible". Accordingly, the participation of private investors in that case "cannot rule out the possibility of the capital injection being a State aid" since there was hardly any economic significance that could be attached to their investment.[39]

12.31   (d) *Iberia.*[40] Although most state aids cases are controversial, not least when the aids are authorised, the recent capital injection of Pta 87bn into Iberia was particularly controversial because Iberia had previously been authorised to receive an aid of Pta 120bn in 1992, subject to the condition that, *inter alia*, it would be the last for the duration of its Strategic Plan of the Iberia Group 1992-96. That aid was accompanied by a restructuring programme that projected a good improvement to traffic conditions, substantial fleet renewal, reduction in personnel and additional investments in Latin America. As a result of the general economic recession and the Gulf hostilities in 1992 and 1993, Iberia's plans suffered a severe setback. The only significant achievement was the reduction in the workforce with a productivity increase of 24 per cent on 1991. By the end of 1994, its debt-equity ratio had spiralled to 14.72:1.

12.32   Therefore, a new restructuring plan was conceived to ensure Iberia's future. It proposed an initial capital injection of Pta 130bn from Teneo, the state holding company. This amount was eventually watered down to Pta 87bn, accompanied by a programme that was less expansionist and based on more prudent assumptions. The exercise would comprise two transactions. One was the creation of a new company, Newco which was later changed to Andes Holding, to acquire Iberia's holdings in Latin American operations and eventually to re-sell them. The company would be created under Dutch law and owned jointly by Teneo (42 per cent) and American merchant banks (52 per cent). The second transaction was the capital injection of Pta 87bn to finance, amongst other things, further staff reductions and restoring the debt-equity ratio. The Spanish Government argued that the adjustment programme was necessary because the implementation of the original strategic plan was affected by "exceptional circumstances, which were unforeseeable and outside the control of the company" including the crisis in the European monetary system that led to a depreciation of the Spanish currency,

---

[39] Commission Decision 94/662, [1994] OJ L258/26.
[40] Commission Decision 96/278, [1996] OJ L104/25.

and the difficulties in privatising its Latin American subsidiary, Aerolíneas Argentinas. In the light of the notification, the Commission appointed an independent consultant to assess the viability of the plan and to consider whether a rational market economy investor would have provided the capital.

The consultant's report in respect of Andes Holding was favourable. According   **12.33**
to the report, the transfer of Iberia's Latin American holdings would practically eliminate all the risks to which Iberia had been exposed. In this transaction, Iberia would transfer to Andes Holding 13 per cent of its holding in Ladeco Airlines, 100 per cent of its holding in Interinvest which owned 53.35 per cent of the shares in Aerolíneas Argentinas, and 10 per cent of its 30 per cent holding in Aerolíneas Argentinas. The Commission accepted this conclusion. It had particular regard to the financial structure of Andes Holding which was typical in similar cases. It also had regard to the fact that private investors would have effective control of the company, not least because of the participation of American merchant banks. The Commission was also satisfied that the interest rates for financing Andes Holding were comparable for similar transactions; likewise, the prices paid by Andes Holding for the acquisitions. Furthermore, Iberia's buy-back option of these holdings was subject to the dual condition that:

"after any repurchase of this kind the market value of the share capital of the whole of the group is at least 30% of the group's enterprise value and that a private investor also has a sizeable share, directly or indirectly, in the operation in question."

In respect of the capital injection, however, the consultant recommended that   **12.34**
Pta 48bn was sufficient to ensure Iberia's survival in the short- to medium-term, with a rate of return between 30 per cent to 40 per cent by 1999. First of all, on the amount of aid, the Commission discounted the costs of financing staff reduction as "of no consequence to the Commission's assessment". On the basis of the considerations relating to traffic growth, satisfactory reduction of operating costs, and proceeds derived from the sale of holdings, the Commission was satisfied that Iberia's financial position would improve substantially by 1999. Although it accepted that a rate of return at 30 per cent was higher than market rates, that reflected "the distinct possibility that the programme will not go as planned . . . Iberia is still a company with a very high specific risk". However, a minimum rate of return of more than 30 per cent would "be expected by an investor working in the short- or medium-term in a purely financial framework". That Teneo was not seeking to make a profit on its capital within this framework, but was instead pursuing objectives of a long-term economic policy, was sufficient to expect a 30 per cent rate of return. In the light of these findings, the Commission concluded that the transactions were such that they could be expected of a rational market economy investor. Consequently, the capital injection would not constitute an aid.

Loan financing
Loans extended by the state to an undertaking can constitute an aid which is   **12.35**
incompatible with the EC Treaty, if in particular they had been granted on the basis of preferential conditions such as lower interest rate or without security. To

this end, loans extended by the state would be subject to the MEIP to determine whether they had been made on normal commercial terms and whether they were readily available from a commercial bank. If the entire loan would not have been available from a commercial bank, then it would constitute an aid. If, however, it was available at a rate which was above that charged by the state, then the aid element would comprise the difference between the rate which the airline would pay under normal commercial terms and the rate actually paid.

12.36   *Vlaamse.*[41] This issue was considered at length by the Commission in its examination of an interest-free loan of Bfrs 20m granted by the Flemish Region to the Belgian airline Vlaamse Luchttransportmaatschappij NV (Vlaamse). Vlaamse was a public limited company owned by five private companies and four individuals. In this respect, it was a private undertaking although the Commission maintained that this did not affect the possibility of an aid being extended by the state. The key questions were whether the loan amounted to an aid, and if so, whether the whole or part of the loan could be regarded as aid. First, the Commission was satisfied that no private investor under normal market conditions would grant an interest-free loan to "a company in which it had no holding and which was in financial difficulties less than two years after its formation". Indeed, the Commission added that it was immaterial that the decision of the Flemish Region took account of the advantage that would accrue to the economy of the region from the direct connection between Antwerp and London City Airport because it had "nothing whatsoever to do with the behaviour of a rational investor in a market economy".

12.37   As regards the second question, the Commission adopted the approach that the amount of aid was "equal to the interest which VLM would have had to pay in normal market conditions". At the time of the loan, the base rate in Belgium for a six year loan was 7.3 per cent. However, the Commission reasoned that a premium of 2 per cent had to be added to this rate on two grounds. One was to reflect the characteristics and financial position of Vlaamse, and the other to reflect on the fact that no asset was secured against the loan. On this basis, the amount of aid would be "the sum of the interest payments" derived from multiplying the amount of the loan by 9.3 per cent. This reasoning has now given rise to a challenge by Cityflyer Express who initially lodged the complaint of an unlawful aid with the Commission. Cityflyer is claiming that the Commission was wrong to decide that aid was limited to the interest-free element. On the contrary, it asserts that the aid should consist of the interest from the loan as well as the full amount of the loan. It argues further that if the approach of the Commission was upheld, then the application of the MEIP would lead to different results according to whether the state aid takes the form of a capital injection or a loan.[42]

Guarantees

12.38   More common, however, is the giving of loan guarantees by the state rather than actual loans. The guarantees may be made directly by the state or indirectly by

---

[41] Commission Decision 95/466, [1995] OJ L267/49.
[42] Case T-16/96, *Cityflyer Express* v *Commission* [1996] OJ C108/11.

institutions delegated with that responsibility. The Commission insists in its guidelines that guarantees must be accompanied by conditions incorporated into the loan agreement including the compulsory declaration of bankruptcy of the airline company. In the case of public undertakings which cannot legally be declared bankrupt, then the guarantee will be regarded as a permanent aid if that guarantee allows the undertaking concerned to procure loans on more favourable terms than would otherwise be available. Thus, the aid element would be comprised of the difference between the rate which the undertaking would have had to pay under normal commercial terms and the rate actually paid given the guarantee. In the event that no lending institution would have extended the loan without the guarantee, then the entire amount of the loan will be considered as aid.

(a) *TAP*.[43] This issue was considered by the Commission in 1994 in its investigation of a proposal to increase the capital in TAP and to extend to it credit guarantees and tax exemption. Under the Strategic, Economic and Financial Restructuring Plan, the Portuguese Government would guarantee up to a total of Esc 530bn over four years. Having considered the financial position of TAP, the Commission decided that no financial institution would extend any credit facility to TAP without any state guarantee. In particular, it had accumulated heavy losses which accounted for its weak financial structure. It was also beset with the problems of failing to adapt its route structure to market conditions, of an inefficient mix of fleet and of low productivity. 12.39

(b) *Olympic Airways*.[44] Immediately prior to TAP's case, the Commission had been considering, *inter alia*, loan guarantees which had been given to Olympic Airways by the Greek Government. The substantive assessment of the guarantee was, however, clouded by procedural issues that the Greek authorities had failed to notify the Commission of the guarantees. Consequently, the guarantee was declared illegal. Nevertheless, the Commission referred to the action of the Greek authorities in "guaranteeing all the carrier's new borrowings indiscriminately" given the magnitude of the risks that stemmed from the Olympic Airways' debt/equity ratio of 3:1 and its severe financial difficulties. In applying the MEIP, the Commission said that no private investor would consider lending money to Olympic Airways even at a high rate of interest. Accordingly, the guarantee had to be regarded as a state aid. In such cases, guarantees which are derived by virtue of the state's holding in a financially troubled undertaking have to amount to an open-ended guarantee, and must therefore be regarded as an aid, if they effectively keep the undertaking in operation. 12.40

Other forms of aid

Capital injections, loans and guarantees are by no means the only kind of state measures which can be classified as state aids. On the contrary, both the Commission and the European Court of Justice have examined a variety of measures which they subsequently deemed to constitute aid. 12.41

---

[43] Commission Decision 94/698, [1994] OJ L279/29.
[44] Commission Decision 94/696, [1994] OJ L273/22.

Tax exemption

12.42   In 1994, the Commission examined the tax exemption facilities maintained by the Greek Government in favour of Olympic Airways as part of its wider review of a proposal to increase the capital of the airline. The nature of a tax exemption is such that the undertaking benefiting from it will enjoy such advantages which are not available to its competitors. Given, therefore, the competitive and cross-border nature of Community air transport, such facilities have the potential of distorting competition. Unless it can be exempted by virtue of the EC Treaty, a tax exemption is likely to be regarded as an unlawful aid contrary to the Treaty.

12.43   Special tax concession may also take the form of a right to operate duty-free shops. In its 1992 Report, the Commission noted the arrangements at Copenhagen airport (SAS), Luxembourg airport (Luxair), Schipol airport (KLM) and Lisbon–Porto–Faro airports (TAP).

Most Member States extend a special tax exemption in respect of fuel to its airlines. This is recognised by Article 24 of the ICAO Convention.

Deferred tax collection

12.44   A special tax deferral system operated in Germany whereby German airlines could deduct 30 per cent in addition to the usual tariff of asset depreciation in respect of aircraft purchased. The Commission took the view that such a preferential treatment was capable of providing the airline with a larger than usual surplus through a fleet investment programme. It is willing to consider the deferral of fiscal contributions as a general measure "unless it confers a competitive advantage to specific undertakings to avoid having to bear costs which would normally have had to be met out of the undertaking's own financial resources", in which case it would probably constitute an aid.[45]

12.45   Following this observation, the Commission initiated an inquiry into the compatibility of this tax scheme with the EC Treaty.[46] This revealed further that the special depreciation scheme was applicable only to aircraft used for commercial purposes and for international services. However, the aircraft had to be registered in Germany and could not be sold for six years following its purchase. Whether the entire 30 per cent allowance was applied in the first year following acquisition or spread over a number of years was left to the discretion of the taxpayer.

By referring to the mechanics of the tax scheme, the Commission decided on two principal grounds that it amounted to an aid. First of all, it noted that the scheme could be applied at any time during the first five years following acquisition which meant that beneficiary airlines had considerable flexibility and advantage, for instance, to make fleet changes more readily. More importantly, it allowed them to increase the amount of depreciation at their discretion during highly profitable years. In this way, they had the flexibility to determine the level of taxable income, or indeed in certain cases to eliminate taxation altogether. However, this financial advantage would ultimately be borne by the budget of the German State.

---

[45] [1994] OJ C350/5, para. 13.
[46] Commission Decision 96/369, [1996] OJ L146/42.

The second ground for its finding centred on the difference between a state aid   **12.46**
and a tax measure of general applicability. There was no doubt that the special
depreciation scheme was available only to "certain clearly defined depreciable
assets to the exclusion of all other assets". Furthermore, they had to comply with
certain conditions relating to usage, place of registration and period of ownership.
These considerations must therefore be regarded "as derogating from the general
measures of accelerated or straight-line depreciation" which were the two general
depreciation methods available in Germany. In this respect, it was not founded
on objective criteria. The Commission pointed out that the scheme had no "indef-
inite temporal scope" and were in no way indispensable to the smooth functioning
of the general tax system. In the final analysis:

> "Neither the physical characteristics of the aircraft nor their conditions of use on the
> market nor any other factor warrants recourse to a method of depreciation other than
> accelerated or straight-line."

Concessions

Special concessions or total exemption from airport charges or air traffic charges   **12.47**
may also constitute an aid if the concessions were the result of state action or measure. The Commission noted the need to examine such privileges in its 1992
Report, in particular the general exemption extended by France in respect of all
domestic flights.

Compensation

Compensation provided by the state to airlines in return for certain obligations   **12.48**
may be treated as aid "save as otherwise provided in this Treaty". Such
obligations may include public service obligations as provided for by Article 4 of
Council Regulation 2408/92 on market access.[47] In such cases, unless the procedures within Article 4 of that Regulation are adhered to, compensation to an
airline may be taken as an aid. It is also possible for such compensation to be
classified as an aid but one which may be exempted if it facilitates certain activities
or promotes the development of certain areas in accordance with Article 92(3)(c).

Likewise, Article 5 of Council Regulation 2408/92 provides for Member States   **12.49**
to grant exclusive concessions on domestic routes either by law or contract with
possible reimbursement. Unless the selection was conducted by a process of open
tender, any reimbursement may be regarded as an aid. Aid of such a nature
which is not directly linked to a restructuring programme will be regarded as an
operating aid. According to the Commission's guidelines, operating aids are per-
missible only if they satisfy the provisions of Article 92(2)(a) on aids with a social
character which are granted to consumers, or alternatively if they satisfy the
conditions of compensation under Article 4 of Regulation 2408/92 on public
service obligations.

The Commission had the occasion to explore this point further in its investi-   **12.50**
gation into the subsidies provided for the operation of air services under the Law

---

[47] [1992] OJ L240/8.

of the Autonomous Region of Sardinia.[48] The subsidies were intended to compensate carriers for the provision of third-level air services which were defined by Sardinia as air services provided by aeroplanes or helicopters with a capacity of between nine and 30 passengers. Specifically, the payments were to compensate for the empty seats on regional routes with low traffic density. However, these were restricted to a maximum of 55 per cent of the seats offered on the routes specified by the Sardinian Regional Executive. In addition, these subsidies were available only for three consecutive years from 1994 with a diminishing rate of compensation: 100 per cent of fares in 1994, 75 per cent in 1995 and 50 per cent in 1996.

12.51   On these facts, the Commission had little difficulty in concluding that the subsidies amounted to a state aid. In particular, it pointed out that the subsidies distorted or had the potential for distorting competition by favouring those airlines which benefited from the subsidies. Furthermore, recipients of the subsidies were prevented from altering the fares which were approved by the Executive. In this respect, the subsidies took no account of the revenue and costs incurred by the recipients in operating the routes. Therefore:

> "there is no guarantee that the carriers will not realize an excessive profit, likely to be transferred to routes where they are in competition with other Community carriers."

In the light of this assessment, the aid could only be authorised if one of the exemptions provided in Article 92(2) or (3) could be invoked.

Aircraft use

12.52   Grants for the use or purchase of a specific aircraft type is considered a direct operational aid. For 1985 and 1986, for example, Air France was granted a total of FF 126m for the operation of Concorde. This scheme, however, was terminated in 1987.

Distortion of competition

12.53   Having established the existence of an aid, the Commission must next determine whether the aid is compatible with the common market since the handing-out of an aid *per se* is not an infringement of Article 92(1). This is done by reference to the effect of the aid, and if the effect is such that it distorts competition or threatens to distort competition, or favours certain undertakings rather than a more general class, then the aid may be considered as incompatible with the EC Treaty. In the significant case of *Philip Morris* v *Commission* involving the grant of aid to a cigarette manufacturer, the European Court of Justice had the occasion to examine the scope of this provision. It reasoned that the aid from the Dutch Government had the effect of reducing "the cost of converting the production facilities and has thereby given the applicant a competitive advantage over manufacturers who have completed or intend to complete at their own expense a similar increase in the production capacity of their plant".[49]

---

[48] Commission Decision 96/110, [1996] OJ L26/29.
[49] Case 730/79, *Philip Morris* v *Commission* [1980] ECR 2671, at 2689.

An important consequence of such an approach is to imply that the state 12.54
measure entails a certain degree of discrimination so that it favours certain undertakings or the production of certain goods. Thus, provided the measure is indis-
criminate and benefits a larger class of undertakings, it is likely to distort competition by virtue of its preferential effect. In the recent *Olympic Airways* case, the
Commission decided that the various categories of aid proposed by the Greek
Government would distort competition on the ground that "they are granted to
only one undertaking which is in competition with the other Community airlines
on the greater part of its European network".[50] In *TAP* too, the Commission
reasoned that it was an airline operating on a network of competitive routes and
consequently, any capital increase or credit guarantees will mean "a direct competitive advantage over its competitors who do not enjoy such facilities".[51]

The Commission has formed the view that Community air transport is a highly 12.55
competitive sector and on a number of routes, the competition is particularly
intense and notable. It seized on the opportunity in 1991 when examining the
case of *Sabena* to reason that the liberalisation measures adopted by the
Community were likely to lead to increased competition, no less in the case of the
routes operated by Sabena. Accordingly, it was highly possible that any aid
granted to Sabena would distort competition in Community air transport.[52] Again,
in *Aer Lingus* and *Air France*, the Commission referred to the characteristics of the
markets in which the carriers operated and concluded that the intense competition
on those markets could be affected adversely by reason of certain preferential
measures which were not generally available.[53]

Effect on intra-Community trade

There is a substantial overlap between the foregoing analysis of the distorting 12.56
effect of an aid on competition and the extent to which intra-Community trade
will be affected by that measure. In particular, if an aid was deemed to distort,
or threatened to distort, competition, then given the cross-border characteristic of
air transport, trade between Member States will almost inevitably be affected. The
Commission has already remarked in the case of *TAP* that trade within the common market will be affected by an aid which has been granted to "a company
which operates in the air transport sector which involves by its nature trans-
border operations".[54] The importance of having regard to the characteristics of
the activity and the relevant geographic market in which the undertaking was
operating was aptly represented in the opinion of the European Court of Justice
in *Philip Morris* v *Commission*:

---

[50] Commission Decision 94/696, [1994] OJ L273/22.
[51] Commission Decision 94/698, [1994] OJ L279/29.
[52] Commission Decision 91/555, [1991] OJ L300/48.
[53] Commission Decision 94/118, [1994] OJ L54/30 and Commission Decision 94/653, [1994] OJ
L254/73.
[54] Commission Decision 94/698, [1994] OJ L279/29.

"When State financial aid strengthens the position of an undertaking compared with other undertakings competing in intra-Community the latter must be regarded as affected by that aid. The aid . . . was for an undertaking organized for international trade and this is proved by the high percentage of its production which it intends to export to other Member States. The aid in question was to help to enlarge its production capacity and consequently to increase its capacity to maintain the flow of trade including that between Member States."[55]

12.57   Trade between Member States must, of course, be seen in its proper context. As Community air transport progressively becomes more competitive as a consequence of the liberalisation measures on market access and fares, it will be irrelevant that the effect of an aid was only confined to domestic boundaries of the Member State concerned. By 1 April 1997, Member States are required to abolish any cabotage or domestic restrictions in accordance with Council Regulation 2408/92, thus paling the notion of trade between Member States into insignificance. In addition, the increasing cross-border ownership of carriers, through mergers and the right of establishment, is creating a new dimension for "trade between Member States".

12.58   On the other hand, where an aid has the effect of diverting international traffic to the Member State in question, which therefore transfers the difficulties of that airline to its competitors established in the Community, the Commission will regard that as affecting trade between Member States.[56] In *Tubemeuse*, the European Court of Justice had the occasion to make an analysis of the issue of "international" trade and the extent to which trade within the common market will be affected by an activity that was largely focused on international trade. In that case, the Belgian Government had extended an export aid to a manufacturer of seamless tubes. Although it was not disputed that 90 per cent of its production was exported to non-EC countries, the Court was less convinced that the export aid would not affect intra-Community trade. It said:

"having regard to the interdependence between the markets on which Community undertakings operate, it is possible that aid might distort competition within the Community even if the undertaking receiving it exports almost all its production outside the Community. The exportation of part of the undertaking's production to non-member countries is only one of a number of circumstances which must be considered."[57]

12.59   Since there were world-wide restrictions on the importation of seamless tubes, an export aid would therefore improve the competitive advantage of the undertaking over other undertakings engaged in similar export activities.

Nevertheless, the Commission is prepared to recognise that in certain circumstances involving international air transport with non-EC countries, foreign airlines may be receiving aid from their respective governments so that it distorts competition and affects the competitiveness of Community carriers. In these

---

[55] Case 730/79, [1980] ECR 2671, at 2688–9. See also *Aer Lingus* [1994] OJ L54/30 and *Air France* [1994] OJ L254/82.
[56] *e.g. Sabena* [1991] OJ L300/48 and *Aer Lingus* [1994] OJ L54/30.
[57] Case 142/87, *Tubemeuse: Belgium* v *Commission* [1990] ECR I-959, at 1013–4.

instances, the Commission may be willing to authorise an aid to the Community carrier provided that it is transparent to demonstrate the link between the aid and the objectives, and is clearly ring-fenced for the market or route in question. In the 1994 guidelines, the Commission explained that:

> "The Commission is aware that State aids granted by third countries to non-Community airlines may affect the Community carriers' competitive position in the routes upon which they compete."[58]

However, the Commission is not prepared to accept the fact of non-Community carriers receiving aids as a reason for not applying the binding provisions of the EC Treaty since their application must be irrespective of whether third countries operate schemes of state aid.   12.60

De minimis rule

The European Court of Justice also rejected in *Tubemeuse*[59] the argument that there should be a *de minimis* rule or a concept of "appreciable extent" when assessing the effect of an aid on trade between Member States. In adopting this approach, the court applied its previous opinions in *Philip Morris* v *Commission* and *Belgium* v *Commission*[60] in which it remarked that a relatively small amount of aid or a relatively small size of the undertaking which received the aid did not as such exclude the possibility that intra-Community trade might be affected. The effect, rather than the aim or cause, of the aid was therefore the material consideration.   12.61

---

[58] [1994] OJ C350/5, para. 11.
[59] Case 142/87, *Tubemeuse: Belgium* v *Commission* [1990] ECR I-959.
[60] Case 730/79, [1980] ECR 2671 and Case 234/84, [1986] ECR 2263. See also Case 259/85, *France* v *Commission* [1987] ECR 4393 and Ch. 14 *infra* on the notification procedures in respect of state aids below a certain threshold.

Chapter 13

STATE AIDS: THE EXEMPTIONS

An aid that has been found to be incompatible with Article 92(1) of the EC Treaty can nevertheless be authorised if it falls within the scope of one or more of the exemptions provided in Article 92(2) and (3). Exemptions under Article 92(2) are mandatory so that if the characteristics of an aid satisfy its requirements, the exemption must be granted automatically. On the other hand, Article 92(3) provides only for discretionary exemptions. Some of these exemptions have been successfully invoked, but not without controversy. Applications for judicial review against decisions of the Commission in this area have grown exponentially over the last few years. There is indeed a detectable juridification of state intervention in the air transport sector. **13.1**

1. Automatic exemptions: Article 92(2)

Article 92(2) sets out three categories of aids which must be exempted if they fall within the scope of those provisions. However, any aid which is alleged to qualify for exemption under Article 92(2) must still be examined by the Commission in order to confirm its compatibility with that Article. **13.2**

Aid with a social character granted to consumers

Article 92(2)(a) provides a derogation for "aid having a social character, granted to individual consumers, provided that such aid is granted without discrimination relating to the origin of the products concerned". **13.3**

This derogation is rarely used in air transport, since most aids that can be justified under this paragraph can normally be justified on other grounds. However, in limited circumstances it may be invoked to justify an aid which subsidises services on specific routes provided that the aid can ultimately be linked to a benefit to consumers; for instance, aid which is used to provide access to air transport services for the elderly or handicapped. The Spanish Government operates a compensation scheme for the provision of services by Iberia between the mainland and the Canary, Melilla and Balearic Islands. This scheme entitles all Community residents in the islands to a 33 per cent reduction in air fares (25 per cent for residents of the Balearic Islands) In addition a 10 per cent reduction is available for flights between the Canary Islands and between the Balearic Islands. In its 1992 evaluation, the Commission noted that these "consumer-oriented" aids were based on public service and regional policy considerations, and since all Community residents on the islands were treated equally, the Commission was satisfied that there was no discrimination.[1]

Aid for natural disasters or exceptional occurrences

13.4   Paragraph (b) of Article 92(2) allows for "aid to make good the damage caused by natural disasters or exceptional occurrences".

Such aids are permitted since they do no more than repair the damage caused although they cannot be applied beyond that purpose. This has never been used in air transport.

Aid to certain areas of Federal Republic of Germany

13.5   Aid granted "to the economy of certain areas of the Federal Republic of Germany affected by the division of Germany, in so far as such aid is required in order to compensate for the economic disadvantages caused by that division" is deemed compatible with the common market under Article 92(2)(c). This provision was designed to assist those areas of Germany during the period of separation. It is now only of historic importance since the unification of East and West Germany.

2. Discretionary exemptions: Article 92(3)

13.6   Discretionary exemptions by their nature require formal approval from the Commission. To effect this, aids which fall or are deemed to fall within the scope of Article 92(3) must be notified to the Commission as required by Article 93(3).

Article 92(3) provides for five categories of aid which "may be considered to be compatible with the common market":

(a)   aid to promote the economic development of areas where the standard of living is abnormally low or where there is serious underemployment;

(b)   aid to promote the execution of an important project of common European interest or to remedy a serious disturbance in the economy of Member States;

(c)   aid to facilitate the development of certain economic activities or of certain economic areas, where such aid does not adversely affect trading conditions to an extent contrary to the common interest;[2]

---

[1] *Report on the Evaluation of Aid Schemes Established in Favour of Community Air Carriers* (SEC(92) 431), para. 5.
[2] This continues: "However, the aids granted to the shipbuilding as of 1 January 1957, in so far as they serve only to compensate for the absence of customs protection, be progressively reduced under the same conditions as apply to the elimination of customs duties, subject to the provisions of the Treaty concerning common commercial policy towards third countries".

(d)   aid to promote culture and heritage conservation where such aid does not affect trading conditions and competition in the Community to an extent that is contrary to the common interest;[3]

(e)   such other categories of aid as may be specified by decision of the Council acting by a qualified majority on a proposal from the Commission.

Both (d) and (e) have not been applied in air transport. In practice, aid for economic activities or areas under (c) has been the most common ground for justifying aid in air transport, although both (a) and (b) have had some relevance in a number of cases.   13.7

In exercising its discretion, the Commission applies a general rule that the exemptions are to be construed narrowly since the norm is to prohibit the grant of state aids which distort competition. In 1980, the Commission noted the growing number of state aids and the increasing tendency not to notify. Accordingly, in an effort to formulate a more stringent approach to state aids, it said:

> "if the Commission has to use its discretionary power not to raise objection to an aid proposal, it must contain a compensatory justification which takes the form of a contribution by the beneficiary of aid over the effects of normal play of market forces to the achievement of Community objectives as contained in derogations of Article 92(3)."[4]

This formulation was tested in the case of *Philip Morris* v *Commission* in which the European Court of Justice agreed with the Commission's submission that the derogation could be applied only in cases where it can be shown that the aid would contribute to the attainment of one of the objectives in Article 92(3).[5]   13.8

Promoting economic development of areas

Aids which are designed to assist regions which suffer under abnormally low standards of living or serious unemployment may be declared by the Commission as compatible with the common market. To that extent, there is a degree of overlap between this paragraph and paragraph (c) which relates to aid designed to facilitate the development of certain economic areas. This was recognised by the European Court of Justice in *Germany* v *Commission* in which it also sought to explain the scope of paragraphs (a) and (c). On paragraph (a), it held that the parameters of "abnormally" and "serious" applied to an economic situation which was "extremely unfavourable in relation to the Community as a whole". On the other hand, paragraph (c) was wider in scope so that it permitted aid for the development of certain areas without being restricted by the parameters in paragraph (a), except that the aid must not affect trading conditions to an extent contrary to the common interest. Hence: 13.9

---

[3] This was inserted in 1992 by the Treaty on European Union.
[4] *Tenth Report on Competition Policy* (1980), para. 213.
[5] Case 730/79, [1980] ECR 2671.

"provision [(c)] gives the Commission power to authorise aid intended to further the economic development of areas of a Member State which are disadvantaged in relation to the national average."[6]

13.10   In a 1988 guidance, the Commission referred to regions with abnormally low standards of living or serious unemployment as those with a Gross Domestic Product (GDP) threshold of 75 per cent or lower than the Community average.[7] Thus, for instance, in the transfer of the RLS pilot school to KLM, the Commission was not satisfied that Schipol and Eelde, where the school was located, were regions which suffered from abnormally low standards of living and serious unemployment.[8] GDP is measured in terms of "Purchasing Power Standards" (PPS) which make a comparison of prices for the same sample of goods or services. For aids within paragraph (a), regions are also assessed on the basis of the "Nomenclature of Statistical Territorial Units" (NUTS) and according to the relative level of regional development compared to the Community average. A list of approved regions is also annexed to the guidance. The intensity of the regional aid is also capped at 75 per cent of the initial value of investment.

13.11   The application of this derogation on its own to air transport is uncommon, and is usually invoked simultaneously with the derogation in paragraph (c). Nevertheless, the proposal for £Irl 175m capital injection into Aer Lingus in 1993 raised the issue of whether the aid in question could be exempted by virtue of paragraph (a). The Irish Government had argued that its existing policy of requiring every trans-atlantic flight to land at Shannon International Airport for technical reasons had supported employment for over 50 years and as a result contributed to the development of mid-west region. In addition, Ireland was an Objective 1 region within the terms of European Regional Development Fund being a region with a per capita GDP of less than 75 per cent of the Community average. The Commission, however, rejected these arguments on the footing that the aid was not "a general scheme from which all the airlines based in Ireland, linking it with the rest of the world, may benefit". It considered the aid as an *ad hoc* measure designed to assist a state-owned carrier to overcome its deep financial crisis.[9]

13.12   By contrast, the Commission was disposed to accept the submission of the Portuguese Government in *TAP: Azores–Madeira* that the aid provided to TAP was a form of compensation that could be regarded as a regional aid under paragraph (a) as a result of the latter being required to perform services to the Autonomous Regions of Azores and Madeira. In its analysis, the Commission said that the application of paragraph (a) involved a consideration of the relative level of development of different zones and of regional development compared to the Community average. In a case where the GDP/PPS was below 75 per cent of the Community, it was prepared to accept that as an indication of abnormally low standards of living and serious unemployment. Since none of the Portuguese

---

[6] Case 248/84, [1987] ECR 4013, at 4042.
[7] *Commission Communication on the Method for the Application of Article 92(3)(a) and (c) to Regional Aid* [1988] OJ C212/2, as amended by [1989] OJ C78/5 and [1990] OJ 163/6.
[8] Commission Decision 94/996, [1994] OJ L379/13.
[9] Commission Decision 94/118, [1994] OJ L54/30.

regions had a GDP/PPS of more than 75 per cent, the Commission concluded that the aid could be characterised as a regional aid under Article 92(3)(a). It added that:

> "Given the degree of access to the market, the compensation of TAP's deficit is the only way to maintain life-line connections with the Autonomous Regions. The compensation of TAP's deficit is an operating aid of regional character, being designed to overcome a permanent and structural disadvantage caused by the remote location of the Autonomous Regions."[10]

The Commission also took a favourable view of the direct operational aids granted by German regional authorities to support specific domestic routes: Hof–Bayreuth–Frankfurt; Saarbrücken–Munich; Saarbrücken–Hamburg; Stuttgart–Friedrichshafen. It reasoned that the aids did not have the effect of diverting significant volumes of international traffic into Germany to the detriment of other Member States or of allowing the carriers in question to cross-subsidise their international operations. Aid granted to Lufthansa's pilot school at Bremen was also approved by the Commission as a regional aid for the special development programme "to create jobs and to overcome the current shortage of pilot licences".[11]   **13.13**

However, in a later decision concerning TAP, the Commission was less convinced that a capital increase and credit guarantees extended to TAP should be treated as a regional aid under paragraph (a) on the ground that the aid was not a general scheme available to every undertaking operating in Portugal. This was despite the submission that Portugal was "a peripheral, less-favoured country in the context of the Community", and the detrimental consequences of unemployment if TAP had to cease its operations.[12]   **13.14**

In the Commission's analysis of the aid granted to carriers operating on specified routes in Sardinia, paragraph (a) was considered as a possible exemption for authorising the aid.[13] The Commission was willing to accept that the entire Sardinian region was covered by Article 92(3)(a). In this respect, the air services, albeit with low traffic density, provided an important means for linking the region with the rest of the Community and consequently promoting the economic development of the island. Although the Commission reasoned that an operating aid may be authorised under Article 92(3)(a), the creation of the common air transport market implied that "direct aid for the operation of regional air services cannot in principle be exempted". In that case, the potential for carriers to cross-subsidise, the method of calculating the subsidies which took no account of revenue and operating costs, and the restrictive procedures for awarding the subsidies outweighed the benefits that may be derived from applying the exemption.   **13.15**

---

[10] Commission Decision 94/666, [1994] OJ L260/27.
[11] SEC(92) 431.
[12] Commission Decision 94/698, [1994] OJ L279/29. See also the decision on *Olympic Airways* [1994] OJ L273/22.
[13] Commission Decision 96/110, [1996] OJ L26/29.

Project of common European interest or to remedy a serious disturbance

13.16   This derogation has two parts, although it is rarely applied to air transport since the aid must be shown to benefit a project of common interest to the Community or to correct an aberration to the economy. Aid granted to a particular carrier is unlikely to be regarded as intended to serve the common interest of the Community if other carriers object to the aid being given. Where, however, the promotion of such interest can be established such as the Airbus Project, the Commission may be prepared to recognise its significance and accordingly grant an exemption. Airbus Industrie is comprised of a consortium of Aérospatiale (France), Daimler-Benz (Germany), British Aerospace (United Kingdom) and Casa (Spain).

13.17   In 1994, the Greek Government attempted to rely on the second part of the derogation in its proposal to increase the capital of Olympic Airways by claiming that the aid was intended to remedy a serious disturbance to the economy. The Commission refused to accept this submission claiming that the aid was "aimed chiefly at preventing the airline from going bankrupt. It relates to only one undertaking and could not possibly have either as its object or effect the remedying of a serious disturbance in the Greek economy", the existence of which the Commission nevertheless acknowledged.[14] This contrasts with the Commission's more liberal approach in respect of external factors which affect the economy or the financial health of carriers when it announced that it was favourably disposed towards state aids which were intended to compensate carriers for increased costs directly related to the Gulf War.[15]

Development of certain economic activities or areas

13.18   The derogation provided under this paragraph is the most commonly cited to justify aid in air transport either on the basis of regional aid (together with paragraph (a) derogation) or sectoral aid. However, an aid will only be approved under this derogation if it can be established that it does not adversely affect trading conditions to an extent contrary to the common interest.

The issue of regional aid has already been discussed at length above. It must be said, however, that regional aid under this paragraph is governed by different "principles of method". While regions will be assessed on the basis of NUTS, the socio-economic situation of a region will be assessed by reference to two criteria: either per capita GDP or Gross Value Added (GVA), and structural unemployment. In general, a region in which the GDP income is at least 15 per cent below the national average and unemployment is at least 10 per cent above the national average, will be entitled to aid under this paragraph. The applicable ceilings for aid intensity are either 20 per cent, 25 per cent or 30 per cent of the initial investment required.[16]

---

[14] Commission Decision 94/696, [1994] OJ L273/22.
[15] COM(91) 59.
[16] *Commission Communication on the Method for the Application of Article 92(3)(a) and (c) to Regional Aid* [1988] OJ C212/2, as amended by [1989] OJ C78/5 and [1990] OJ 163/6.

Article 92(3)(c) which provides for aids to facilitate the development of certain **13.19** economic activities has been given a restrictive interpretation so as to exclude aid which merely serves to benefit the activities of the carrier concerned. On the contrary, the aid programme must be shown to be capable of contributing to the sector as a whole. The European Court of Justice has already given its blessing to this line of interpretation so that "the intervention must also contain a compensatory justification for the aid in the form of a contribution by the beneficiary or to the development of the sector as a whole on a Community level by a reduction of its presence in the market".[17] The Commission itself has ruled on this distinction in an attempt which sought to reinforce the natural interpretation of the derogation, that is to facilitate the development of the sector as a whole, not the individual undertaking. It said:

> "Since . . . it will then be a matter of granting aid to companies which, although basically viable, have run into difficulties threatening their survival, it follows that the operation must not result in their being left in a stronger competitive position vis-à-vis industries and other Member states than would otherwise occur had those difficulties not arisen in the first place. Accordingly the aid must not promote the expansion of production capacity nor must it merely shift the problem without finding a genuine solution to the social and industrial problems facing the Community as a whole or even aggravate the situation even further in the medium or long-term future."[18]

This opinion encompasses the two conditions which are laid down in Article **13.20** 92(3)(c) before an aid may be granted to remedy the serious financial difficulties experienced by the undertaking:

- the aid must facilitate the development of certain economic activities;
- the aid must not adversely affect trading conditions to an extent contrary to the common interest.

Over time the Commission has been able to develop a more coherent policy for **13.21** state aids in air transport in the application of these provisions, even in spite of the lack of a Council Regulation pursuant to Article 94 of the EC Treaty. Its case law in respect of aid under this derogation is well illustrated in the six leading cases involving Sabena, Aer Lingus, Air France, Olympic Airways and TAP. The case of Iberia did not reach this stage of the assessment because the Commission had decided that the capital injection was not an aid. The 1994 guidelines epitomise the position of the Commission and the applicable principles which have evolved over a number of years.

The aid must facilitate the development of certain economic activities
To assess whether a particular aid has the consequence of facilitating the **13.22** development of air transport, the Commission applies the following conditions.

---

[17] Cases 278-290/92, *Spain* v *Commission* [1994] ECR I-4103, at 4166.
[18] Commission Decision 88/167, [1988] OJ L76/18.

• The aid must form part of a comprehensive restructuring programme which aims to restore the financial health of the airline so that within a reasonable period it can be expected to operate viably without the need for further aid.

13.23   (a) *Viability*. The requirement of a restructuring programme is part of the compensatory theory which the Commission announced in 1980. Typically, the restructuring plan will set out the ways in which the airline can be returned to operational viability including plans for market development, cost reductions, route rationalisation, productivity improvements and re-investments. These will need to be verified against general and specific market trends and the potential for growth in the sector. This is an essential requirement if the MEIP is to have sense. As the European Court of Justice has opined:

> "although the conduct of a private investor with which the intervention of the public investor pursuing economic policy aims must be compared need not be the conduct of an ordinary investor laying out capital with a view to realizing a profit in the relatively short term, it must at least be the conduct of a private holding company or a private group of undertakings pursuing a structural policy – whether general or sectoral – and guided by prospects of profitability in the longer term."[19]

The plan must clearly be workable and be founded on pragmatic assumptions.

13.24   (b) *Necessity of link*. A restructuring plan on its own will not of course suffice. According to the Commission, the aid must be linked to the plan so that the ultimate effect of the aid is not simply to ensure the survival or continuity of the airline, but will in fact allow for implementation of the objectives of the plan. In *Air France: CDC-P*, for example, the Commission was not convinced that the bond subscriptions were directly linked to the restructuring plan put forward by Air France. On the contrary, they represented operating aids intended for ensuring the survival of an airline in a financial crisis.[20] By contrast, the Commission had previously authorised the restructuring aid totalling £Irl 175m to Aer Lingus in which decision it accepted that the aid would be used to finance voluntary redundancies and to reduce outstanding debt. Moreover, the Commission was satisfied that the aid was linked to the restructuring programme by virtue of the second and third tranches of payment being made conditional upon Aer Lingus achieving cost reductions. The Commission concluded that it was "beyond doubt that the capital injection [was] directly linked to the restructuring of the airline".[21] This has now been questioned by Ryanair in its application to the Court of First Instance for a review of the Commission's decision authorising the payment of the second tranche.[22] Ryanair alleges that, by the time the second tranche was due, Aer Lingus had failed to implement its restructuring plan properly and, more significantly, had failed to achieve the cost reductions envisaged.[23]

---

[19] Case C-305/89, *Alfa Romeo: Italy* v *Commission* [1991] ECR I-1603, at 1640.
[20] Commission Decision 94/662, [1994] OJ L258/26.
[21] Commission Decision 94/118, [1994] OJ L54/30. See also *Sabena* [1991] OJ L300/48; *Air France* [1994] OJ L254/82; *Olympic Airways* [1994] OJ L273/22; *TAP* [1994] OJ L279/29.
[22] Commission Decision 94/C399, [1994] OJ C399/1.
[23] Case T-140/95, *Ryanair* v *Commission* [1995] OJ C248/14.

The Commission has indicated, in line with the recommendation of the Comité   13.25
des Sages, that aids should be limited in duration and be subject to a one-off-and-
last-time condition. It stated in the 1994 guidelines:

> "the programme must be self-contained in the sense that no further aid will be neces-
> sary for the duration of the programme and that given the objectives of the programme
> to return to profitability, no aid is envisaged or likely to be required in the future."[24]

The difficulty with this condition rests with its legal ambiguity, since the EC
Treaty does not expressly provide for such a constraint nor empower the
Commission to adopt it. On the contrary, the language of Article 93(3) on notification of aid is such that the Commission is obliged by law to examine each
proposed aid on its merits. Nevertheless, given the nature of a restructuring
exercise, the Commission will need to have regard to the fact of the first aid if it
should be called to examine another proposed aid to the same undertaking. Thus,
it "will not allow any further aid unless under exceptional circumstances, unforeseeable and external to the company [and] under very stringent conditions".[25] In
the series of aids to Air France, for example, including the refusal to authorise the
bond subscriptions, the Commission made frequent references to the serious
deterioration of Air France's financial position and structure as a basis for considering further state aids to the airline.[26]

(c) *Proportionality*. In addition, the aid must be proportionate to the needs of the   13.26
restructuring programme so that no excess aid is provided for other purposes such
as the acquisition of shareholdings, increase in capacity or subsidisation of fares
which have the effect of distorting trading conditions to an extent contrary to the
common interest. At any rate, the Commission expects the aid to be granted
degressively. This was stated in the *Sabena* case, and in that particular case, to be
achieved through the greater participation of private investors. Whether the aid
is proportionate to the needs of the restructuring plan or otherwise, the intensity
is measured by reference to the size of the underlying problem facing the airline.
In Sabena's case, the Commission noted that the aid was to be applied for two
purposes. By 1981, the airline's debt had increased to Bfrs 43bn and the amount
of aid would consequently improve its debt-equity ratio so that it can be restored
to commercial viability. The Commission was also satisfied that the amount of aid
was necessary to allow Sabena to implement its fleet modernisation programme
costing Bfrs 46.2bn so that it could achieve lower operating costs and comply with
new laws governing aircraft noise.

Again in *Aer Lingus*, the Commission stressed the importance of the aid being   13.27
proportionate to the aims of the restructuring plan so that it would not lead to
over-capitalisation, and distort competition as a consequence. The Commission

---

[24] [1994] OJ C350/5, para. 38.
[25] *Ibid.*
[26] Commission Decision 94/653, [1994] OJ L254/73; Commission Decision 94/662, [1994] OJ
L258/26. The Commission had earlier authorised a FF 2bn grant to Air France as part of FF 5.8bn
capitalisation programme on the basis that it was a normal commercial transaction in accordance with
the MEIP: *Twenty-First Report on Competition Policy* (1991), p.179.

was satisfied that the aid to Aer Lingus was intended for financing voluntary redundancies and reducing debts to restore its financial ratios.[27]

• The aid must be structured so that it is transparent and readily verified.

13.28   This condition is designed to prevent the difficulties of detecting interference in the management of the airline by the state as the provider of the aid except to the extent of its ownership in the company. To that end, it will make the relationship between the state and the airline receiving the aid more transparent. So in *Aer Lingus*, for example, the Commission said that transparency was important to ensure that the capital injection was directly linked to the restructuring of the airline.[28] Transparency would also ensure that the Commission was able to monitor the implementation of the aid and the restructuring plan more effectively. This would be particularly relevant in cases involving several tranches of aid payments, for example in the case of aid granted to Aer Lingus and Air France, so that authorisation for subsequent payments could be assessed according to whether the objectives of the plan were being achieved. Most important of all, transparency and verifiability would enable the Commission to ensure that the aid was not leading to a transfer of the difficulties of that airline to its competitors. This requirement represents the second condition laid down in Article 92(3)(c) prohibiting aids which adversely affect trading conditions which are contrary to the common interest.

The aid must not adversely affect trading conditions to an extent contrary to the common interest

13.29   Given the nature of air transport and a certain inevitability of aid affecting trading conditions between Member States, the typical way in which this condition is satisfied is by imposing further conditions on the approval of the aid including transparency and reporting requirements. There is considerable discretion in the application of this part of the derogation on the ground that there is no *de minimis* rule which structures the extent to which the common interest becomes adversely affected. Hence, it is possible for the Commission:

> "without exceeding its discretionary power, to form the view that the aid granted . . . could not come within the exemption provided for in Article 92(3)(c) of the Treaty in favour of aid designed to facilitate the development of certain economic activities or of certain economic areas, where such aid did not adversely affect trading conditions to an extent contrary to the common interest."[29]

13.30   In that case, the European Court of Justice had reasoned that the aid granted to Compagnie Boussac which manufactures textiles, clothing and paper products, would lower its costs "and thereby reduced the competitiveness of other manufacturers within the Community, at the risk of forcing them to withdraw from the

---

[27] Commission Decision 94/118, [1994] OJ L54/30.
[28] *Ibid.*
[29] Case 301/87, *Boussac: France v Commission* [1990] ECR I-307, at 364.

market even though they had hitherto been able to continue their activities by virtue of restructuring and improvements in productivity and quality, financed by their own resources".[30]

However, in the case of state aids to airlines, the Commission has typically   13.31
required that the state gave the undertakings that the recipient airline would not use the aid to the disadvantage of its competitors. In the 1994 guidelines, the Commission set out its view that aid cannot be used for anti-competitive purposes such as the violation of the competition principles set out in Articles 85 and 86, nor can it be used in a manner detrimental to the liberalisation programme of Community air transport.[31] Thus, aid which is used to increase, rather than reduce, capacity by offering more seats on all or specific routes will be regarded as incompatible with the common interest. In *Olympic Airways*, for example, the Commission required an undertaking from the Greek authorities that "the increase in the number of seats offered annually by OA within the EEA would be proportional to the growth rate of the market". This, the Commission opined, was to prevent OA from offering a number of seats that was in excess of the growth of the overall market so that its expansion was carried out at the expense of its Community competitors. Accordingly, the Commission set the reference capacity at 3,518,778 seats for operations within the Community.[32] Similarly, in *Aer Lingus*, the Commission decided that while Aer Lingus could not increase its capacity either on the United Kingdom–Ireland market as a whole or on the Dublin–London (Heathrow) route, it was not precluded from increasing capacity should the traffic grow in that particular geographical market.[33] A decision was adopted later in that year by the Commission to allow Aer Lingus to revise its capacity for those markets.[34]

In addition to the restriction on capacity, it is also common for the Commission   13.32
to impose a restriction relating to fares. Typically, this means that the carrier receiving the aid would be prohibited from acting as the price leader in the relevant market. Therefore, in the case of *Olympic Airways*, the Commission reasoned that:

"this renunciation of a price leader role implies that OA will not be offering fares lower than those offered by its competitors on the routes in question, when account is taken of the nature of the services and the conditions and restrictions attached to the individual fares."[35]

The routes in question were Athens–London and Athens–Stockholm. The   13.33
FF 20bn aid to Air France was also subject to the condition that the carrier would not act as the price leader on routes within the Community. The Commission took the view that this commitment meant that "Air France will, during the period of the restructuring, be limited in its commercial strategy and will not be

---

[30] *Ibid.*
[31] [1994] OJ C350/5, para. 38.7.
[32] Commission Decision 94/696, [1994] OJ L273/22.
[33] Commission Decision 94/118, [1994] OJ L54/30.
[34] Commission Decision 94/997, [1994] OJ L379/21.
[35] Commission Decision 94/696, [1994] OJ L273/22.

able to introduce lower tariffs than generally offered by its competitors".[36] TAT has applied for judicial review to annul the decision of the Commission to authorise the second tranche of this aid on the ground that Air France had breached its undertaking on price leadership. It alleges that Air France had been "deviating between 15% and 74% relative to other fares on some routes in which Air France takes advantage of a price leadership".[37]

In authorising aid to airlines, the Commission has also consistently and explicitly insisted that the aid cannot be used for the acquisition of shareholdings in other Community carriers. Such acquisitions were characteristic of expansion, rather than consolidation through the restructuring plan. Thus, in *TAP*[38] and *Olympic Airways*,[39] the Commission required undertakings from the Portuguese and Greek authorities that any expansion of such a nature would not be funded by the aid.

3. Conclusion

13.34   The control of state aids has had and will continue to have an instrumental role to play in Community air transport. As the sector makes its way towards more competition, it becomes more crucial to ensure that aids can only be seen as exceptions lest they have a disproportionate effect on the aims of the common market. Where they have to be authorised, strict conditions will need to be imposed such as a comprehensive restructuring programme which may either prohibit expansion through acquisitions, or require fares and capacity reduction. This would avoid the danger of the aid being used to secure additional market share, contrary to the published guidelines that aids must be aimed at restoring the enterprise to competitiveness and economic viability.

13.35   Although the Commission has no powers to require that publicly-owned airlines be privatised since Article 222 of the EC Treaty provides for a neutrality concept in respect of ownership, it has shown a disposition to authorise aids which are linked to increasing participation by private investors. It has also stated in the 1994 guidelines that it believes the way to achieve greater competitiveness and better financial performance in European air transport is to adopt more commercial management so as to avoid the difficulties of state aids. One of these is no doubt the application of the MEIP in determining whether an aid is justified. Another is the difficulty of detecting the granting of aid to undertakings whose relationship with the state is not always transparent. It may be that privatisation will gradually emerge as a consequence of stricter control over state aids so that access to capital will be subject to a more obvious level playing field. Air France, for instance, has already indicated that it now expects to be privatised by 1998.[40]

---

[36] Commission Decision 94/653, [1994] OJ L254/73.
[37] Case T-236/95, *TAT European Airlines* v *Commission* [1996] OJ C64/20.
[38] Commission Decision 94/698, [1994] OJ L279/29.
[39] Commission Decision 94/696, [1994] OJ L273/22.
[40] *Financial Times*, 13 May 1996.

Chapter 14

STATE AIDS:
THE PROCEDURES

An examination of the framework governing state aids will be incomplete without   14.1
a brief reference to the applicable procedures. This is all the more so where the
breach of procedural requirements can give rise to a substantive outcome without
the merits of the aid in question being actually considered. To that end, this
chapter is devoted to an examination of the procedural issues.

1. Enforcement and procedure

The enforcement procedure for state aids is set out in Article 93 of the EC Treaty.   14.2
In essence, it charges:

- the Commission with the duty to monitor existing aid schemes and to initiate
  the procedure to determine whether an aid is compatible with the common market;
- the Member States with the duty to notify the Commission of any plans to
  grant or alter aid.

Two types of aid are distinguishable from the provisions of Article 93: new aids
which include alteration to an existing aid, and existing aids which have been
expressly authorised by the Commission previously or by default.

New aid: Article 93(3)

Article 93(3) of the Treaty requires that the Commission: 14.3

"be informed, in sufficient time to enable it to submit its comments, of any plans to
grant or alter aid. If it considers that any such plan is not compatible with the common market having regard to Article 92, it shall without delay initiate the procedure
provided for in paragraph 2. The Member State concerned shall not put its proposed
measures into effect until this procedure has resulted in a final decision."

The intention of this provision is to enable the Commission to conduct a   14.4
preliminary investigation to ascertain whether the full procedure under Article
93(2) needs to be initiated.[1] If a *prima facie* case cannot be established, the case will

---

[1] Case 84/82, *Germany* v *Commission* [1984] ECR 1451.

then be closed under Article 93(3). When the Commission should decide to adopt the full procedure will depend on whether it "has serious difficulties in determining whether an aid is compatible with the Common Market".[2] This includes circumstances in which the Commission is unable to overcome the difficulties in determining whether the aid is compatible with the EC Treaty. However, it is for the Commission to decide, on the basis of the factual and legal circumstances of the case, whether the difficulties involved in assessing the compatibility of the aid warrant the initiation of the full procedure.

Where the Article 93(2) procedure has been initiated, and the Commission subsequently comes to the conclusion that the aid is not prohibited by Article 92(1) or that it falls within the scope of Article 92(3) exemptions, the case will be closed under Article 93(2).

Un-notified aids

14.5 Over time, the case law of both the European Court of Justice and the Commission suggests that new aids may be classified into notified or un-notified new aids. In the case of un-notified new aids, Article 93(3) has stated explicitly that unless and until the Commission has given a clearance to the aid in accordance with Article 93(3) or issued a decision pursuant to Article 93(2), Member States cannot implement a new aid. New aids are un-notified for a number of reasons, including a genuine belief that the aid is compatible with the EC Treaty, or automatically exempt by Article 92(2), or a deliberate defiance of the Treaty provision to avoid Commission scrutiny or delay stemming from the investigation. In 1994, the Commission held that the subscription by CDC-P to two bonds issued by Air France was an unlawful aid by reason of the failure of the French Government to notify the Commission of the proposed measure.[3]

14.6 However, not every un-notified new aid is automatically incompatible with the common market. Indeed in *Boussac*, the European Court of Justice implied that the failure to observe procedural requirements by Member States, that is, in notifying the Commission of the proposed aid under Article 93(3), was not always tantamount to a substantive illegality, and consequently declared as void, regardless of whether it is ultimately compatible with the common market or falls within the scope of the exemptions. This was possible because the rules on state aids presuppose that "conservatory measures may be taken to counteract any infringements of the rules laid down in Article 93(3)". Nevertheless:

> "Once it has been established that aid has been granted or altered without notification, the Commission therefore has the power, after giving the Member State in question an opportunity to submit its comments on the matter, to issue an interim decision requiring it to suspend immediately the payment of such aid pending the outcome of the examination of the aid and to provide the Commission, within such period as it may specify, with all such documentation, information and data as are necessary in order that it may examine the compatibility of the aid with the common market."[4]

---

[2] Case C-198/91, *William Cook* v *Commission* [1993] ECR I-2487.
[3] [1994] OJ L258/26.
[4] Case 301/87, *Boussac: France* v *Commission* [1990] ECR I-307, at 356.

Furthermore, the Court in taking a punitive attitude towards un-notified aids,   **14.7**
explained that there was no procedural infringement by the Commission if it
allowed itself a period for considering and investigating the aid prior to notice
being served on the Member State under Article 93(2), if it had not been informed
in sufficient time. Indeed, it could not be faulted for having allowed a lengthy
period to elapse before issuing a final decision in cases where owing to the attitude
of that Member State, it was not given the available documentation and information to initiate the investigation. During this time too, the prohibition will
continue to apply.

Notified aids

Article 93(3) requires that the Commission be informed in sufficient time. A letter   **14.8**
was sent from the Commission to Member States setting out the system of stan-
dardised notification and the publication of annual reports.[5] In return, the
Commission is required to initiate the Article 93(2) procedure "without delay" if
it believes that the new aid is not compatible with the common market. Although
Article 93 does not define the period within which the Commission is to complete
its preliminary investigation, it should be "guided by Articles 173 and 175 of the
Treaty which, in dealing with comparable situations, provide for a period of two
months".[6] Thus, the Commission is required to submit its comments or initiate the
full procedure within two months of the notification. There is, however, a divergence of opinion as to precisely when the two-month period begins. The European
Court of Justice has been drawn into this debate in a number of its decisions as
to when the Commission is regarded as "informed" of the plan. In the view of the
Commission, the period begins when all the relevant information for the purposes
of the case has been received. In *Van der Kooy*, regarding preferential tariff for
natural gas to glass house growers, the commencement of the two-month period
began at the end of exchange of data between the Dutch authorities and the
Commission.[7] The Court has also given its blessing to this line of interpretation.[8]

It is, however, clear that within the two months when the preliminary investi-   **14.9**
gation is taking place, the aid cannot be implemented. During the two months,
however, the Commission is expected to act diligently.[9] At the end of the two
months, the Commission can either clear the aid as compatible with the common
market, or initiate the full procedure. As with un-notified aids, once the full
procedure has been initiated by the Commission, the Member State concerned
continues to be prohibited from implementing the aid until a final decision has
been reached, which must obviously continue to apply if the aid was deemed by
the Commission as incompatible with the common market. Decisions of the
Commission whether to give a clearance or initiate the full procedure are subject
to review by the European Court of Justice under Article 173 of the Treaty

---

[5] SG(94) D/284.
[6] Case 120/73, *Lorenz* v *Germany* [1973] ECR 1471, at 1481.
[7] Commission Decision 92/C344, [1992] OJ C344/4.
[8] Case 301/87, *Boussac: France* v *Commission* [1990] ECR I-307, *Tubemeuse: Belgium* v *Commission* [1990]
ECR I-959.
[9] *Lorenz* v *Germany* [1973] ECR 1471.

although it is less clear whether the "comments" of the Commission in accordance with Article 93(3) are subject to review so that they can be regarded collectively as an "act" within the terms of Article 173.

14.10   Where, at the end of the two months, the Commission fails to take any action, the prohibition lapses in which case the Commission can only investigate that aid as an existing aid. This has been confirmed by the European Court of Justice in *Germany* v *Commission*.[10] Furthermore, in *Produits Bertrand* v *Commission*, the Court held that in circumstances where the Commission's inaction had detrimentally affected the interests of the recipient's competitors, the injured competitor may bring an action under Article 215 for damages.[11] In addition to this action for damages, it is also possible for a Member State to seek a judicial review of the Commission's inaction under Article 175.

14.11   In its 1994 Guidelines, the Commission set out an accelerated clearance procedure for proposed aids which have been notified. Under this procedure, the Commission will issue a decision within 20 working days from the time of "complete notification". The new procedure will apply only in cases where the amount of the proposed aid is no more than ECU 1m over a three-year period and where the aid is linked to specific investment objectives. Operating aids are thus excluded. The Commission believes that the ceiling of ECU 1m reflects the characteristics of the air transport industry which is capital intensive and which would consequently exclude a large number of aids. Indeed, the Commission states that the objective of the new procedure "is to speed up the approval of the small aids given mainly for regional purposes not covered by public service obligations"[12] However, the accelerated clearance procedure has no bearing on the substantive issue of whether a particular measure constitutes an aid. This was held by the Commission in its decision relating to an aid from the Flemish region to a Belgian carrier, Vlaamse.[13]

Existing aids: Article 93(1)

14.12   The Commission, in co-operation with Member States, is required by Article 93(1) to:

> "keep under constant review all systems of aid existing in those States. It shall propose to the latter any appropriate measures required by the progressive development or by the functioning of the common market."

In *Lorenz* v *Germany*, the European Court of Justice listed three categories of existing aids envisaged by Article 93(1). First, those aids which were already in existence when the EC Treaty came into effect, and for the United Kingdom, Denmark, Greece and Spain those in existence at the time of their accession to

---

[10] Case 84/82, *Germany* v *Commission* [1984] ECR 1451, at 1488.
[11] Case 40/75, [1976] ECR 1.
[12] [1994] OJ C350/5, para. 50.
[13] Commission Decision 95/466, [1995] OJ L267/49.

the Community. Secondly, those aids which had been lawfully introduced or previously authorised by the Commission. The third category includes aids which had been notified, but were implemented as a consequence of the Commission's failure to act within two months of the notification.[14] Existing aids which are no longer compatible with the common market will be subject to the full procedure under Article 93(2).

The full procedure: Article 93(2)

The procedure under Article 93(2) is contentious. It provides: 14.13

> "If, after giving notice to the parties concerned to submit their comments, the Commission finds that aid granted by a State or through State resources, is not compatible with the common market having regard to Article 92, or that such aid is being misused, it shall decide that the State concerned shall abolish or alter such aid within a period of time to be determined by the Commission."

Once this procedure has been initiated, the Commission is expected to reach its findings expeditiously. Although in *RSV* v *Commission*, the Court did not lay down a time limit within which the substantive investigation must be concluded, it stated nevertheless that the 26 months taken to reach a decision prohibiting the aid was unsatisfactory and without due justification. The Court added that the delay by the Commission in issuing its decision had established a legitimate expectation on the part of the recipient so as to prevent the Commission from requiring the refund of the aid; *a fortiori*, if the recipient had reasonable grounds for believing that the Commission would not object to the aid by virtue of a previous authorisation.[15]

Direct effect under Article 93

The notion of direct effect, which enables an individual third party to enforce its   14.14
rights in the national courts, is assuming an increasing significance as cross-border ownership becomes more common, and greater liberalisation of Community air transport markets takes place. It is a legal concept which legitimises the greater vigilance exercised by competitors against any illegitimate practices contrary to the common market.

In Article 93(3) on preliminary investigation, Member States are expressly   14.15
prohibited from putting their "proposed measures into effect until this procedure has resulted in a final decision". The European Court of Justice has interpreted this provision as giving rise to direct effects so that affected parties may have recourse to the remedies provided by national courts against a Member State who has failed to notify the Commission of the proposed aid or who has implemented an aid before the end of the preliminary period or before a final decision has been reached by the Commission under the full procedure. In *Lorenz* v *Commission*, the Court stated in its judgment that:

---

[14] Case 120/73, [1973] ECR 1471, at 1481.
[15] Case 223/85, [1987] ECR 4617.

235

"The direct effect of the prohibition extends to all aids which have been implemented without being notified and, in the event of notification, operates during the preliminary period, and where the Commission sets in motion the contentious procedure, up to the final decision."[16]

14.16   In respect of existing aids, the Court said in an earlier opinion in *Capolongo* that the prohibition laid down in Article 92(1) was intended to have effect in the national legal systems of Member States so that it may be invoked before national courts.[17]

The jurisdiction of the national courts is clearly limited to the determination of whether the proposed measure is an aid, and if so, whether due notification has been given to the Commission. The question of whether the aid is compatible with the common market is the exclusive responsibility of the Commission. This was so held in the *French Salmon* case:

"National courts do no more than preserve, until the final decision of the Commission, the rights of individuals, faced with a possible breach by State authorities of the prohibition laid down by the last sentence of Article 93(3) of the Treaty. When those courts make a ruling in such a matter, they do not thereby decide on the compatibility of the aid with the common market, the final decision of that matter being the exclusive responsibility of the Commission."[18]

14.17   This approach has been applied by the English courts in *R* v *Attorney-General ex parte ICI*, relating to an application for judicial review by ICI against the British Government. The Court of Appeal in reversing the High Court's judgment acknowledged that the role of national courts was to determine whether in that case the valuation rules which benefited certain undertakings, but not others, was an aid measure. The question of compatibility was to be determined only by the Commission.[19]

2. Review of Commission decisions

14.18   The review of Commission decisions on state aids does not differ from the general principles of judicial review applicable in other areas of the EC Treaty. Four fundamental grounds of review are stipulated in Article 173 which consist of the lack of competence, infringement of an essential procedural requirement, infringement of the Treaty or any rule of law, and misuse of powers.

Typically in state aids cases, insufficient reasoning by the Commission contrary to Article 190 has been cited as a ground for review.[20] Other grounds of review

---

[16] Case 120/73, *Lorenz* v *Germany* [1973] ECR 1471, at 1483.
[17] Case 77/72, *Carmine Capolongo* v *Azienda Agricola Maya* [1973] ECR 611.
[18] Case C-354/90, *Fédération Nationale du Commerce Extérieur des Produits Alimentaires* v *France* [1991] ECR I-5505, at 5528.
[19] [1986] 1 CMLR 588.
[20] *e.g.* Case 102/87, *France* v *Commission* [1988] ECR 4067.

include incorrect finding of facts,[21] delay in arriving at a decision[22] and failure to adhere to the procedural requirement of hearing.[23]

Recipient of aid

There is no doubt that an undertaking which is the proposed beneficiary of an aid, but which has not been authorised by the Commission, will have the right to impugn the decision of the Commission under the terms of Article 173. 14.19

Third party

Third parties will have to establish that the decision of the Commission is "of direct and individual concern" to them. The second paragraph of Article 173 states: 14.20

> "Any natural or legal person may, under the same conditions [as paragraph one], institute proceedings against a decision addressed to that person or against a decision which, although in the form of a regulation or a decision addressed to another person, is of direct and individual concern to the former."

Whether a decision bears the characteristics of being of direct and individual concern depends on a variety of factors. In *Cofaz I*, the European Court of Justice reiterated its opinion set out in *Plaumann* v *Commission*[24] which held that third parties could only claim to be directly and individually concerned: 14.21

> "if that decision affects them by reason of certain attributes which are peculiar to them, or by reason of circumstances in which they are differentiated from all other persons, and by virtue of these factors distinguishes them individually just as in the case of the person addressed."[25]

These may include, for instance, whether the measure in question is of concern to the complainants, and whether they were at the origin of the complaint which led to the investigation such that it can be established that the decision of the Commission may "adversely affect their legitimate interests by seriously jeopardising their position on the market in question".[26]

More significantly, in 1993, Air France brought an action under Article 173 to annul the decision of the Commission to allow the merger of British Airways and TAT. Although there was no dispute that Air France was directly concerned with that decision, the crucial question on the admissibility of the action was whether Air France was also individually concerned. Referring to its previous decisions, the Court upheld the principle that an applicant would only be individually 14.22

---

[21] *e.g.* Case 169/84, *Cofaz II: Société CDF Chimie Azote et Fertilisants* [1990] ECR I-3083.

[22] *e.g.* Case 223/85, *RSV* v *Commission* [1987] ECR 4617.

[23] *e.g.* Case 301/87, *Boussac: France* v *Commission* [1990] ECR I-307.

[24] Case 25/62, *Plaumann* v *Commission* [1963] ECR 95.

[25] Case 169/84, *Compagnie Francaise L'Azote* v *Commission* [1986] ECR 391, at 416.

[26] *Ibid.*

concerned if its circumstances were such as to differentiate itself from all other persons. In that case, it referred to three factors which it considered were pertinent to the assessment. First, Air France had been involved in the proceedings, particularly through its criticisms of the Commission's definition of the relevant market which the Commission admitted were seriously taken into consideration. Secondly, in assessing the relevant the market, the Commission was mainly preoccupied with the position of Air France and the effect that merger would have on its operations. It took into particular account the 84.9 per cent share of the French passenger market enjoyed by Air France. Thirdly, Air France had been required by the Contrat de Plan of 1990 to divest itself from TAT by 30 June 1992. This was followed four months later by the BA-TAT merger proposal. On the basis of these factors, the Court was satisfied that the decision was of direct and individual concern to Air France.[27] Again, in respect of Air France's later challenge to the decision of the Commission to decline jurisdiction over the BA–Dan Air takeover, the Court upheld the submission that it was directly and individually concerned.[28]

14.23   Judicial review under Article 173 is, of course, conditional upon a "final act" on the part of the Commission without which there would be no basis for challenge. In *Spain* v *Commission*, the Court pointed out that the prohibition issued by the Commission against the aid in question was "a considered decision" on its part and an act for the purposes of Article 173.[29] In particular also, the Court of First Instance has said in the merger case between BA and Dan Air that a measure which has binding legal effects and is capable of affecting the interests of the complainant so as to bring about a change in his legal position constitutes an "act".[30]

Council veto

14.24   In addition, Article 93(2) provides a power of veto to the Council to authorise an aid in exceptional circumstances which is under investigation by the Commission:

> "On application by a Member State, the Council may, acting unanimously, decide that aid which that State is granting or intends to grant shall be considered to be compatible with the common market, in derogation from the provisions of Article 92 or from the regulations provided for in Article 94, if such a decision is justified by exceptional circumstances. If, as regards the aid in question, the Commission has already initiated the procedure provided in the first paragraph, the fact that the State concerned has made its application to the Council shall have the effect of suspending that procedure until the Council has made its attitude known."

The Council must, however, formulate a decision within three months failing which the Commission will continue with its investigation.

---

[27] Case T-2/93, *Air France* v *Commission* [1994] ECR II-323.
[28] Case T-3/93, *Air France* v *Commission* [1994] ECR II-121.
[29] Case C-312/90, *Spain* v *Commission* [1992] ECR I-4117.
[30] Case T-3/93, *Air France* v *Commission* [1994] ECR II-121.

3. Recovery of unlawful aid

Aids which have been granted in breach of the provisions of the EC Treaty or   14.25
decisions of the Commission pursuant to Article 93 can be subject to a recovery
order. Despite the fact that neither Article 92 nor Article 93 provide for aid to be
recovered, the European Court of Justice has explicitly recognised the competence
of the Commission to order the Member State concerned to recover an unlawful
aid from the recipient. In an action brought by the Commission against Germany,
the latter had argued that an action for recovery was not admissible, and in any
event, the Court must limit itself to finding a failure to fulfil an obligation. It had
no power to order that Member State to take any specific measures, so that it is
the responsibility of that Member State to determine the appropriate measures to
comply with the judgment and consequently eliminate the results of its non-
compliance. The Court rejected this view. It said:

> "The Commission is competent, when it has found that aid is incompatible with the
> common market, to decide that the State concerned must abolish or alter it. To be of
> practical effect, this abolition or modification may include an obligation to require
> payment of aid granted in breach of the Treaty, so that in the absence of measures
> for recovery, the Commission may bring the matter before the Court."[31]

Nevertheless, the process of recovering the aid is to be pursued within the   14.26
framework of the applicable national law, although the latter must not operate in
such a manner as to frustrate the recovery.[32] This is in accordance with the narrow interpretation which the Court has adopted in the application of the recovery
principle. In *Commission* v *Belgium*, for example, it took the view that the responsible Member State was not absolved of the responsibility to recover the aid even
if that would put the recipient in bankruptcy,[33] or indeed had serious consequences for the state's economic and monetary policy.[34]

Air France: CDC-P

Aid granted through the subscription of bonds in Air France by CDC-P was also   14.27
the subject of a recovery order. In that decision, the Commission ordered the
French authorities to retrieve within two months the sum of FF 1.5bn from Air
France, minus any interest already paid by the latter to CDC-P, in order "to re-
establish the status quo by eliminating all financial advantages from which the
recipient of aid illegally granted has unduly benefited".[35] This decision, however,
became the subject of an application for judicial review by Air France.[36] The

---

[31] Case 70/72, *Commission* v *Germany* [1973] ECR 813, at 829. See the guidelines issued by the
Commission [1983] OJ C318/3.
[32] Case C-5/89, *Commission* v *Germany* [1990] ECR I-3437.
[33] Case 52/84, [1986] ECR 89.
[34] Case 63/87, *Commission* v *Greece* [1988] ECR 2875.
[35] Commission Decision 94/662, [1994] OJ L258/26.
[36] Case T-358/94, *Air France* v *Commission* [1994] OJ C370/16.

applicant argued that the Commission had misconstrued the status of CDC and misapplied the MEIP. It also impugned the substantive analysis of the Commission, in particular that the subscriptions by other private shareholders were economically irrelevant because they did not reveal the proportion of risks assumed by the shareholders. The case has now been rejected by the Court of First Instance.[36a]

14.28   As a result of these proceedings, the Commission was requested to revise its earlier decision relating to recovery. Moreover, the French authorities were "facing difficulties in implementing the Decision".[37] Since the recovery of unlawful aid must be pursued in accordance with national law, a straightforward recovery of the aid under French law would require Air France to terminate its contract with CDC-P. Similarly, as "Obligations Remboursables en Actions" were only reimbursable in shares, and not cash, repayment of the amount subscribed by CDC-P would require a modification to the contract. Because this modification would prejudice CDC-P, it was unlikely that their agreement would be forthcoming. In addition, they argued that the cancellation of the whole subscription would prejudice the interests of private investors whose participation was legitimate and did not constitute aid. At any rate, repayment of the amount subscribed by CDC-P would also prejudice the position of other parties in past subscriptions who were not offered a similar possibility of reimbursement.

14.29   Accordingly, an interim recovery scheme was proposed pending the final outcome of the judicial review application. This was to prevent an irreversible exercise of repayment by Air France to the participants in the event that the European Court of Justice annulled the Decision of the Commission because Air France would not legally be able to impose on the participants the obligation to reinvest the same amount under the same conditions. The interim scheme provided for the setting up of a bank account into which the funds released by CDC-P would be deposited. The key feature of the scheme was that Air France would not be given access to the funds for the duration of the proceedings, and that the bank would release the funds to CDC-P if the Commission's decision was confirmed.

14.30   Although the Commission referred in its Decision to the principle that a Member State may not plead provisions existing in its internal legal system in order to justify a failure to recover an unlawful aid, it noted that the Commission had a degree of discretion in applying that principle. This may be necessary in cases where, in giving effect to a Commission decision, "a Member State encounters unforeseen and unforeseeable difficulties or perceives consequences overlooked by the Commission". In the present case, the Commission accepted that the aid involved "particularly complex financial instruments", in addition to which:

"the implementation of the contested decision before a final decision of the Court would bring about irreversible consequences overlooked by the Commission . . . it will be impossible to re-establish the *status quo ante* if the decision is annulled by the Court of Justice."

14.31   Given these considerations, the Commission must nevertheless ensure that its initial decision remained effective. Since the objective of a recovery is to deprive

---

[36a] Case T.-358/94, *Air France* v *Commission* (Transcript of 12 December 1996).
[37] Commission Decision 95/367, [1995] OJ L219/34.

the recipient of the aid which it was granted, the Commission was satisfied that it was immaterial to the effectiveness of its decision if CDC-P was not immediately reimbursed, provided that Air France was denied access to the aid.

The power of the Commission to order recovery is, however, conditional upon **14.32** a non-compliance with its earlier decision having been established, and it must be exercised in accordance with the procedures laid down in the EC Treaty. Article 93(2) provides that:

> "If the State concerned does not comply with this decision within the prescribed time, the Commission and any other interested State may, in derogation of Article 169 and 170, refer the matter to the Court of Justice direct."

In *British Aerospace*,[38] the European Court of Justice distinguished between aid **14.33** which had been granted in defiance of a Commission decision and aid which had been granted to the same recipient but which fell outside the scope of the decision. British Aerospace and the Rover Group had challenged the decision of the Commission to order the recovery of the alleged £44.4m aid. That decision was taken on the ground that the British Government had acted contrary to an earlier decision of the Commission authorising aid to the Rover Group as part of its acquisition by British Aerospace. The authorisation was, however, subject to the conditions that no further aid in the form of capital contributions would be granted. Subsequent findings revealed that British Aerospace was granted a number of financial concessions although these were not covered by the earlier decision. The crucial question was whether the Commission had adopted the appropriate procedure and was permitted to order recovery. The Court took the view that if the Commission considered that its earlier decision had not been complied with, it ought to initiate proceedings against the Member State before the Court directly. If, however, the Commission considered that a new aid had been given, and had not been previously examined, it was obliged to initiate the full procedure under Article 93(2).

---

[38] Case C-294/90, *British Aerospace & Rover Group* v *Commission* [1992] ECR I-493.

Part V

BEYOND THE COMMUNITY

Chapter 15

EXTERNAL RELATIONS POLICY

Air transport is an international industry. By virtue of this characteristic, countries   15.1
which engage in the provision of air transport services through their respective air
carriers will usually adopt an external relations policy to map out the details of its
participation. The Community (Union) is no different in this respect. The achievement of a common policy for intra-Community air transport is necessarily incomplete, for the single market which has been created cannot exist in splendid
isolation. Indeed, much of the air transport activities of the Community are
"international" so that Community airlines depend heavily on air transport services to destinations outside the Community.

However, the formulation of an external relations policy in air transport for the
Community has been a thorny issue.[1] Like all else in air transport, the EC Treaty
itself is silent on matters relating to the external relations of this sector. This is no
surprise, bearing in mind the difficulties which surrounded the adoption of a
common air transport policy for the Community and the reasons behind the
deliberate decision of the founders of the Treaty to accord special treatment to
air transport. At the time the Treaty was concluded, international air transport
was very much in its infancy. Hence, the lack of detailed policy content.

This chapter seeks to address a number of matters. First, to identify the claims   15.2
made to justify the need for a common policy on external relations in air transport, by turning to some of the relevant provisions in the EC Treaty and the two
Communications of the Commission to the Council. Secondly, it will attempt to
examine the extent to which progress has been achieved in constructing such a
policy and related issues. Thirdly and finally, it will seek to piece together the
persistent problems facing the formulation of a common policy

1. International air transport and the EC Treaty

According to Article 75 of the EC Treaty, the transport sector has distinct and   15.3
unique characteristics which require special treatment and consequently a separate common policy. This special treatment is expressed in highly discretionary
language in Article 84(2):

---

[1] See J.Goh, "External Relations in Community Air Transport: A Policy Analysis" (1996) 2 *European
Public Law* 451 and M. *Von Zebinsky, European Union External Competence and External Relations in Air
Transport* (1996).

"The Council may, acting by a qualified majority, decide whether, to what extent and by what procedure appropriate provisions may be laid down for . . . air transport."

In *Ministère Public* v *Asjes*, the European Court of Justice ruled that the effect of this special treatment was to exclude air transport from the general provisions of Article 75.[2]

15.4   Although a common air transport policy has since been adopted over a period of 10 years, it applies only to intra-Community air transport and does not extend to air transport relations beyond the Community. But since Member States are bound by the provisions of the EC Treaty and relevant measures adopted under it, they are legally required to ensure that their air transport relations with third countries are not contrary to their Treaty obligations. Most significant in this respect is the provision in Article 234 which requires Member States to "take all appropriate steps to eliminate the incompatibilities established" by agreements concluded prior to the Treaty coming into force. Since international air transport continues very much to be governed by bilateral agreements which typically express national interests, it is therefore possible for agreements between Member States and third countries to fall foul of the Treaty or relevant measures under it. There is therefore an implied logic from this provision that the avoidance of any possible contravention or incompatibilities in the future could be achieved, or at least minimised, by vesting the authority to conclude agreements with third countries in Community institutions, unless a derogation is provided otherwise; though this consideration is by no means exhaustive. To that end, the founders of the EC Treaty made provision for such agreements to be concluded at the Community level, including international air transport agreements. However, the ability to conclude agreements or assume contractual obligations must first be preceded by the legal personality to do so. This is provided for by Article 210 of the Treaty.

15.5   The legal authority of the Community to conclude international agreements is derived from Article 228 which provides that:

"(1) Where this Treaty provides for the conclusion of agreements between the Community and one or more States or an international organisation, such agreements shall be negotiated by the Commission. Subject to the powers vested in the Commission in this field, such agreements shall be concluded by the Council, after consulting the Assembly where required by this Treaty.
(2) Agreements concluded under these conditions shall be binding on the institutions of the Community and on Member States."

The important pre-requisite in Article 228 is therefore the existence of a provision under the Treaty for agreements to be concluded by the Community. Arguably, this existence may be express or implied, and in the latter respect, the role of the European Court of Justice has been highly significant especially for its expansive interpretation of the powers of the Community under the Treaty.

---

[2] Cases 209-213/84, [1986] ECR 1425, at 1466.

2. A Community policy on external relations in air transport

Purposes of a Community policy

The difficulties which underlie efforts to create a common external policy for air   15.6
transport are complex, though it is clear that the arguments for this policy can be
highly attractive. With such a policy, the framework will enable the Community
to conduct negotiations with third countries on the basis of Community rather
than national objectives. Notions of nationality between Member States, a characteristic so dominant in international air transport, would be eliminated in
accordance with the requirements laid down in the third phase of the air transport
liberalisation programme. Among other things also, in as much as Community
interests will be systematically promoted, negotiations at the Community level
may produce better overall results. The advantages are in abundance.

To that end, the Commission issued two Communications to the Council in an   15.7
effort to initiate the formulation of a common policy: *Community Relations with Third
Countries in Aviation Matters* of 1990 and *Air Transport Relations with Third Countries* of
1992. Both represent the most significant step towards a Community policy and
point quite appropriately to the "gradual development of the internal market" and
the emerging demand for the Community to act collectively in its relations with
non-Community countries.[3] And in the case of air transport specifically, the countries of primary concern are the USA and Japan since the density of trade and
air traffic between the Community and these countries are rather significant.
Other world-wide developments, in particular the General Agreement on Trade
and Tariffs (GATT) and the limited inclusion of air transport in the General
Agreement on Trade in Services (GATS), and their consequences have also
required an urgent consideration of the Community's policy on external relations
in air transport.

The common policy on external relations in air transport would consist of three   15.8
principal objectives:

- to promote the interests of Community air carriers and their workers;
- to promote the interests of consumers;
- to promote the interests of airports or Community regions.[4]

EC Treaty objective

The Communications appear to suggest that the general basis for a Community   15.9
policy stems from the EC Treaty itself. The interests of Community carriers would
not be properly served if the conditions were not established by a Community

---

[3] COM(90) 17 and COM(92) 434. For ease of reference, both Communications will be treated as a
single document, unless otherwise specifically cited.
[4] COM(92) 434, paras. 26–36.

policy to enable these carriers to compete efficiently and effectively in the global market. Nor would the interests of users be served by a weak internal and external air transport market. Both will not be compatible with the Treaty. Collective actions must therefore prevail. The Commission argued that, unlike North America, intra-Community services represent a very small part of the total operations of Community carriers. The dependence on markets beyond the Community was therefore vital to the success of these carriers. The North Atlantic and Asia-Pacific markets provide considerable opportunities for Community air carriers, but these could only be exploited to their maximum if concerted and co-ordinated efforts on the part of Community authorities were possible. This is consistent with the observation of the Comité des Sages for Air Transport on the actual and potential prospects of existing and developing markets.[5]

Legal certainty under the EC Treaty

15.10   The main issue here is the compatibility of bilateral agreements concluded between a Member State and a third country with the provisions of the EC Treaty. In the absence of a Community policy and the ability of the Community to negotiate on behalf of Member States with third countries, bilateral agreements between Member States and the latter would continue to be concluded. The Commission argued in the Communications that there was a high probability of such agreements being incompatible with the provisions of the Treaty and the obligations of Member States under the Treaty.

Nationality

15.11   The most obvious area in which Member States run the risk of contravening the Treaty and having their bilateral agreements invalidated on the ground that they discriminate against other Community carriers is the use of the nationality clause, a feature so fundamental to international air transport. Typically, a bilateral agreement would require that an air carrier to be designated under the agreement must be "substantially owned and effectively controlled by nationals" of the Contracting State. This would be a clear infraction of Community law since it would be contrary to the right of establishment as recognised under the Treaty, the freedom of market access under Council Regulation 2408/92 and the common criteria for the licensing of Community air carriers under Council Regulation 2407/92.[6] A corollary of this common clause is the allocation or distribution of traffic rights secured from the third country among Community air carriers particularly on routes where the demand to operate exceeds the permitted capacity. These will have to be allocated in a non-discriminatory manner and a procedure will have to be developed by which the traffic rights can be distributed fairly and in accordance with Community objectives. This is considered in due course.

---

[5] *Expanding Horizons* (1994), pp.33–36.
[6] [1992] OJ L240/8 and [1992] OJ L240/1 respectively.

Existing bilateral agreements, however, which incorporate such a provision or   15.12
have the effect of discriminating on the ground of nationality between Community
air carriers "shall not be affected by the provisions of this Treaty". Article 234
preserves the rights and obligations of a Member State arising from an agreement
with a third country but only to the extent that the agreement was concluded
"before the entry into force of this Treaty". In so far as the incompatibilities continue to apply, Member States are required by the Article to eliminate them by
modifying the agreement.

In accordance with this requirement, Member States were informed in 1989 by   15.13
a letter from the Transport Commissioner (then Karel van Miert) of the need to
amend all existing bilateral agreements as soon as possible.[7] To what extent this
can be achieved unilaterally remains unclear since the agreement of the third
country is always necessary for any amendment to a bilateral air service agreement. This was duly recognised by the Commission in its Communications to the
Council although it stated further that agreements concluded after the coming
into force of the EC Treaty could only be tolerated "when Member States agree
on an appropriate consultation and authorisation procedure whereby on a case
by case basis steps are developed to remedy the situation".[8] This statement very
clearly indicates the transitional nature of any incompatible provisions and the
conditions under which they will be accepted for the time being.

In respect of future agreements with third countries, the Commission proposed   15.14
in its Communication of 1990 that the following clause on nationality should
appear instead:

> "The ownership of the air carriers designated to operate the services provided for in
> the Annex to this Agreement on behalf of the Party that is a member of the European
> Communities must have its central administration and principal place of business in the
> Community, the majority of whose shares are owned by nationals of Member States
> and/or Member States and which is effectively controlled by such persons or states."[9]

Community competition rules

Although the competition rules of Articles 85 and 86 of the EC Treaty apply to   15.15
air transport by virtue of the first package of liberalisation measures adopted in
1987, they do not apply to extra-Community air transport. In defining their
scope, the European Court of Justice said in *Ahmed Saeed* that:

> "the Community rules which have been adopted with regard to air transport apply
> only to international air transport services between Community airports. It must be
> inferred from this that domestic air transport and air transport to and from airports
> in non-member countries continue to be subject to the transitional provisions laid
> down in Articles 88 and 89."[10]

---

[7] See COM(90) 17.
[8] COM(92) 434, para. 41.
[9] COM(90) 17, para. 14.
[10] Case 66/86, *Ahmed Saeed Flugreisen and Silver Line Reisebüro GmbH* v *Zentrale zur Bekämpfung Unlauteren Wettbewerbs* [1989] ECR 803. This has now changed as regards domestic air transport with the advent of the Council Regulation 2408/92 on market access: see Ch. 7 *supra*.

15.16   The effect of this judgment was such that the Commission could not enforce the competition provisions of Articles 85 and 86, nor more importantly grant exemptions under Article 85(3), in respect of anti-competitive practices involving extra-Community air transport. World-wide practices such as tariff co-ordination under the auspices of the International Air Transport Association are consequently open to challenge as an infraction under the EC Treaty, as are restrictive provisions of a bilateral agreement. According to the Commission, concluding an agreement in the future which, for instance, had an anti-competitive effect or had not been duly exempted under Article 85(3) would violate the Treaty obligations of the Member State under Article 5 as "Member States are not competent bilaterally to accept obligations which furthermore may infringe Community law".[11] Thus, the Commission cautioned that "to remove legal uncertainty and to ensure the benefit of the application of the competition rules, the Commission would have no alternative, in the absence of proper enforcement powers, but to make use of its residual powers under Article 89".[12] Consequently, the climate of serious uncertainty could be avoided so that air carriers knew what practices and arrangements they may legitimately have on such routes if the Commission was vested with the relevant powers of enforcement and authority to negotiate air service agreements with non-Community countries.

A coherent strategy in international air transport

15.17   The Commission submitted that if Member States continued to negotiate air service agreements individually and bilaterally with third countries, then the best interests of the Community might not be served. The actual and potential fragmentation under this approach would lead to greater complexity and uncertainty. The number of bilateral agreements based on the Chicago Convention between Member States and third countries is already in excess of 700, and the cost of such fragmentation, if not the undue repetition, on the ability to compete effectively in the provision of international air transport services may be significant.[13] Although fundamentally similar in their general principles, some air service agreements will vary considerably in their nature and philosophy: from restrictive agreements, to more liberal agreements, to "open skies" agreements. Memoranda of Understanding or Exchanges of Letters are commonly annexed to the agreements detailing routes, fares, capacity and designated carriers, and the like. These number in hundreds. The dynamics of the industry require frequent changes to these agreements some of which are concluded after lengthy negotiations. The protracted negotiations between the United Kingdom and the USA since 1990 which have yet to conclude are instructive of this point. The diversity of these agreements, and the ability of Member States to continue negotiating with third countries possibly without regard to their obligations under the EC Treaty, may result not only in legal uncertainty as to the compatibility of certain agreements

---

[11] COM(92) 434, para. 16.
[12] *Ibid.*, para. 37.
[13] *Ibid.*, paras. 10–12.

with the Treaty but will also undermine the strength of the Community in inter-national air transport relations.

The Commission thus argued that the fragmentation of air service agreements   15.18
was a likely cause of information being obscured and therefore leading to a weak-er negotiating position in respect of other dominant countries in the provision of international air transport services such as the USA, Japan and other countries of the Asia-Pacific region. Eliminating such fragmentation would enable areas in which it would be most "useful to concentrate action at Community level" to be identified, and would ensure that the agreements which continue to be negotiated and concluded by Member States are compatible with existing and evolving Community policy.[14]

Developing a Community asset

Co-ordination at Community level in the negotiation and conclusion of air service   15.19
agreements with third countries would also ensure that Member States do not diminish the value of traffic rights unilaterally to the detriment of the Community and its users. In particular, the Commission subscribes to the view that fifth freedom rights for third country air carriers derived from traffic *between* Member States must be regarded as "a Community asset" since it provided them in a sense with cabotage traffic rights to operate essentially "domestic" services within the Community. At present, a third country air carrier is permitted to exercise fifth freedom rights within the Community as long as two Member States have given the relevant authorisation, for example Tokyo–Frankfurt–London. This could not be in the interest of Community air carriers unless reciprocal traffic rights were also secured from such third countries. The need was therefore evident to create a "Community cabotage area".[15]

Regional development

The Commission maintained that the fragmentation of bilateral agreements in the   15.20
Community also means that "market opportunities are very unevenly distrib-uted".[16] The consequence of this unevenness does not only affect the air carriers but may have repercussions on the regional development policy of the Community. As the tradition of international air transport tended to focus on national interests and national air carriers, economic development has the propen-sity of being concentrated at relatively few gateways leading to congestion and environmental problems at those airports and regions while other regions which are less popular suffer from the lack of adequate air links.

---

[14] COM(90) 17, para. 12.
[15] *Ibid.*, paras. 37–42.
[16] *Ibid.*, para. 1.

3. Progress towards an external relations policy

15.21   The first signs of a Community policy on external relations appeared in the form of Council Decision 69/494.[17] This Decision was adopted to standardise agreements concerning commercial relations between Member States and third countries. A procedure was established by which such agreements could be negotiated by the Community so that eventually national agreements would be replaced by Community agreements. The generality of the Decision, however, augured ill for the subsequent difficulties in applying its provisions to air transport.

15.22   Little was done in respect of air transport until the adoption of Council Decision 80/50 to set down a consultation procedure relating to international air transport "to make allowance for developments affecting air transport and for their consequences for the Member States".[18] Immediately prior to the Decision, there had been sufficient evidence for the Commission to propose a measure on the basis that it was "probably correct to say that the interests of member States and European airline companies may quite often not be identical (or, indeed considerably diverge)".[19] The principal aim of the Decision was therefore to establish a framework within which the exchange of information and consultation on matters which pose problems of common interest could be facilitated and to consider whether actions taken by Member States in international organisations need to be co-ordinated. Such a need could not be disputed, and the aims of a single European air transport market would clearly demand it.

15.23   While its importance as an initial step could not be denied, a consultation procedure designed for the communication of information and experience was no substitute for a coherent Community policy. The absence of such a policy necessarily meant the continuing use of bilateral negotiations for the conclusion of international air service agreements between Member States and third countries, consequently compounding the fragmentation of air transport relations with third countries. Accordingly, the Commission embarked in 1990 on the unenviable task of proposing a framework for a common policy. Several key issues of the proposals were highly complex, particularly that relating to the Commission's argument that it had exclusive competence on external relations in air transport. This generated an abundance of substantive objections, predictably from the Member States and the European Parliament.

15.24   The Communication of 1990, *Community Relations with Third Countries in Aviation Matters*,[20] was essentially a basis for the Commission to propose the adoption by the Council of a Decision on the consultation *and* authorisation of agreements concerning commercial aviation relations between Member States and third countries. The preamble to the proposed Decision noted that although Council

---

[17] [1969] OJ L326/39.
[18] [1980] OJ L218/24.
[19] *Contribution of the European Communities to the Development of Air Transport Services*, (1979) *EC Bulletin*, Supplement 5, para. 89.
[20] COM(90) 17.

Decision 69/494 extended to all modes of transportation on the standardisation and negotiation of agreements on commercial relations with third countries, "it is necessary that commercial relations with third countries in the field of civil aviation are governed by special provisions replacing the provisions of Decision 69/494". In an almost identical, but much more comprehensive, Communication of 1992, the Commission again proposed a Council Decision to be adopted on consultation and authorisation. There is little doubt that this Communication, *Air Transport Relations with Third Countries*,[21] was a deliberate response to the lack of action by the Council to adopt the proposal of 1990.

Competence and legal base: Article 113 v Article 84(2)

The main difficulty with the Commission's proposals stems from its decision to adopt Article 113 of the EC Treaty as the legal base for its proposed legislation, instead of Article 84(2). The crucial provision in Article 113 is stated in paragraph (3) which provides that:

> "Where agreements with third countries need to be negotiated, the Commission shall make recommendations to the Council, which shall authorise the Commission to open the necessary negotiations."

15.25

The language used in this paragraph connotes a mandatory obligation on the part of the Council to authorise the Commission to negotiate as and when recommendations from the Commission have been received. By contrast, Article 84(2) confers a large measure of discretion on the Council "to decide whether, to what extent and by what procedure appropriate provisions may be laid down for air transport". As such, air transport matters would remain in the hands of the Member States given the nature of the Council's membership. In proposing Article 113 as the legal base then, the Commission was asserting exclusive authority for concluding air transport agreements with third countries.

15.26

Regardless of the merits of exclusive or concurrent competence, the real difficulty lies with the proper scope of Articles 113 and 84(2). Article 113 sets out the basis for a *common commercial policy* in which uniform principles would apply to "changes in tariff rates, the conclusion of tariff and trade agreements, the achievement of uniformity in measures of liberalisation, export policy and measures to protect trade". The problem with the Commission's assertion is immediately apparent. Its argument is premised on the assumption that external relations in air transport are a commercial subject, not dependent on the provision laid down in Article 84(2). By any reasonable standard of measure, this is clearly a significant turning-point in the development of Community air transport policy. In particular, a historical analysis will reveal that all previous measures relating to air transport have had Article 84(2) as their legal base, albeit that these measures were concerned with intra-Community air transport. Furthermore, a bold assertion of exclusive competence of the Community to conclude air transport

15.27

---

[21] COM(92) 434.

agreements with third countries ignores the cautious approach which has been a dominant feature of Community air transport policy development and the unique characteristics of the sector which have explained the extreme difficulties of achieving consensus between Member States. The underlying legal rationale for the shift in the legal base in respect of extra-Community air transport is therefore not readily apparent, although the Commission pointed out that Council Decision 69/464 was adopted on the basis of Article 113; consistency was therefore important.[22] Indeed, the Commission expressed its concern that the procedures laid down in Council Decision 69/494 on Community negotiations with third countries "have not been respected by Member States" against whom the Commission "has so far refrained from starting infringement proceedings, in order to allow for open discussions on the development of a commonly agreed approach".[23]

15.28   More importantly, the Commission argued further that the legal rationale for adopting Article 113 was consistent with the jurisprudence of the European Court of Justice by citing a series of judicial decisions on the express and implied powers of the Community. In *Re European Road Transport Agreement*, otherwise known as the *ERTA* case,[24] the Court had recognised that there were two sources from which the exclusive competence of the Community may be derived. First, where it has been expressly provided by the EC Treaty, and secondly where it can be implied as flowing from "other provisions of the Treaty and from steps taken, within the framework of these provisions, by the Community institutions".[25] Accordingly, as Title IV of the Treaty on Transport does not provide expressly for treaty-making powers by the Community, it was therefore necessary to consider whether exclusive competence of the Community could be implied. In the opinion of the Court, this could be achieved in a case where the Community has laid down a common policy as envisaged by the Treaty. The effect of adopting such measures then was to vest in the Community an exclusive competence, as Member States would "no longer have the right, acting individually or even collectively, to contract obligations towards non-member States affecting these rules".[26] The basis for this proposition is simply one of integrity and consistency because the category of measures internal to the Community cannot be separated from that of external relations – at least not satisfactorily.

15.29   This principle was later adopted in the case of *Cornelis Kramer and others*[27] and again in an Opinion of the European Court of Justice in 1976 relating to Article 228(1) of the Treaty.[28] In both cases, the Court took the view that, by virtue of Article 210 which confers on the Community a legal personality to conclude or enter into international commitments, the Community had the authority to do so either from an express provision in the EC Treaty, or impliedly from other provisions of the Treaty, provided of course the exercise of the authority was for the attainment of a Treaty objective or objectives. In Opinion 1/76, the Court stated that:

---

[22] COM(90) 17, para. 36.
[23] COM(92) 434, para. 52.
[24] Case 22/70, *Re The European Road Transport Agreement: Commission v Council* [1971] ECR 263, 3 [1971] CMLR 335.
[25] *Ibid.*, at 354–355.
[26] *Ibid.*, at 355.
[27] Cases 3, 4 and 6/76, [1976] ECR 1279.
[28] [1977] ECR 741.

"whenever Community law has created for the institutions of the Community powers within its internal system for the purpose of attaining a specific objective, the Community has authority to enter into the international commitments necessary for the attainment of that objective even in the absence of an express provision in that connexion."[29]

The scope of these principles was further expanded in Opinion 2/91 on the issue of compatibility between the International Labour Organization Convention and the EC Treaty. The Court held that while Member States were prohibited from assuming international commitments which might affect or alter the scope of Community rules within the framework of a common policy: 15.30

"The Community's tasks and the objectives of the Treaty would also be compromised if member-States were able to enter into international commitments containing rules capable of affecting rules already adopted in areas falling outside common policies or of altering their scope."[30]

Since a large number of measures have already been adopted to regulate intra-Community air transport, from competition to aircraft noise, the strict application of these European Court of Justice opinions would appear to vest in the Community the competence to conclude international agreements, although the difficulty of whether the competence was exclusive remained. For the argument of exclusive competence to stand, the Commission had to bring Article 113 into sharper focus. It would need to establish that external relations in air transport was part of the common commercial policy. To that end, the Commission stated in its Communication that there were certain clear cases where Article 113 would apply since "in international relations it is nowadays widely recognised that trade in services forms part of the commercial policy and that aviation activities can be considered as services in this respect".[31] In other cases, Article 84(2) in Title IV of the Treaty would continue to apply.   15.31

This observation was made in accordance with an opinion of the European Court of Justice in 1978 on the International Agreement on Natural Rubber which noted, *inter alia*, that commercial policy in Article 113 had an evolutionary characteristic which embraced all that may be considered as commercial. The Court said: 15.32

"the enumeration in Article 113 of the subjects covered by commercial policy is conceived as a non-exhaustive enumeration which must not, as such, close the door to the application in a Community context of any other process intended to regulate external trade. A restrictive interpretation of the concept of common commercial policy would risk causing disturbances in intra-Community trade by reason of the disparities which would then exist in certain sectors of economic relations with non-member countries."[32]

---

[29] *Ibid.*
[30] *Re I.L.O. Convention on Chemicals at Work* [1993] ECR I-1061, at 1077.
[31] COM(90) 17, para. 20.
[32] Opinion 1/78, [1979] ECR 2871, at 2913.

15.33   On the strength of these authorities, the Commission was able to argue that the commercial aspects of air transport relations with third countries would include:

> "all measures directly related to market access, to capacity offered by the enterprises and to prices and all accessory measures . . . All the other aspects of aviation relations with third countries, i.e. social, environmental, technical, security problems etc. are governed by Article 84(2), as far as they are not accessory to the commercial aspects."[33]

15.34   This assertion is not without difficulty. Justifying a measure on extra-Community air transport on this basis would create a degree of artificiality in separating the issues of air transport. In as much as it represents a significant departure from past practice in intra-Community air transport of adopting Article 84(2) as the legal base for, say, market access and the like, it will also present an insuperable task of having to neatly divorce economic and non-economic issues in air transport, no less so than in attempting to draw the boundaries of what are or are not accessory to the commercial aspects of air transport. When, for example, is an environmental issue not accessorial to air transport? Or to what extent would the costs of providing airline security be regarded as commercial?

15.35   The differences in opinion as to the appropriate legal base and, hence competence, have been the major stumbling block so far to the adoption of a policy for the external relations of Community air transport. In particular, Member States were highly cautious of enabling the Community to act exclusively in an area so jealously guarded in the past. Divorced from the political realities, there are nevertheless arguments of consistency for adopting Article 84(2) as the legal base for air transport, and of pragmatism so that the monstrous task of classifying commercial, non-commercial and accessorial aspects of air transport can be avoided. Further, the resources and expertise to carry out such a task are not yet fully available within the Commission, a point which the Commission specifically acknowledged in its Communication.[34] The concern with the proposal of the Commission to adopt Article 113 was also objected to by the European Parliament on the footing that such a step would exclude its contributions in extra-Community air transport as a matter of legal requirement[35] and therefore "lacks democratic legitimation".[36]

15.36   More significantly, in a recent opinion of the European Court of Justice in *Uruguay Round Treaties* on the ratification of GATT, the Commission was held to have lacked the exclusive competence to conclude or negotiate agreements in certain trade areas such as transport, in certain services and in intellectual property rights. The effect of this opinion is that the Commission must share the responsibility for these matters with Member States.[37] The principle of subsidiarity then becomes crucially important.

According to Article 3B of the EC Treaty, the principle of subsidiarity provides that:

---

[33] COM(90) 17, paras. 22–23.
[34] *Ibid.*, para. 33.
[35] Report of the Committee on Transport and Tourism, Doc A3-192/90.
[36] Report of the Committee on Transport and Tourism, Doc A3-306/90.
[37] Opinion 1/94 [1995] 1 CMLR 205.

"In areas which do not fall within its exclusive competence, the Community shall take action, in accordance with the principle of subsidiarity, only if and in so far as the objectives of the proposed action cannot be sufficiently achieved by the Member States and can therefore, by reason of the scale or effects of the proposed action, be better achieved by the Community."

The question is therefore whether the responsibility for concluding air transport agreements with third countries should be vested in the Community or Member States in a given case although it is expected that the Commission and Member States will co-operate to carry out the task of negotiating with third countries to avoid the need for a complex legal determination on the application of the subsidiarity principle. However, there would be a *prima facie* assumption that the Community should take responsibility for negotiating all such agreements. This would be on the grounds that: 15.37

- it would give a better economic result than negotiations at Member State level although there would be initial difficulties of judgement. Relevant factors would include the strength of the negotiating partner, existing balance of traffic rights, size of market and overall trade relationship with the third country in question;
- it would avoid a Member State being placed in an unacceptable position where there was an insistence on the application of Community principles such as the prohibition of discrimination on the basis of nationality.[38]

The Member State concerned may be authorised to negotiate subject to a directive from the Council, primarily to ensure compliance with Community law, and Community co-ordination "to safeguard the interests of other Member States and of the Community as a whole".[39]   15.38

A resolution was adopted in 1996 to give the Commission the mandate to negotiate an agreement creating a common aviation area with the USA. All Member States, except the United Kingdom, agreed to the mandate.[40]

International legal personality in air transport

While Article 210 of the EC Treaty confers a legal personality on the Community to conclude international agreements, several problems relating to the public international law of air transport remain. First and foremost is the uncertainty surrounding the legal status of the Community within the international legal order. To what extent would third countries be willing or reluctant to recognise the Community as a sovereign state since the central assumption in international air transport is the existence of state sovereignty? Without entering into the political debate of whether the Community, or in this particular context the European Union, represents a sovereign state, the doubts surrounding that existence are   15.39

---

[38] COM(92) 434, para. 57.
[39] *Ibid.*, paras. 54–64.
[40] See *infra*.

sufficiently instructive of the proposition that the Community may lack the necessary sovereignty or requisites of a "Contracting State" for the purposes of international air transport. Any derogation from this proposition will have to take the form of an express commitment by a third country to accept the jurisdiction of the Community. In his evidence to a UK parliamentary committee, Frederik Sorensen of DG-VII cited Article 77 of the ICAO Convention in support of Community actions. Article 77 of the Convention states that:

"Nothing in this Convention shall prevent two or more contracting States from constituting joint air transport operating organisations or international operating agencies and from pooling their air services on any routes or in any regions, but such organisations shall be subject to all the provisions of this Convention, including those relating to the registration of agreements with the Council."

15.40   In the case of the Community, he submitted that Member States have come together and decided to act together under the EC Treaty in their capacity as sovereign states.[41]

A further related complication is the lack of Community competence in some areas of international air transport under the ICAO Convention. Although the Community enjoys competence in a substantial number of areas in air transport, there also remains a large number of areas in which it lacks competence. An example is aviation security. Thus, even if the Community assumes the status of a "contracting State", the lack of competence in these areas may render Community representations questionable, although the European Court of Justice has said in Opinion 2/91 that in circumstances where the Community is precluded from concluding an international agreement by virtue of the constitution of that international organisation rather than Community rules, "its external competence may, if necessary, be exercised through the medium of the member-States acting jointly in the Community's interest".[42] The Community at present assumes only an observer status at the ICAO.

Cabotage

15.41   One of the most difficult areas in international air transport is the issue of cabotage, which in essence is the provision of domestic services by a carrier not registered in that territory. Such services have long been the preserve of national carriers. Article 7 of the Chicago Convention expressly recognises this:

"Each contracting State shall have the right to refuse permission to the aircraft of other contracting States to take on in its territory passengers, mail and cargo carried for remuneration or hire and destined for another point within its territory."

---

[41] House of Lords Select Committee on the EC, *Conduct of the Community's External Aviation Relations* (1990–91) HL39, Q.59.
[42] *Re I.L.O. Convention on Chemicals at Work* [1993] ECR I-1061, at 1076.

Traffic rights to carry domestic passengers, even as an integral part of an inter-   15.42
national service, are very rarely granted. Where such traffic rights are to be granted, they are often used as a bargaining instrument to extract equivalent, if not
more valuable, reciprocal rights. The provision of cabotage services is perhaps
most relevant in the USA where there is sufficient and sustained demand for
domestic air travel. The provision of cabotage services in a small-sized country,
which often has no sufficient demand to justify the provision of such services, is
not likely to be attractive.

The Commission argued that the traffic rights between Member States should   15.43
be given a high premium since these are basically cabotage rights to provide
"domestic" services within the Community, notwithstanding that they are
technically fifth freedom rights granted by two Member States. As such, they must
be protected as a Community asset and be granted only under a systematic
procedure so that the interests of the Community are not prejudiced. Under this
procedure, "Member States are no longer competent to grant new fifth freedom
rights to third countries but they will have to refer requests for such fifth freedom
rights to the Commission for consideration under Community procedures
according to the Article 113".[43] This is a thorny issue. Even if Member States may
have collectively waived their sovereign prerogative to grant traffic rights, there
has to be an express and formal acceptance by third countries of the alteration
from fifth freedom rights to the decidedly more protected cabotage rights. It is
unlikely that any third country would willingly agree to this conversion without
the offer of significantly attractive benefits.

Air traffic distribution

The Commission also proposed a procedural framework and a set of criteria by   15.44
which traffic rights secured from non-Community countries may be distributed
between Member States. Essentially, these rights would be allocated by bids. The distribution would be made in accordance with a range of considerations in terms of:

- the service to the public;
- the competition in the relevant market;
- the use of scarce resources;
- established Community policy such as slot allocation and public service
  obligation.

Carriers would be expected to submit proposals containing detailed information   15.45
in support of the request which would then be assessed according to the criteria
to decide which "can best make use of the traffic rights".[44] In cases where the
carrier to whom the traffic rights have been allocated fails to optimise their value,
the Commission proposed that a substitution should apply. It stated that:

---

[43] COM(90) 17, para. 42.
[44] COM(92) 434, para. 67.

"It might be possible that a designation would have to be withdrawn when the results of the operation do not meet reasonable expectations and better candidates are interested in operating the route."[45]

15.46   Inevitably, the manner in which these rights are to be distributed will always remain a difficult issue since demand is always likely to exceed the available supply. It will not attract universal acceptance; not when there is a great disparity in the popularity of airports and therefore differing values of traffic rights into these airports which are not necessarily quantifiable. A right into London (Heathrow) for instance is unlikely to have a similar value to a right into, say, Athens.

4. Special cases

15.47   In spite of the difficulties surrounding the issue of the Community's external competence in air transport, a number of agreements have nevertheless been made between the Community and other, principally European, countries.

Agreement with Norway and Sweden

15.48   Given the affinity between the Danish air transport system and those of Norway and Sweden, represented in the main by their joint airline, the Scandinavian Airlines System (SAS), a logical step was to extend the air transport law and policy of the Community to Norway and Sweden. To arrive at an agreement to that effect, formal negotiations had to be entered into, for which the Commission sought the necessary mandate from the Council. The Council in 1990 agreed to authorise the Commission to commence negotiations with Norway and Sweden subject to a number of directives.[46]

15.49   The Agreement which was entered into in July 1992 provides, *inter alia*, that:

- the rules contained in the Agreement do not prejudice the application to the parties of the rules in the EC Treaty and in particular Articles 85 and 86 including any subsidiary measures adopted under them;
- the rules on state aids shall also be applicable to the parties;
- questions on the validity of Community decisions shall fall within the exclusive competence of the European Court of Justice;
- there shall be established a Joint Committee to oversee the administration and implementation of the Agreement. Certain disagreements relating to the Agreement are to be referred to the Joint Committee;
- there shall be a consultation exercise between the parties on air transport matters dealt with in international organisations, on the developments which have taken place in relations between Contracting Parties and third countries, and on the application of any significant provisions in such air transport agreements;

---

[45] *Ibid.*
[46] Council Decision 92/384, [1992] OJ L200/20, as amended by [1993] OJ L212/17.

- where relevant, bilateral agreements between Norway and Sweden, and Member States of the Community shall be superseded by the Agreement.

Both Norway and Sweden are members of the European Free Trade Area (EFTA), with which the Community was also seeking to conclude various agreements, including agreements in the field of air transport. Accordingly, the Agreement provided in Article 19(3) that it "shall cease to be in force from the date an agreement between the Community and the EFTA countries on the European economic area enters into force". Sweden joined the EC in 1995.   15.50

The agreement with Norway and Sweden is unique in some respects in the exercise of the Community's external competence in air transport, and would in any case transcend the debate on the exclusive competence of the Community in this area. First, the legal base adopted for the Agreement was Article 84(2), preceded by an agreement of the Council to authorise the Commission to commence negotiations. Secondly, the SAS arrangement will not be not recurrent in that a party to that arrangement is a Member State of the Community, unlike a case in which the third country carrier was entirely independent of the Community. It would be illogical to expect Denmark, Norway, Sweden and SAS to be subject unwillingly to different sets of rules when SAS was regarded as a Community carrier for the purposes of Community air transport legislation.

Agreement with EFTA

The land-mark agreement for the European Economic Area (EEA) between the Community and the European Free Trade Area (EFTA) entered into force in January 1993.[47] Its aim is to facilitate greater economic co-operation between the Community and EFTA countries by enabling the free movement of goods, services, persons, and capital along the lines envisaged by the EC Treaty. Most significant among its provisions is the emphasis on competition which is represented by the competition principles of the Treaty. The institutional framework of the EEA which also takes on a similar set up as the Community is made up of: 15.51

- an EEA Council, the supreme body consisting of members from the Community and governments of the EFTA countries;

- an EEA Joint Committee consisting of Community and EFTA representatives and which main purpose is to facilitate the exchange of information, formulate decisions relating to new measures, administer and ensure the proper application of the Agreement;

- an EEA Joint Parliamentary Committee, an advisory body consisting of members from the European Parliament and parliaments of EFTA countries;

- an EEA Consultative Committee.

Prior to the conclusion of the EEA, a Commission proposal was submitted to the Council to authorise the former to commence negotiations on air transport   15.52

---

[47] The EFTA countries are Austria, Finland, Iceland, Norway, Sweden and Switzerland.

with the EFTA countries.[48] The proposal had come in the light of requests from the EFTA countries to conclude an agreement between them and the Community on scheduled passenger air services. In respect of Norway and Sweden, their interests clearly stemmed from the link with Denmark and SAS, while the remaining EFTA countries referred to the "integrated character of international civil aviation" where harmonised solutions on a European-wide scale were essential and of mutual interest.[49]

15.53   The proposal identified several advantages attendant in an agreement with the EFTA countries:

- The creation of extra traffic rights for Community and EFTA carriers and the development of hubs within the EC–EFTA area. These additional rights could "provide States with new opportunities in the countries when rights are currently denied or restricted".

- The extension of the zonal system of approving fares to EC–EFTA journeys would enable Community carriers to innovate on fares as the extension of the capacity sharing criteria would provide these carriers with greater flexibility and freedom on capacity decisions.

- The provision of specific procedures for the resolution of conflicts involving international law and air transport competition.

- The projection of a liberal image in international air transport signifying that the Community is open to exchanges with third countries. This is "politically valuable".[50]

15.54   The negotiations for an agreement with EFTA countries were, however, superseded by the conclusion of the EEA Agreement which incorporated provisions dealing with transport generally and air transport specifically. The Agreement sets out the provisions governing air transport by reference to Community legislation on air transport competition and other harmonisation measures.

15.55   Regardless of the supersession of the air transport negotiations by the EEA Agreement, the authorisation of the Council to the Commission to open negotiations with the EFTA countries on air transport does not indicate an exclusive Community competence in extra-Community air transport. Indeed, the Commission recognised in its own proposal that there was a difference between the EFTA countries and other third countries:

"Therefore, there is no immediate reason to link the pursuit of these negotiations with the development of an external relations policy with other countries. On the contrary, it is to the advantage of the Community to start the negotiations without undue delay, since this would give the Community an opportunity to take account of the results of these negotiations in the further development of the external relations policy."[51]

---

[48] COM(90) 18.
[49] *Ibid.*, para. 3.
[50] *Ibid.*, para. 6.
[51] *Ibid.*, para. 8.

The negotiating brief was therefore separate from the broader issue of exclusive competence in air transport relations with third countries.

Agreement with Eastern European countries

In 1991, several agreements were entered into independently between the Community and Poland, Hungary and (formerly) Czechoslovakia, which became known as the "European Agreements". Although these agreements by no means represent a mandate for the Commission to commence formal negotiations with these countries, they sought to establish a number of conditions between the parties to co-ordinate the provision and development of air transport services. They provide a framework within which political dialogue could take place, to ensure a gradual integration of these countries into the Community.

15.56

General Agreement on Trade and Tariffs

The most recent Uruguay Round of GATT in 1994 included for the first time within its ambit the GATS, an explicit though very preliminary acknowledgement of the increasing importance of global trade in services including civil aviation and the need for a multilateral framework. In the event though, civil aviation was not included within GATS since it was felt that its inclusion would produce a considerable impact on the existing bilateral system, particularly the so-called "hard rights" such as traffic rights.

15.57

The involvement of the Community in the entire GATT negotiations had been significant. This was clearly so because the GATT was essentially an agreement on trade in goods, until of course more recently when limited trade in services was annexed to it. As trade in goods was part of the common commercial policy, the jurisdiction to negotiate fell exclusively within the Community's competence.[52] But where trade in services is involved, particularly transport services, the European Court of Justice has already ruled that competence will be concurrent, suggesting that services of this nature do not fall within the common commercial policy and hence Article 113 of the Treaty. It must therefore be logical to infer from this decision that competence for extra-Community air transport has not as yet become exclusive to the Community.[53]

In addition to the mandate to negotiate on the Uruguay Round of the GATT, the Community has also been expressly charged with the responsibility of ensuring "the maintenance of all appropriate relations with the organs of the United Nations, of its specialised agencies and of the General Agreement on Tariffs and Trade" under the provisions of Article 229 of the EC Treaty. The ICAO is a specialised agency of the United Nations, at which the Community has an observer status. Article 229 also requires the Commission to maintain "such relations as

15.58

---

[52] See for instance, Council Decision 92/496 on the conclusion of Agreement between the Community and the USA on the application of the GATT on trade in civil and large aircraft which adopted Article 113 as its legal base: [1992] OJ L301/31.
[53] Opinion 1/94 [1995] 1 CMLR 205.

are appropriate with all international organisations". To that end, links have already been established with the European Civil Aviation Conference and Eurocontrol, the body responsible for air navigation in Europe, for the Community's contributions.

Agreement with the USA

15.59   One of the most important developments in recent years has been the resolution of 1996 to assign the negotiating responsibility with the USA to the Community. The mandate charges the Commission with the responsibility of negotiating with the USA an agreement creating a common aviation area. It is, however, a special authorisation which does not represent an exclusive competence to negotiate on the part of the Community, nor a blanket authorisation to negotiate future agreements. Indeed, the mandate had no universal agreement between the Member States. The United Kingdom submitted strong objections against it, but will nevertheless be bound under the rules of majority voting.

Although the mandate includes a negotiating responsibility for traffic rights, the Commission will only be negotiating on issues such as investment and antitrust regulation within the general framework of the mandate. The authority to negotiate traffic rights will depend on the progress of negotiations in these areas and, more importantly, on "an explicit instruction from the Council".[54]

5. Conclusion

15.60   It must be a logical progression now that the die is cast for a single European air transport market for Member States and the Community to focus their efforts on the development of a policy for external relations in air transport; to create a systematic procedure which will facilitate a process of decision-making and negotiation that transcends national boundaries. Whatever may be the practical and legal obstacles, the incentives of acting as a Community must outweigh the costs of national protection. Sir Christopher Chataway, a past chairman of the UK Civil Aviation Authority has aptly reminded us that "This endless debate ignores the obvious fact that geography has already made the decision for us".

---

[54] Press Release IP(96) 520.

Appendix I

LEADING CASES

Airline mergers

Air France – Sabena
[1994] 5 CMLR M1

British Airways – British Caledonian
[1988] 4 CMLR 238

British Airways – Dan Air
[1993] OJ C68/5

Pan Am – Delta Airlines
[1992] 5 CMLR M56

Air France v Commission
Case T-2/93, [1994] ECR-II 323
BA-Dan Air merger – partial acquisition – calculation of turnover

Air France v Commission
Case T-3/93, [1994] ECR-II 121
BA-TAT merger – analysis of relevant market

Market access

Orly Airport
Commission Decision 95/259, [1995] OJ L162/25
Traffic distribution rules

TAT: Paris–Marseille–Toulouse
Commission Decision 94/290, [1993] OJ L127/22
Authorisation – exclusive concession

TAT: Paris–London
Commission Decision 94/291, [1993] OJ L127/32
Authorisation – traffic distribution

Viva Air: Paris–Madrid
Commission Decision 93/347, [1993] OJ L140/51
Authorisation – traffic distribution

State aids

Aer Lingus
Commission Decision 94/118, [1994] OJ L54/30
Capital injection – exemption – Article 92(3)(c) – authorisation

Air France
Commission Decision 94/653, [1994] OJ L254/73
Capital injection – exemption – Article 92(3)(c) – authorisation

Air France: CDC-P
Commission Decision 94/622, [1994] OJ L258/26
Bond subscription – Article 93(3) – unlawful aid

Iberia
Commission Decision 96/278, [1996] OJ L104/25
Capital injection – market economy investor principle – no aid

Olympic Airways
Commission Decision 94/696, [1994] OJ L273/22
Loan guarantees – exemption – Article 92(3)(c) – authorisation

Sabena
Commission Decision 91/555, [1991] OJ L300/48
Capital injection – exemption – Article 92(3)(c) – authorisation

TAP
Commission Decision 94/698, [1994] OJ L279/29
Capital injection – loan guarantee – tax exemption – exemption – Article 92(3)(c) – authorisation

TAP: Madeira–Azores
Commission Decision 94/666, [1994] OJ L260/27
Compensation – Madeira and Azores regions – Article 92(3)(a) – authorisation

Appendix II

IMPACT OF THE THIRD PACKAGE OF AIR TRANSPORT LIBERALIZATION MEASURES (COM (96) 514)

General Evaluation and follow-up

Liberalisation of civil aviation in Europe was established between 1993–96. Certain experts believe that three years is too short a period to carry out an objective evaluation of its impact. However, with only six months before the complete liberalisation of the market, with unrestricted cabotage, the Commission feels it necessary to present a first evaluation.

The fact, which certainly hits the average traveller, is that the single aviation market has not occurred with a "Big Bang": there has been no spectacular reduction in the fares, nor any dramatic disappearance of the more important carriers, nor a substantial penetration of the domestic markets by foreign competitors. Liberalisation has happened in a progressive way and without major upsets. This contrasts with the situation that the United States experienced at the time of the deregulation of the aviation market. The Community has found the correct balance between competition and control mechanisms. Competition and consumer have both benefited.

The effects of this process, although slow, are nevertheless quite clear and it is satisfactory the note that in the end almost all operators have made use of the new possibilities offered by the third package.

For example, when the third package was introduced there were 490 routes, there are now approximately 520. This increase contrasts with the situation which prevailed in the United States. 30% of the Community routes are served by two operators and 6% by three operators or more. It should be noted that out of the 64% of routes operated as a monopoly a large number of them have low levels of traffic and are of no interest to most other carriers. Furthermore a certain number of the other routes experience real competition from neighbouring routes, from charter services or from other modes of transport. One of the most interesting developments certainly is the fact that the number of operators, on a significant number of domestic routes, passed from one to two. Moreover, the dominant carrier's market share often fell to the advantage of the second carrier.

The possibilities of access to the market have been used: there are now 30 routes operated on a fifth freedom basis as opposed to 14 in January 1993; routes operated with cabotage traffic grew from 0 in 1993 to 20 today. The public service obligations have been used on a hundred routes in Ireland, Sweden, the United Kingdom, Portugal, France and Norway.

Capacity increased but did not reduce the load factors in an unacceptable way.

It is certainly in respect of the creation of new airlines that market dynamics have been most visible. Over the three years 800 licences have been granted, the majority going to small operators: 80 companies have been created, for the most part private companies, while 60 have disappeared. Increased competition from the charter companies on regular routes should also be highlighted. More important, new entrants appeared on the markets of the United Kingdom, France, Germany, Denmark, Ireland, Spain, Italy, Greece, Austria and Belgium. Their entry into the market has often contributed to a fall in the fares.

The downside of liberalization is that the fall in air fares has been felt only on the routes where competition has been fully realised, *i.e.* where more than two airlines operate. Certain categories of fares have fallen significantly on routes such as Barcelona/Madrid, UK/Ireland, Paris/London, certain domestic routes in Germany, France, Italy, UK and Belgium towards a number of European destinations. In general, the structure of the fares on scheduled flights remains complex and sometimes seems non-transparent thus preventing the users from benefiting from the competition.

If the third package has been implemented in 1993 and 1994 because of the economic recession, the pace has accelerated since 1995 and 1996 and results are encouraging. However, it is clear that, if the "foundations" of liberalization have been well established, much still remains to be done to make it a complete success.

Four grey areas can be identified:

Air Fares

Liberalization is not an end in itself. The opening of the markets is only meaningful if the increased competition brings to the consumer better goods and services at lower costs. Expected beneficial effects of competition on fares has not materialized. An impressive number of promotional fares has developed and the share of the passengers travelling on scheduled flights with tickets at reduced prices has passed from 60.5% in 1985 to 70.9% in 1995 and, taking into account that the share of the charter market accounts for approximately 50–55% of the total market, it is estimated that 85–90% of the passengers travel at reduced prices. A sharp drop of almost 20% of the yield also confirms this tendency. However, these tickets are often accompanied by restrictions with regard to schedules' flexibility and are available only for a limited number of seats. The new distribution techniques (Internet *etc.*) should facilitate access to these fares by the individual traveller: however, the existence of these techniques must be known and access to them must be established. The Commission is examining ways of informing the public on this subject to ensure the necessary transparency for the consumer and to avoid differences in tariffs which cannot be justified on objective grounds.

In contrast to the promotional fares most of the fully flexible fares have continued to increase. On certain routes these fares can be described as excessive. A detailed examination will consequently be necessary in order to pinpoint the cases of excessive fares under Regulation 2409/92 and the rules of competition. Where necessary the Commission will use the powers of enquiry conferred by this regulation to put an end to excessively high fares. The Commission could in certain cases examine potential abuse of dominant position under Article 86 of the Treaty.

Capacity restrictions

It would be unrealistic to seek to liberalize civil aviation in Europe, with the consequent increase in traffic, without envisaging adjustments to the capacity available. In recent years the majority of airports have had to re-examine their development plans, both as regards capacity of terminals and use of runways. Similar problems exist with air traffic control, where the fragmentation of the European airspace continues to pose serious management problems. The Commission is active in these areas:

- As regards airports, the Commission has just conducted a series of consultations on the question of slot allocation. In the light of these discussions it will present, during the last quarter of 1996, a proposal for amendments to Regulation 95/93. One of the objectives sought by the system of slot allocation is to allow optimum use of capacity while encouraging increased competition.

- With regard to air traffic control, the Commission published in March a White Paper on "the management of air traffic". One of the fundamental ideas proposed by this document is to guarantee that common rules apply at the widest possible European level and cover the largest possible geographical space in order to abolish the artificial capacity restrictions connected with the administrative/political parcelling out of the airspace.

The costs of air transport

When the aim of liberalization is to give operators more choice and provide users with better services at competitive prices, it is necessary to examine the costs. It has been estimated the infrastructure charges alone account for 25% of total operational costs these are believed to be 40% higher than in the United States. These costs not only concern air traffic control but also airport fees and ground handling:

- A directive on the liberalization of ground handling has been adopted by the Council on 15 October 1996. The aim is to open the market for ground handling and should, in the long term, reduce prices for these services.

- With regard to air traffic management, the aim of the above mentioned White Paper is to improve service levels and recommends the separation of regulatory activities from the provision of services to the users. This should give more freedom to the airlines and reduce costs. Indeed until now the system of air traffic management has been such that the ATM service providers are not at all encouraged to seek the best cost/effectiveness ratio. Decentralised services will encourage rigorous management and a better control of the costs.

• Lastly, as regards airport fees, the Commission plans to submit a proposal before the end of 1996. It will be based on three major principles: non-discrimination, transparency and cost-effectiveness.

Access to the market

The internal market remains fragile in so far as it remains incomplete. External relations continue to be subject to bilateral agreements between the Community Member States and non-member countries. These agreements always contain provisions incompatible with the internal market, such as the nationality clauses, and their existence is partly responsible for the loss of competitive pressure on the Community market, it is to preserve the internal aviation market and to be in a position to control the impact that the bilateral agreements can have on the Community market that the Commission proposes negotiations with third countries. Based in part on such considerations, the Council has granted a Community negotiating brief with the United States in several fields. The Council has granted a negotiating brief with the associated countries of Central Europe.

The effects on competition of the alliances, which have increased rapidly, can only be appreciated on a case by case basis. Certain of these alliances have ended fairly quickly whilst others are too recent to evaluate. Nevertheless their association with the practice of code-sharing, coupled with the frequent flyer programmes, can cause a number of difficulties in respect of access to the market for the small operators who are not in a position to cope with such dominant positions. Similarly, by using such practices, certain non Community carriers can overcome the barriers of entry to the Community market by making use of the services of a Community carrier which is permitted to operate without restrictions between Community airport to the detriment of certain Member States. These practices merit examination by the Commission under the competition rules.

We have seen that public service obligations (PSO) have been used frequently. It will be advisable to check that PSOs do not become a disguised means of restricting the market. In this context the Commission will have to ensure that the provisions concerning PSOs are carefully monitored.

Access to the market will only be completely liberalised in April 1997, when the last restrictions on cabotage traffic are removed. However, it is prudent, as of now, to take the necessary measures, as described above, in order to prevent obstacles for access to the market being retained. There are still numerous routes which are not operated, or are operated with low traffic densities, where the lack of competition provides very good opportunities for a new carrier to take advantage. The Community market is not yet optimal: its restructuring in ongoing privatisations continue. During this restructuring exercise, it will be the

Commission's role to ensure that competition rules continue to be applied rigorously. With the completion of the single aviation market in 1997 "the Commission will not be able to authorise restructuring aid unless under very stringent conditions".[1]

The Commission is also conscious of the potential implications of the liberalization of air transport on employment. In this context, a study of the social impact of the liberalization of air transport is underway.

Lastly, and although it is not the purpose of this analysis, it is important to recall that improvements in the Community aviation system will have to be accompanied by more stringent safety measures and better consideration of the environment. Proposals will be tabled to this end.

---

[1] With regard to this, see the guidelines of the Commission on the Application of articles 92 and 93 of the Treaty and article 61 of the EEA agreement to state aids in the aviation sector (OJ C350 du 10.12.94).

INDEX